21

FROM WHENCE I CAME

To Kevin,
I hope you will enjoy
this book about one of
Boston's best known
Irish-American families.
Best wishes,
Brian Murphy.

In memory of Noel Whelan, 1968–2019

'What he leaves to us is what he said, what he did, and what he stood for.'

Senator Edward M. Kennedy speaking at the public memorial service for

Robert F. Kennedy at St Patrick's Cathedral, New York, 8 June 1968.

FROM WHENCE I CAME

THE KENNEDY LEGACY, IRELAND AND AMERICA

BRIAN MURPHY AND
DONNACHA Ó BEACHÁIN

MERRION
PRESS

First published in 2021 by
Merrion Press
10 George's Street
Newbridge
Co. Kildare
Ireland
www.merrionpress.ie

978-1-78855-141-0 (Paper)
978-1-78855-142-7 (Kindle)
978-1-78855-143-4 (Epub)
978-1-78855-144-1 (PDF)

A CIP catalogue record for this book is
available from the British Library.

Typeset in Adobe Garamond Pro 11/14.5 pt

Merrion Press is a member of Publishing Ireland.

CONTENTS

BIOGRAPHICAL NOTE
ON CONTRIBUTORS

Brian Murphy is a director of the Kennedy Summer School and a director of the John F. Kennedy Trust. He is a lecturer and member of the Academic Council at Technological University Dublin. He holds a PhD in Modern Irish History from the School of History and Archives, University College Dublin. Brian's monograph *Forgotten Patriot: Douglas Hyde and the Foundation of the Irish Presidency* was published in 2016 by the Collins Press. He previously co-edited *Brian Lenihan: In Calm and Crisis*, the best-selling book on the public career of the former Minister for Finance. Brian is a former speechwriter and special adviser to two Taoisigh.

Donnacha Ó Beacháin is Professor of Politics at the School of Law and Government, Dublin City University where he lectures on the post-Soviet region, unrecognised states, foreign policy and Irish studies. His books include *Destiny of the Soldiers: Fianna Fáil, Irish Republicanism and the IRA 1926–1973*, *Political Communication in Ireland* (co-edited with Mark O'Brien) and *From Partition to Brexit: The Irish Government and Northern Ireland*, which is the 2019 recipient of the Brian Farrell book of the year award from the Political Studies Association of Ireland. He has twice (2012 and 2017) been awarded the accolade 'Champion of European Research' by Ireland's National Support Network for FP7 and Horizon 2020 in award ceremonies hosted by President Michael D. Higgins and the Minister of State for Training and Skills. The citation reads that 'as leaders of major research projects in the EU Framework Programme for Research and Development [these] researchers … are deemed to have reached the pinnacle of the European Research System'.

Mary E. Daly is Professor Emerita of History at University College Dublin and a former Principal of the UCD College of Arts and Celtic Studies. She has also held visiting positions at Harvard, Boston College and the European University Institute (EUI) in Fiesole. Professor Daly served on the National Archives Advisory Council, the Irish Manuscripts Commission and the Higher Education Authority. In 2015 she was appointed as a member of the Commission to Inquire into Mother and Baby Homes. Elected to the Royal Irish Academy in 1991, Mary served as Secretary of the RIA from 2000 to 2004 and was the first woman elected as President of the Royal Irish Academy, 2014–17. Her recent publications include *Sixties Ireland: Reshaping the Economy, State and Society, 1957–1973* (2016); and with Eugenio Biagini, *The Cambridge Social History of Modern Ireland since 1740* (2017).

Tad Devine is a media consultant, writing, directing and producing television and radio advertising for leading Democratic and Independent candidates in the United States and providing strategic advice for national campaigns in Europe, the Middle East and Latin America. In the United States, Tad has worked at the highest levels of campaigns for President of the United States. He served as senior adviser to the Bernie Sanders campaign for president in 2016. In 2000, he acted as senior strategist to the Gore/Lieberman campaign. In 2004, he served as a senior adviser and strategist to Senator John Kerry's campaign. A 2011 Fellow at The Institute of Politics at Harvard University's Kennedy School of Government, Tad has taught campaign management and strategy courses at New York University, University of Pennsylvania, Boston University and the George Washington University.

Larry Donnelly is a director of the Kennedy Summer School. From a Boston Irish political family, he is an attorney and was active in local politics there before relocating to Ireland. He is a lecturer and director of Clinical Legal Education in the School of Law at the National University of Ireland, Galway. He is also a frequent commentator in the broadcast media about politics, law and current affairs in the United States and Ireland and a political columnist with *TheJournal.ie*.

Howard Keeley is the director of the Centre for Irish Research and Teaching at Georgia Southern University in Savannah, Georgia. He is also a member of the university's Department of Literature. He has published articles on the representation of middle-class houses in post-Famine Irish literature. Dr Keeley (PhD Princeton) is the principal investigator on the Wexford–Savannah research project, which examines the mid-nineteenth-century trade-and-migration axis that operated between County Wexford, Ireland, and Savannah. His efforts have resulted in Georgia Southern University's establishment, in November 2019, of an overseas learning facility in a heritage building in the town of Wexford.

Cody Keenan is a speechwriter who has worked with President Barack Obama for more than a decade, rising from a campaign intern in Chicago to Director of Speechwriting at the White House. He helped President Obama craft remarks on every topic for every audience – from tiny backyards in Iowa to the biggest stadiums in the country; from a sermon in Selma to his farewell address. Educated at Northwestern University and Harvard University, Cody's passion for public service was sharpened as a young aide to Senator Edward M. Kennedy. Upon leaving the White House, President Obama asked Cody to continue their partnership as his post-presidential speechwriter. He is a visiting professor at the Department of Political Science, Northwestern University, a Fellow of American University's Sine Institute of Policy and Politics and a board member of the Edward M. Kennedy Institute for the United States Senate.

Kerry Kennedy is the President of Robert F. Kennedy Human Rights. Since 1981, she has worked on diverse human rights issues including child labour, disappearances, indigenous land rights, judicial independence, freedom of expression, ethnic violence, impunity, women's rights and the environment. Kerry founded RFK Compass, which convenes biannual meetings of institutional investors to address the impact of human rights violations on investment outcomes. She serves on the boards of the United States Institute of Peace, Human Rights First, Ethics in Action, SDG USA, Sustainable Development Goals Center for Africa, Health eVillages, and the Kailash Satyarthi Children's Foundation as well as several public companies. A graduate of Brown University and Boston College Law School, Kerry received the Medal for Social Activism from the World Summit of Nobel Peace Laureates along with many other awards and honorary degrees.

Michael Kennedy is the Executive Editor of the Royal Irish Academy's Documents on Irish Foreign Policy Series. Since 1998, under Dr Kennedy's direction, the series has published eleven volumes of select documents from the archives of the Department of Foreign Affairs and Trade covering 1919 to 1957. For over twenty-five years, Michael has also published widely on the history of Irish foreign policy and Irish military and political history. Recent publications include *Ireland, the United Nations and the Congo (2014)* and *Ireland and Japan, 1957–2017: diplomatic, economic and cultural connections* (with Dr Eoin Kinsella) (2017).

Felix M. Larkin is a former academic director of the Parnell Summer School, and a co-founder and former chairman of the Newspaper and Periodical History Forum of Ireland. He has written extensively on the press in Ireland in the late nineteenth and early twentieth centuries and has had a particular interest in historical cartoons. His publications include *Terror and Discord: the Shemus Cartoons in the Freeman's Journal, 1920–1924* (2009). Having studied history at University College Dublin, Felix was an Irish public servant for thirty-six years before reverting to the role of non-stipendiary historian in his retirement.

Alison Meagher earned her PhD from the School of History, Anthropology, Politics and Philosophy at Queen's University Belfast in 2017. Her research considers United States foreign policy towards Northern Ireland under President Jimmy Carter. A former QUB Convocation Scholar and recipient of the Centre for Cross Border Studies' Universities Ireland scholarship, her work has been featured in such publications as *Diplomatic History*. She is currently Vice Consul at the Consulate General of Ireland in Shanghai.

Celestine Murphy is a former librarian with Wexford County Council Public Library Service. She was involved in the management and development of the library's Local Studies Collections and in the delivery of its publishing programme. Educated at Maynooth NUI and University College Cork, Celestine is well known in her native Wexford as a lecturer, researcher, family history specialist, writer and publishing supervisor. She has contributed to several local history journals and publications and is the author of *Publish and be damned: some practical advice for the community publisher* (2002), and

Between place and parish: a guide to the historical administrative divisions of County Wexford (2004), both published by Wexford County Council Library Service. Celestine retired from Wexford Library service in July 2019 and now works as a freelance history and family history consultant/researcher, writer, tutor and publishing specialist.

Harvey O'Brien teaches film studies at University College Dublin. He is the author of *Action Movies: The Cinema of Striking Back* (Columbia University Press) and *The Real Ireland: The Evolution of Ireland in Documentary Film* (Manchester University Press). He has served on the board of directors of The Irish Film Institute and is former associate director of the Boston Irish Film Festival. He has contributed to numerous international journals and edited volumes, writing on diverse interdisciplinary topics including Irish cinema, animation, horror, Neo-Victorian studies, trash culture, literary adaptation and documentary. He is a frequent guest on Irish national radio and a well-known speaker and interviewer at public events at the Irish Film Institute and the Dublin International Film Festival. He is currently involved in the development and delivery of the BA in Humanities Pathway in Music, Film and Drama at University College Dublin and recently served as Head of Film.

Robert Schmuhl is the Walter H. Annenberg–Edmund P. Joyce Chair in American Studies and Journalism at the University of Notre Dame and an Adjunct Professor in the School of Law and Government at Dublin City University. Schmuhl is the author or editor of over a dozen books. He joined the Notre Dame faculty in 1980, teaching at the University of Notre Dame of Australia in 1997, serving as the inaugural Naughton Fellow at University College Dublin in 2000, and being Visiting Professor of Media Ethics at St Augustine College of South Africa in 2003. In 2004 and 2012, he was on the faculty of Notre Dame's London Centre, and in 2009 he was the first John Hume Visiting Research Fellow at University College Dublin.

Robert M. Shrum is the director of the Jesse M. Unruh Institute of Politics and the Carmen H. and Louis Warschaw Chair in Practical Politics at the University of Southern California. Bob is also a former political strategist and consultant who served as senior adviser to the Kerry–Edwards campaign in 2004 and to the Gore–Lieberman campaign in 2000. The *Atlantic Monthly* described him as 'the most sought-after consultant in the Democratic Party'. Bob served as speechwriter to New York Mayor John V. Lindsay from 1970 to 1971, speechwriter to Senator George McGovern's 1972 presidential campaign and speechwriter and press secretary to Senator Edward M. Kennedy from 1980 to 1984 and political consultant until 2009. Internationally, he was a senior adviser to the campaign of Prime Minister Ehud Barak of Israel and to the British Labour Party in the 2001 General Election campaign.

INTRODUCTION

Brian Murphy and Donnacha Ó Beacháin

On 27 June 1963, the Freedom of Wexford was conferred upon the thirty-fifth President of the United States. At Redmond Place, along the quayside in Wexford town, 'a special platform had been dressed in the national colours of America and Ireland' for the occasion and 'from its four corners the Stars and Stripes and Tricolour made a brave display in the seaside breeze'.[1] John Fitzgerald Kennedy was 'obviously moved' as he leaned forward to sign the Roll of Freemen, making him only the thirteenth freeman of the ancient Irish borough.[2] To 'a tumult of cheering', the Mayor of Wexford, Councillor Thomas Byrne, handed the roll, placed in a silver casket, to the United States President. However, 'a hush' quickly 'then descended on the thousands who stood craning their heads forward in expectance of the President's speech. President Kennedy came to the microphone'.[3] The population of Wexford had temporarily swollen by 250 per cent to 30,000 and 'the narrow streets of the former Danish stronghold were early packed with people who had driven in from many parts of the south, using many modes of conveyance, even to horse traps'.[4] In opening his acceptance speech to the assembled crowd, President Kennedy simply said: 'I want to express my pleasure at being back from whence I came'.[5]

Kennedy's presence in Wexford was a family homecoming of sorts. He had spent part of the morning with distant relatives in Dunganstown, outside New Ross, drinking tea and, in the President's own words, toasting 'all the Kennedys who went and all the Kennedys who stayed'.[6] He had also made a short speech in New Ross, the small port town, where his great-grandfather had taken his last steps on Irish soil. In Maier's words, 'as if coming full circle, as if completing some generational journey begun by his forefathers more than a century ago,' Kennedy had returned to New Ross as the first serving President of the United States of America to visit Ireland.[7] Reflecting on his impoverished ancestor's emigrant voyage and his own Irish heritage, Kennedy said:

> I am glad to be here. It took 115 years to make this trip, and 6,000 miles, and three generations. And I am proud to be here and I appreciate the warm welcome you gave to all of us. When my great grandfather left here to become a cooper in East Boston, he carried nothing with him except two things: a strong religious faith and a strong desire for liberty. I am glad to say that all of his great-grandchildren have valued that inheritance.[8]

Rapid population growth was at the root of the catastrophe that devastated Ireland in the 1840s. Between 1741, the date of the previous big famine, and the coming of the potato blight in 1845, the population of Ireland had tripled. Feeding so many was already a problem before the Great Famine, with the bulk of the Irish population surviving on a subsistence diet. In October 1848, Patrick Kennedy joined the mass exodus from an Irish nation stricken by starvation, disease and death.

Escaping the Great Famine and leaving behind forever his native, rural Wexford and an Ireland devastated by deprivation and British misrule, Patrick Kennedy boarded a ship in New Ross. He journeyed initially to Liverpool 'living by his wits, until he could secure passage to Boston.'[9] On 20 March 1849, Patrick Kennedy boarded the *Washington Irving*, a White Diamond Line ship that had been built by Donald McKay, one of the most famous shipbuilders of the time, with a steerage class ticket bought at the offices of Train & Co. on Waterloo Road, Liverpool.[10]

After enduring over a month of sordid and perilous conditions, which saw vessels like the *Washington Irving* labelled 'coffin ships', Patrick Kennedy disembarked at Noodle's Island, East Boston on 28 April 1849.[11] He was part of a massive Irish influx into the capital city of Massachusetts. The author Roger Abrams has noted that in the decade between 1840 and 1850 Boston's population swelled from 85,475 to 136,881. This demographic surge was rooted in the problems of Ireland. In 1847 alone, the worst year of the Great

Famine in Ireland, more than 37,000 immigrants arrived in Boston, many fleeing from starvation. By 1855, more than a third of Boston's population was Irish. At the turn of the twentieth century, Boston had become one of the largest Irish populated cities in the world, outside of Dublin.[12]

When Patrick Kennedy first landed in Boston, he was part of an emigrant class, which was despised by many Americans for their alien religion, their strange language and their readiness, born out of desperation, to work for low wages. Before emigrating, Patrick Kennedy had been employed by Cherry Brothers Brewery in New Ross and the skills that he learned there stood to him in the United States. He found employment as a cooper at Daniel Francis's on Sumner Street, Boston, where he made beer and whiskey barrels. Patrick Kennedy did his best to provide for the young family he started in the United States, having married another Wexford emigrant, Bridget Murphy, only five months after arriving in America. Despite his meagre income, he financially contributed to Irish separatist organisations and he battled discrimination. As Klein notes,

> Many want ads in the Boston papers read, 'None need apply but Americans.' When Irish men and women showed up for jobs, they encountered notices that read, 'No Irish Need Apply,' which eventually became shortened to 'NINA' ... Even skilled workers like Patrick did not avoid the virulent anti-Catholic nativism that was fomented by the infamous Know-Nothing Party. In 1854, five years after Patrick's arrival, the Know-Nothing Party captured the governor's office and virtually every seat in the Massachusetts General Court. The party harassed Catholic schools, disbanded Irish militia companies, and tried to pass legislation mandating a twenty-one-year wait before a naturalised citizen could vote. All this struck Patrick like a replay of the notorious British Penal Laws in Ireland.[13]

Announcing his candidacy for President of the United States, on 16 June 2015, Donald Trump proclaimed, 'Sadly, the American dream is dead.'[14] For Patrick Kennedy, the tragedy was that his American dream of greater opportunity and prosperity never became a reality. His life in the New World was as impoverished as it had been in New Ross and, hampered by prejudice and a deteriorating economic situation, by 1856 his annual family income had declined to only \$100.[15] The hunger, deprivation and disease that Patrick Kennedy thought he had fled from in leaving Ireland were never far away in the immigrant tenements of East Boston. During the previous year, 1855, Patrick and Bridget had endured the nightmare of losing a child, their eldest son, John Kennedy, who died from cholera, a disease associated with the squalid living conditions that typically accompany poverty. According to Abrams,

> The crowded housing available to the new arrivals offered few comforts ... The slums were dark and noisy with a fetid odour. Without adequate sewerage or drainage, with oppressive heat during the summer and no heat during the winter, life for Irish immigrants was frightful. Disease, particularly among children, was rampant. Cholera caused a ghastly toll.[16]

The children of immigrant Irish Catholics, mostly 'living in the vermin-infested confines' of East Boston experienced by far the highest levels of infant mortality in the city.[17] Adult life-expectancy was also devastatingly low in the immigrant community. Exploited, overworked and undernourished, 'the average Irishman who immigrated to America', according to Maier's research, 'survived only fourteen years after he came ashore'.[18] Even by that grim statistic, Patrick Kennedy fared badly. He died 'virtually penniless', aged just 35, less than a decade after he first set foot on American soil.[19] 'The first Kennedy to arrive in the New World, he was the last to die in anonymity'. Patrick Kennedy's death occurred on 22 November 1858 – exactly 105 years to the day when the entire world would be stunned by the murder of his great-grandson.

When Patrick Kennedy died, the prospects for his wife and their surviving children were bleak. Patrick Kennedy is often referred to as the 'founding father' of the Kennedy dynasty,[20] but without the perseverance, work ethic and ingenuity of Bridget Murphy, the Kennedy family may well have perished. To keep her family from starving, Bridget took in lodgers and she worked long hours as a maid, 'an occupation so often filled by Irish Catholic women that the jobs were known derisively as "bridgets" or "biddys"'.[21]

In this book, local Wexford historian and genealogist Celestine Murphy provides significant new details on Bridget's family origins in Cloonagh,

Ballycullane and she traces the life stories of Bridget and her immediate relatives across the landscapes of nineteenth-century County Wexford, Boston and beyond. Bridget Murphy was born into grinding poverty on a small holding twelve miles from New Ross, before emigrating to the United States. Blessed with endurance and entrepreneurial skills, Bridget was also 'industrious and personable'[22] and, though faced with adversity as a young widow, she ensured that the Kennedys not only survived, but began to thrive. Through endeavour and hard work, she managed to get enough money together to buy and build up a flourishing grocery business, which 'apparently sold liquor as well as food to local Irish labourers'.[23] As Celestine Murphy documents in this book, Bridget Murphy lived long enough to witness her son, Patrick Joseph 'P.J.' Kennedy become a member of the Massachusetts House of Representatives and state Senate, and the birth of her grandson, Joseph Kennedy, JFK's father.

P.J. Kennedy was a shrewd businessman. He had started out working on the docks, but he eventually became the owner of three pubs and, before he was 30, he owned his own whiskey importing business.[24] By the time of his death in 1929, the upward mobility of his family had seen the Kennedys join 'the ranks of the cut-glass set' with an attractive home on 'Jeffries Point'. P.J. died a wealthy man with an interest in a coal company and a substantial shareholding in a bank – the Columbia Trust Company.[25] P.J.'s son, Joseph P. Kennedy, would bring the family's wealth and level of influence into a new stratosphere. Joseph P. Kennedy was ambitious and driven. By 1914, he was, by his own claim, 'the youngest bank president in America'.[26] Throughout the 1920s, he ruthlessly played the stock market and profited enormously. He survived the Wall Street crash of 1929 by getting out of stocks in time and investing in real estate. He later said he knew it was time to get out of the overheated market when he received a 'stock tip from a shoeshine boy'.[27] By 1935 his personal fortune was over $180 million, making Joseph P. Kennedy a billionaire by modern standards.[28]

Joseph P. Kennedy also nurtured unrestrained political ambitions. He had supported Franklin D. Roosevelt's successful campaign for the presidency in 1932 and served the New Deal administration as Chairman of the Securities and Exchanges Commission and later as Chairman of the US Maritime Commission, before being appointed the United States Ambassador to Great Britain. On 16 March 1938, the grandson of Irish famine emigrants presented his credentials to King George VI at Buckingham Palace. Kennedy wished to succeed Roosevelt at the 1940 presidential election and, as ambassador, he was not averse to using his new position and his wealth to encourage media support for his potential candidacy.[29]

In a provocative contribution to this book, Michael Kennedy assesses the role that Joseph P. Kennedy played during the Anglo-Irish negotiations of the late 1930s. While historians have argued that Roosevelt appointed Joseph P. Kennedy as Ambassador to Great Britain in an attempt to influence Neville Chamberlain, Michael Kennedy cogently argues that, despite Joseph P. Kennedy exaggerating or positively spinning his impact on the negotiations, he made little tangible difference and that de Valera entertained an unjustified optimism about the role the United States Ambassador could play. Michael Kennedy concludes that Joseph P. Kennedy's non-involvement in the 1938 negotiations demonstrated that de Valera and the Department of External Affairs would have to act more strategically to engage the United States in Anglo-Irish relations.

Joseph P. Kennedy's presidential ambitions ran aground because of his support for appeasement and United States isolationism. Following the death in August 1944 of his eldest son, Joe Jnr, in a secret military mission to guide B-17 drone planes loaded with explosives into Nazi V-2 rocket bases, Joseph P. Kennedy shifted the focus of his ambition to his next-eldest son, who himself had been seriously wounded in the Pacific when his patrol boat was cut in two by a Japanese destroyer. John Fitzgerald Kennedy (JFK) did not initially want a political career, his father recalled many years later, 'he felt he didn't have the ability ... But I told him he had to.'[30]

In his chapter in this book, 'Electing Kennedy', Donnacha Ó Beacháin charts how JFK rose through national politics, from winning a place in Congress during his late 20s, a Senate seat during his mid-30s and the presidency while still in his early 40s. Ó Beacháin demonstrates how Joseph Kennedy's influence and fabulous riches facilitated JFK's meteoric rise but that despite Kennedy's profound wealth he managed to present himself as an outsider.

During his career on Capitol Hill, John F. Kennedy was never a political insider. In the words of his long-serving secretary Evelyn Lincoln, Kennedy was 'a loner' and 'despite his warm friendships with many of the other senators of both parties', Kennedy 'did not belong to any of the so-called cliques within the Senate'.[31] Kennedy had never 'learned to grease the wheels of power in Washington … [and] never had the patience to learn the fine art of horse-trading for votes'. This was a failing that Kennedy privately admitted to when he was elected President. 'When I was in Congress, I thought all the power was down at the other end of Pennsylvania Avenue, at the White House,' Kennedy told Jim Deakin, a reporter from the *St. Louis Post-Dispatch*. 'Now I am down here, and am amazed at all the power those bastards have.'[32] Kennedy's closest friend in the Senate was Florida's Senator George Smathers, who had served as an usher at his wedding. Smathers and Kennedy were of a similar age and they had an easy relationship. Smathers recalled, 'we'd walk to the floor together to vote, talking about legislation, events of the day, girls, and so on'.[33] In his chapter in this book, Howard Keeley assesses President Kennedy's engagement with the influential senator from Georgia, Richard Russell, who was from almost the same generation as Kennedy's father. In doing so, Keeley demonstrates how, despite fundamental differences on race, the two men enjoyed a very productive and warm relationship characterised by generosity and mutual respect.

The warmth of the reception that President Kennedy received in Ireland, during his visit in June 1963, had a deep impact on him. Seán Lemass, the Taoiseach who welcomed Kennedy to Ireland, was not a man who did hyperbole, but he later observed:

> I think he was very, very, very deeply moved by the warmth of the reception he got here. It wasn't so much the enthusiasm of the crowd, the cheers, the general outpouring of welcome to him as what he sensed in them … They weren't beseeching anything from him; they weren't asking for anything; it was just enthusiasm for himself as a person. He broached it to me on one occasion when we were out on the streets. He said that he had addressed many large meetings in the United States, he was very well received and welcomed by enormous crowds in many United States cities, but that he always realised that half of those who were there were Republicans and had qualifications about him. But he sensed in the reception in Ireland that there was no such qualification.[34]

The welcome accorded to Kennedy in Ireland re-affirmed the President's pride in his Irish heritage, a point noted by Lemass, who recalled that the United States President was 'intensely interested in his Irish ancestry'.[35] Harvey O'Brien's chapter in this book illuminates how JFK's visit was a major event for the relatively young Irish state. As a public and media spectacle, it was widely viewed as both a homecoming for the Irish diaspora and an affirmation of how Ireland and its people had succeeded across the globe.

Kennedy's visit also underlined that the independent Irish state was finally getting into its stride. In his address to the Joint Houses of the Oireachtas, Ireland's national parliament, the President lauded the modernisation of the Irish economy and Irish society:

> And it is the present and the future of Ireland that today hold so much promise to my nation as well as to yours, and, indeed, to all mankind, for the Ireland of 1963, one of the youngest of nations, and the oldest of civilisations, has discovered that the achievement of nationhood is not an end, but a beginning. In the years since independence, you have undergone a new and peaceful revolution, an economic and industrial revolution, transforming the face of this land, while still holding to the old spiritual and cultural values. You have modernised your economy, harnessed your rivers, diversified your industry, liberalised your trade, electrified your farms, accelerated your rate of growth, and improved the living standard of your people.[36]

In an insightful speech at the Kennedy Summer School, New Ross, in 2019, the leader of Fianna Fáil, Micheál Martin, maintained that

> because of the compelling nature of [Kennedy's] story and image, we often miss when looking back at his visit, is what was happening in Ireland at the time. In fact, I believe that the very reason why the visit was so important was that he was welcomed by a country which had itself begun a decisive period of change. It absolutely was not a question of an old country being indulged by a younger one.[37]

In this book, Mary Daly argues that the early 1960s was a time of transitions in Ireland and that these changes were reinforced by John F. Kennedy's brief presidency and his visit to Ireland in 1963. Lemass's government sought to re-orientate Ireland's policies on the economy and towards Northern Ireland. President Kennedy influenced the style of Irish politics, not least in electioneering, and prompted Irish politicians and officials to reappraise their views towards the Irish in America.

The Irish Ambassador to Washington, Thomas Kiernan, who had done much to ensure that Kennedy visited Ireland, believed that the President's trip had boosted national morale and drawn a line under decades of despair and failure. He noted:

> I think his coming back to Ireland was a closing of a chapter that began with the famine ... here was a success at top level. Here was a fellow who came from famine stock on both paternal and maternal sides and who had reached the very top in the United States. That was felt throughout the country.[38]

Lemass's view was similar. He felt that Kennedy's visit to Ireland had been 'a tremendous success' and he recalled that 'national prestige was enhanced, morale was raised and we gained in international influence by reason of the fact that he came here'.[39] Kennedy left Ireland with a renewed sense of personal optimism. On the final day of his visit, Kennedy told a large crowd in Limerick that the four days he had spent in Ireland 'has made the past very real and has made the future very hopeful'.[40] In his chapter in this book, Brian Murphy focuses on the final weeks of John F. Kennedy's presidency from his departure from Shannon Airport on 29 June 1963 to his assassination in Dallas, Texas on 22 November. He argues that this period was among the most action-packed and significant of Kennedy's presidency as he doggedly pursued a peace strategy. Kennedy had entered office as a convinced Cold Warrior, but the Cuban Missile Crisis had altered his views and persuaded him of the need for peaceful co-existence with the Communist world. In this short twenty-one week period, Kennedy concluded a significant nuclear test ban treaty and extended peace overtures to America's Cold War opponents. On the domestic front, civil rights and his re-election campaign were central to the President's busy agenda.

In this period, President Kennedy also welcomed Seán Lemass to the White House. Lemass had met Kennedy on a number of occasions and the private observations of this consummate Irish political leader are of interest. In the 'Lemass Tapes', Lemass stated that Kennedy 'had charm and was a strongly attractive personality. I always felt, however, that he had a motive for everything he did. There was a certain noticeable reservation in his attitude, a mind working away behind the outward façade of the charming personality.'[41]

According to Ronan McGreevy in a paper delivered at the Kennedy Summer School, New Ross, in 2019, 'Lemass was too shrewd and candid a politician to be carried away by the euphoria' generated in Ireland by Kennedy's visit. McGreevy observed that Lemass 'did not warm entirely to Kennedy. He candidly admitted that he preferred Kennedy's predecessor Dwight D. Eisenhower – even if he did not believe that Eisenhower had the "higher intellectual qualities" required.'[42]

Lemass's preference for Eisenhower is surprising. In his chapter in this book, Felix Larkin notes that, as Kennedy's immediate predecessor, Eisenhower was most unfavourably compared with Kennedy during the period of JFK's presidency. Larkin argues that Kennedy's record as president was a positive one and that JFK was a president of substance, who might have become one of the greatest of presidents, but for the brevity of his time in office. John F. Kennedy's presidency lasted just 1,036 days and ended in tragedy when an assassin's bullet in Texas took his life. In this book, Robert Schmuhl assesses Kennedy's legacy and explores how Kennedy changed the unwritten rules of campaigning for the White House by refusing to step aside for more experienced politicians. Schmuhl also suggests that Kennedy's impact on political culture was significant. As the first celebrity president of the modern era, JFK was responsible for bringing the image of a political figure to centre stage in the American consciousness.

The assassination of John F. Kennedy and a few years later, in 1968, of his brother Senator Robert Kennedy would have a traumatic and lasting impact on the American consciousness. Ted Kennedy was then the only Kennedy son left and the mantle of leadership in the family passed to him. In 1957, John F. Kennedy had said, 'Just as I went into politics because Joe died, if anything happened to me tomorrow, my brother Bobby would run for my seat in the Senate. And if Bobby died, Teddy would take over for him.'[43] Ted Kennedy was elected to the United States Senate in 1962 against a backdrop of accusations of nepotism from political opponents, but over an almost forty-seven-year-long career Kennedy earned the sobriquet 'The Lion of the Senate' for his endurance, influence and legislative achievements. On Ted Kennedy's passing in August 2009, President Obama described him as 'the greatest US senator of our time'.[44]

In this book, Larry Donnelly looks at one of the most controversial aspects of Ted Kennedy's long career as the United States Senator for Massachusetts – the Boston busing crisis. This crisis arose in 1974 when Judge W. Arthur Garrity, in an effort to desegregate Boston schools, ordered that white students from mainly white neighbourhoods would have to attend schools in predominantly black neighbourhoods and vice versa. This meant thousands of students being bused back and forth across the city on a daily basis. Ted Kennedy's support for this initiative bolstered his liberal credentials, but it created a deep fissure in his relationship with Boston's Irish community, who had been amongst the most ardent supporters of his brother Jack.

Ted Kennedy's input into the cause of peace in Ireland was crucial. Throughout the key negotiations leading up to the 1998 Good Friday Agreement, the then Taoiseach, Bertie Ahern, kept in regular contact with Senator Edward Kennedy on how the talks were going. 'I was asking Teddy all the time to try and keep [President] Clinton interested and get him to be supportive and keep an eye on the Brits,' Ahern later recalled.[45] In fact, Senator Kennedy's involvement in the Irish peace process had endured over a number of decades. Kennedy had been raising concerns about the conflict from the early 1970s through to the early 1990s when, significantly in the later period, he worked with his sister, the then United States Ambassador to Ireland, Jean Kennedy Smith. Her persuasion of the Clinton administration to grant a visa to Sinn Féin leader Gerry Adams in January 1994 was a major stepping stone towards the IRA ceasefire that occurred later that year.[46]

Senator Kennedy's involvement with the quest for a lasting peace in Ireland continued right through difficult moments in the process up to his death in 2009. In her contribution to this book, Alison Meagher traces Ted Kennedy's engagement with issues relating to Northern Ireland throughout the 1970s, from the early days of the conflict, to the Carter Presidency. Kennedy, alongside Tip O'Neill, Daniel Moynihan and Hugh Carey, successfully lobbied the United States government to break its policy of non-involvement in the Northern Ireland conflict. This opening of the door for

United States government engagement in the Irish peace process would, in later years, prove to be of huge consequence. President Clinton, Senator George Mitchell and Senator Ted Kennedy would all play instrumental roles in the lead-up to and during the negotiations that gave effect to the Good Friday Agreement.

Robert Shrum was one of Ted Kennedy's closest political aides, serving as his campaign speechwriter during Kennedy's presidential run in 1980 and subsequently as press secretary in his senate office. Shrum later worked as a central strategist in Al Gore's campaign for president in 2000 and John Kerry's campaign in 2004 and is a household name in Democratic politics. In his contribution to this book, Shrum provides an intimate and fascinating panorama of United States and international politics from his meeting with JFK as a 16-year-old, while working at the 1960 Democratic National Convention through to assisting Bill Clinton with State of the Union speeches and helping to prepare Bertie Ahern for debates in the 1997 Irish general election. Shrum concludes that while political events can break your heart, politics is a passion that its practitioners cannot set aside.

Shrum was the principal author of Ted Kennedy's famous concession address at the 1980 Democratic National Convention in Madison Square Gardens, which became known as 'The Dream Shall Never Die' speech. In January 2008, Ted Kennedy reworked words from that famous speech and from his brother's even more celebrated presidential inauguration address to endorse Barack Obama in a hard-fought Democratic primary battle with Senator Hillary Clinton. Speaking at the American University, while Obama sat on a tall stool on stage behind him, Kennedy declared Obama ready to lead and, invoking his family's legacy, Kennedy said: 'The torch will be passed again to a new generation of Americans. The hope rises again. And the dream lives on.'[47] Kennedy's carefully choreographed endorsement of Obama – alongside that of JFK's daughter Caroline – was a game-changer in the race for the Democratic nomination.

> David Axelrod, Obama's senior adviser ... [maintained] that the weekend of Kennedy's endorsement 'transformed the campaign.' 'It was like being shot from a cannon,' Axelrod said. The day of the endorsement was, Obama told a Kennedy adviser at the time, the greatest day of his life ... [Kennedy] knew the impact he could have

in 2008. He timed his announcement for the lead-up to a national primary – Super Tuesday – where Obama was struggling to convince millions of voters who had barely heard of him that he was ready to be president. 'Senator Kennedy had an acute understanding of the way politics works and a particularly good understanding of the nominating process,' said the consultant, Tad Devine. 'When Kennedy stepped in the way he did, he essentially credentialed Obama.' Clinton's camp watched the endorsement with dismay. 'It was tremendously important and played a pivotal role in the campaign – as he has in politics and the Senate for decades,' said Clinton's chief strategist, Mark Penn, who had once also polled for Kennedy.[48]

Ted Kennedy's endorsement set Barack Obama on course to be president and, in this office, Obama proved himself to be 'in a league with the most gifted modern presidential public communicators – Franklin D. Roosevelt, John F. Kennedy and Ronald Reagan'.[49] President Kennedy described his brilliant speechwriter Ted Sorensen as 'his intellectual blood bank', while President Obama said that he relied on his wordsmith Cody Keenan 'to help tell America's story'.[50] In 'The Download', Cody Keenan's chapter in this book, he reveals what it was like to write with and for President Barack Obama. Having risen from mailroom intern in Ted Kennedy's office to chief speechwriter in the White House and having composed 3,577 speeches for President Obama, Keenan concludes that there is no magic formula to producing a superior script worthy of a presidential address. His task was helped, however, by the input of President Obama who focused on 'the story' and the choices his administration were trying to present to the American people.

John F. Kennedy had a deep knowledge of the history of the Democratic Party and he took pride in its achievements. At the 1964 Democratic National Convention in Atlantic City, Robert Kennedy recalled:

> President John F. Kennedy ... used to take great pride in telling of the trip that Thomas Jefferson and James Madison made up the Hudson River in 1800 on a botanical expedition searching for butterflies; that they ended up down in New York City and that they formed the Democratic Party. He took great pride in the fact that the Democratic

Party was the oldest political party in the world, and he knew that this linkage of Madison and Jefferson with the leaders in New York combined the North and South, and combined the industrial areas of the country with the rural farms and that this combination was always dedicated to progress and all of our Presidents have been dedicated to progress.[51]

In 2016, Senator Bernie Sanders's quest to become the standard-bearer of the Democratic Party was given a major boost when he won the New Hampshire primary with more votes than any candidate in its 100-year history. In 1960, John F. Kennedy had swept the boards in the New Hampshire primary, but he had only faced token opposition. Sanders's decisive victory in New Hampshire against Hillary Clinton shocked the Democratic Party establishment in a very changed political landscape. In his contribution to this book, Tad Devine, a chief strategist in Bernie Sanders's campaign, offers a unique insider's perspective of how the Vermont Senator's 2016 presidential bid was promoted. While Sanders ultimately failed to win the Democratic presidential nomination, Devine argues that his 2016 campaign had a profound and inspirational impact on the Democratic Party and United States politics that continues to reverberate today. Sanders managed to shift the policy platform of the Democratic Party to the left and to prioritise issues, such as healthcare for all, expanding educational opportunity, the need to protect senior citizens and fighting for working-class interests.

How much the policies of Bernie Sanders have been influenced by the Kennedy legacy has become a matter of contemporary debate. During the 2020 Democratic primaries, Sanders's second effort to secure the Democratic presidential nomination, he launched an advertisement praising President Kennedy, despite the fact that in the past he had uttered critical words about JFK, to the point of saying that he 'physically nauseated' him.[52] A week out from the 2020 New Hampshire primary, Caroline Kennedy penned an endorsement of Joe Biden for president.[53] Biden was perceived to be one of Sanders's main opponents in New Hampshire, but ended up badly trailing Sanders and Peter Buttigieg, the former mayor of South Bend, in that particular race. In March 2016, Robert Kennedy Jr had taken to Twitter to deny 'false and unauthorised media and social media assertions', that he had endorsed Bernie

Sanders.[54] However, Sanders himself, as well as a number of commentators, have argued that his politics draw heavily on the progressive, liberal tradition of Bobby Kennedy espoused during his 1968 campaign for president. Joe Biden, who ultimately defeated Sanders for the 2020 Democratic presidential nomination, is on record as saying that he had two political heroes growing up, Martin Luther King and Bobby Kennedy.[55]

In an interview to mark the fiftieth anniversary of the assassination of Robert Kennedy, his daughter, Kerry said: 'My father spent most of the '68 [presidential] campaign focused on healing the divisions within our country and he saw that this can get a lot worse than it was. Donald Trump came to power as somebody exploiting those divisions, and he has led through exploiting divisions, and that's extremely harmful to our country.'[56] In her contribution to this book, Kerry Kennedy reflects on the values advocated by her father and the wider Kennedy legacy. In particular, she speaks about how Robert Kennedy put peace, justice and compassion for those who had suffered at the heart of his vision for the United States of America. Kerry Kennedy maintains that there is 'a direct line' between her family's Irish heritage and the values advocated by John, Bobby and Ted Kennedy 'to stand up to oppression and to seek, to strive, to create a better world'. Reflecting on Patrick Kennedy's journey from New Ross and a famine-devastated Ireland, Kerry Kennedy contends that this strong and enduring connection with the place from whence the Kennedys came has helped to shape their political leanings.

Arguably no set of political brothers have inspired more people around the globe than John, Robert and Edward Kennedy. Even today, the Kennedy legacy has an enduring appeal. In their ancestral home of Ireland, the Kennedy family are still held in high esteem. Every year, in New Ross, international academics and political figures, media personalities and other interested parties gather to reflect on the Kennedy family's record of public service and to discuss broader themes relevant to Irish, American and global politics. Each of the chapters in this book have their origins in papers delivered at the Kennedy Summer School, which was founded in 2012 as a precursor to the series of events being held in County Wexford the following year to mark the fiftieth anniversary of President Kennedy's historic visit to Ireland in 1963. On his final day in Ireland, Kennedy pledged to 'come back in the springtime'. While tragedy intervened, the Kennedy legacy lives on. The words still have resonance, the hold on our imagination remains strong and the torch still brightly burns.

CHAPTER 1

IN SEARCH OF BRIDGET MURPHY, GREAT-GRANDMOTHER OF JFK

Celestine Murphy

Virtually all of the information we have about Bridget Murphy Kennedy comes from United States primary sources, principally the church registers, censuses, city directories, and birth, marriage and death civil records of Boston.[1] Apart from giving us details of Bridget's life in Boston, these sources can also provide us with clues to her origins and family in Ireland. Therefore, the names of baptismal sponsors, marriage witnesses and those designated in censuses as 'visitors' or 'boarders' in Bridget's Boston household became vital evidence in this research.

Our first glimpse of Bridget is when she marries Patrick Kennedy in the old Cathedral of the Holy Cross, Boston on 26 September 1849.[2] No civil record of this marriage is extant. This is a particularly unfortunate loss as the civil record of a marriage in nineteenth-century Massachusetts often included the ages of both parties and the names of their parents – information that would have made research on both Patrick and Bridget very much easier. The church record does supply the names of the witnesses to the marriage: Patrick Barron and Ann McGowan. I shall return to Patrick Barron in due course; Ann McGowan has not, as yet, been identified.

Patrick and Bridget Kennedy cannot be identified with any certainty in the 1850 United States census in Boston. However, it is possible to trace the couple after that, through the births of their children and through other censuses. As the addresses for the children's births show, the family moved several times in the following years. However, they were never far from the docks areas of East Boston, where Patrick, who was a cooper by trade, found steady employment. The next time we encounter them in official records is for the birth of their first child, Mary, on 6 August 1851 at Meridian Street.[3] Mary Kennedy was baptised at St Nicholas's Church a few days later when her baptismal sponsors were Nicholas Aspill and Joanna Barron.[4] Birth and baptismal details for the other children of Patrick and Bridget Kennedy are as follows:

> Joanna Kennedy, born at Meridian Street[5] and baptised at St Nicholas' church, 28 November 1852. Baptismal sponsors were Patrick Maloy [sic] and Bridget Aspill;[6]
> John Kennedy, born at Bremen Street and baptised at St Nicholas' church, 22 July 1854. Baptismal sponsors were Patrick Barron and Margaret Murphy.[7] John died the following year of cholera and was interred in Cambridge Catholic cemetery;[8]
> Margaret Kennedy, born at Eutaw Street and baptised 22 July 1855 at St Nicholas' church. Baptismal sponsors were John MacKenny and Mary Stafford;[9]
> Patrick Joseph Kennedy, born at Liverpool Street, 14 January 1858 and baptised at Most Holy Redeemer church (formerly St Nicholas' church), 16 January 1858. Baptismal sponsors were Allice Doyle and Mary Doyle.[10]

I have included details of the children's baptismal sponsors because some of their last names – Aspill and Barron in particular – point to a possible County Wexford connection, and because baptismal sponsors were (and are) often related to the parents of the child. However, as Boston-based professional genealogist Richard Andrew Pierce points out in a groundbreaking article published in 1992, no connection has ever been established in United States or Irish records between Patrick Kennedy and the Barrons or Aspills, so some kinship with Bridget Murphy Kennedy seems more likely for some of these sponsors.[11]

Conclusions from Pierce's meticulously researched article may be summarised as follows:

- Nicholas Aspill, one of the baptismal sponsors for Mary Kennedy in 1851, was a cooper from County Wexford, born c.1817 and arrived in the US in the late 1830s. He had a daughter, Bridget who is one of the baptismal sponsors for Joanna Kennedy in 1852. Bridget Aspill was born in the townland of Nash in the Roman Catholic parish of Ballycullane (formerly Tintern), Co. Wexford, in 1835. In the 1850 US census, Nicholas Aspill is living in the household of Patrick Barron.

- Patrick Barron, one of the baptismal sponsors for John Kennedy in 1854 and a witness at Bridget Murphy's marriage in 1849, was a cooper from County Wexford. His father's name was also Patrick Barron and his mother's name was Mary Aspill. His known siblings were James, Thomas and Joanna. Joanna Barron was a baptismal sponsor for Mary Kennedy in 1851.

- In Ireland, the Barrons lived in the townland of Cloonagh, Catholic parish of Ballycullane, Co. Wexford. The Tithe Applotment books[12] for Cloonagh in 1834 show a Patrick Barron on a holding of seventeen acres. Immediately to the east of the Barron holding is the land of a Richard Murphy. This measured sixteen acres. The Barrons left Ireland for Boston in the late 1830s and 1840s. Griffith's Valuation[13] of 1853 shows their former holding was by then in the name of a Patrick Roche. Richard Murphy was still on his holding in 1853.[14]

- Margaret Murphy, baptismal sponsor for John Kennedy in 1854, was Bridget Murphy's sister. She was listed in the Kennedy household in the 1855 census. In September 1857 she married Patrick Cleary, a labourer, in Holy Redeemer church; John Lynch and Joanna Barron witnessed the marriage. When Margaret died in Boston in 1880, Richard and Mary Murphy were named as her parents on her death certificate. When Bridget Murphy Kennedy died in 1888 her parents were also named as Richard and Mary Murphy.

- A search for children of Richard and Mary Murphy in the parish of Ballycullane turned up one result: the baptism of Edward Murphy on 18 May 1831, the son of Richard Murphy and Mary Barron. Baptismal sponsors were James Dunn and Mary Scott. No townland is mentioned. However, a short register of deaths for Ballycullane parish is extant for the period from October 1828 to January 1832. This shows that infant Edward Murphy of Cloonagh died on 5 June 1831.[15]

- The death record (1929) of Bridget Murphy's son, Patrick Joseph Kennedy gave his mother's name as Bridget *Barron*, not Murphy, an error that, as Andrew Pierce puts it, is 'very suggestive'. He concludes from this research that it is highly likely that Richard Murphy and Mary Barron were Bridget's parents and that Patrick and Mary (Aspill) Barron were either Bridget Murphy's maternal grandparents or her uncle and aunt.

Returning to the narrative of Bridget and Patrick's life in Boston, we find that tragedy befell the couple in 1855 when their young son, John, died of cholera. Immigrants in East Boston neighbourhoods endured grinding poverty, overcrowding, poor sanitation and ventilation, and a host of social problems. Outbreaks of cholera were common and consumption (tuberculosis) was a leading cause of death. Patrick's skills as a cooper were probably enough to keep his family from destitution but, when he died of consumption on 22 November 1858, Bridget was left with four young children to rear and without an income.

In the 1860 census Bridget is listed with her four children in a building with seven other families, including her sister Margaret and Margaret's husband, Patrick Cleary. Bridget's personal estate is given in the census as $75, an indication perhaps of her resourcefulness in grim circumstances.[16] Also listed in the household are two visitors, a young girl, Mary Roche and a small boy, aged 6, Michael O'Brien. I will come back to Mary Roche's presence in Bridget's household later.

In the 1865 state census, we find Bridget running a grocery business, something she would build upon and later expand into a bakery and a variety store. From the 1870 census we learn that Bridget could read but not write. By then, her two eldest daughters were old enough to contribute to the family income, with Mary working as a skirt maker and Johanna employed in a jute mill. Bridget's other children, Margaret, aged about 15, and Patrick Joseph (P.J.), aged about 12 years, are absent from the household.

By 1880, Bridget was living at 25 Border Street with her eldest daughter, Mary, and her son P.J. who is described as a brass finisher.[17] Also in the house are two young men, Martin and Laurence Kane, described as 'lodgers' and working as teamsters. The Kane brothers had emigrated to Boston in 1872. They can be traced back to Ballyhackbeg, County Wexford, a townland about eight miles south of Cloonagh and within Ballycullane Catholic parish. Their parents were Philip Kane and Margaret Murphy.[18] Although it is possible that Margaret Murphy Kane and Bridget Murphy Kennedy were related in some way, it cannot have been a near relationship as Margaret Kane's son, Laurence, married Bridget's eldest daughter, Mary, on 1 January 1883, in Holy Redeemer Catholic church.[19] Nevertheless, it seems likely that the presence in Bridget's household of two young men from her home parish in Wexford was not entirely coincidental and that Bridget had somehow remained in contact with her relations back in Wexford.

At this point, my research turned to the possibility of establishing if more of Bridget's siblings might have followed her to the United States.[20] Relying on Andrew Pierce's identification of Richard Murphy and Mary Barron as 'highly likely' to have been Bridget's parents, I searched the Massachusetts death records using the parameters 'born in Ireland' and the parents' names. Two of the results – Ann Murphy Kennedy and Catherine Murphy Roche – fitted these criteria. I then traced both women through United States censuses in the hope that some of their children were also born in Ireland and that their baptismal records might make the important link to Ballycullane or, more specifically, to Cloonagh.

I started with Ann because I was intrigued that she had also married a Patrick Kennedy. Ann first appears in the United States 1880 census. She is a widow and is living with her adult family in Salem, a town on the coast about sixteen miles north of Boston. Her children were all born in Ireland. A search through the Catholic marriage registers for Ballycullane (Tintern) found Ann's marriage to Patrick Kennedy on 23 February 1846. 'Cloonagh' is given as her place of residence and 'Adamstown' for her husband, Patrick Kennedy. James Hennessy and Richard Murphy are witnesses.

I then searched the Adamstown/Newbawn baptismal registers for their children and found the following individuals, all with an address at Misterin, a townland about ten miles north east of Cloonagh and within the Catholic parish of Adamstown: John Kennedy, bp. 8 May 1847; Thomas Kennedy, bp. 17 June 1849; Patrick Kennedy, bp. 3 April 1851; Mary Kennedy, bp. 1 May 1853; Moses Kennedy, bp. 20 November 1857. With the exception of Moses Kennedy, the names of Ann's adult children in the 1880 census correspond with these baptisms.

Moses was a common boys' name in County Wexford in the nineteenth century and well into the twentieth century.[21] However, its uniqueness in the United States proved most useful in searching through the Massachusetts death registers, where I found Moses had died of liver disease in Salem in 1872. This gave me a date before which he moved to the United States, presumably with a parent or older sibling as he was quite young. A search for him in the emigration records found him arriving at Boston in 1871 on board the *Tripoli* out of Liverpool. With him were his mother, Ann Murphy Kennedy and one of his brothers, Patrick. I also discovered that Moses had been buried in St Mary's cemetery in Salem, and that his name is included on a headstone there. It reads: 'KENNEDY Patrick, died in County Wexford, Ireland in 1871 age seventy-seven. His wife ANN died in Salem in 1893, age sixty-five. MOSES died 1872, age thirteen. THOMAS died 2 January 1921'.

Although the ages at death of Patrick, Ann and Moses are incorrect,[22] it is clear that Ann Murphy was considerably younger than her husband, Patrick Kennedy, possibly by as much as twenty-five years. This was a feature of Famine and post-Famine Ireland when parents became the arbiters of who and when their children, especially their female children, would marry. This may explain Richard Murphy's presence as a witness at his daughter Ann's marriage in 1846. According to Griffith's Valuation, Patrick Kennedy's holding in Misterin was of thirty-four acres, he had a sizeable house, and could offer his new wife and prospective children a better life than Richard's sixteen acres could afford.[23]

Ann's sons, John and Thomas, emigrated to the United States in 1866 and 1869 respectively. According to his naturalisation papers filed in 1872, John entered through the port of New York. One of his naturalisation sponsors is a John Roche, most likely one of Catherine Murphy Roche's sons. In contrast, Thomas entered the country through the port of Boston but did not file his naturalisation papers until 1883. One of his sponsors is an Edward Roche, who is also, I believe, one of Catherine Roche's sons. It is not clear when Ann's daughter, Margaret Kennedy arrived in the United States, but she may have arrived with her brother Thomas in 1869. After her husband Patrick died in 1870/1, Ann Murphy Kennedy brought Patrick and

Moses to Boston and on to Salem where her sister Catherine's family was already established.

I followed a similar research path for Catherine Murphy Roche. Unfortunately, at the time that Catherine married, the parish priest did not provide addresses in the marriage register unless one of the parties was from another parish. Therefore, all that could be established was that both Catherine Murphy and Nicholas Roche were from Ballycullane parish. The couple were married on 24 February, 1835, with witnesses Martin Redmond and Mary Murphy. Their nine children, who were all born in Arklow townland in Ballycullane parish, were as follows: Martin Roche, b.1836; John Roche, b.1837; Mary Roche, b.1839; Simon Roche, b.1840; Catherine Roche, b.1842; Richard Roche, b.1844; James Roche born c.1846;[24] Margaret Roche, b.1848; Edward Roche, b.1850.

It is clear from United States censuses and death registers that not all of these children emigrated. Catherine's eldest son, Martin remained in Ireland and I have been unable to trace Simon (b.1840) or Catherine (b.1842) in the United States. Catherine's eldest daughter, Mary definitely emigrated: she is the Mary Roche listed in Bridget Kennedy's household in Boston in the 1860 census. It appears that the family emigrated in stages, beginning before 1857 with Catherine's husband, Nicholas Roche, and possibly their eldest daughter, Mary and their son, John. However, Nicholas died of consumption in June 1857 at Meridian Street, Boston, not far from where Patrick and Bridget Kennedy lived. According to the record of his death, he was 50 years old.

Catherine's second eldest son, John was already in Salem in 1860, working as a factory operative. In 1866 he married Ellen Alice Doherty from St John's, New Brunswick, Canada. By 1870 his mother Catherine, and his siblings Richard, James, Edward and Margaret were living near him in Salem, and by 1880 his aunt, Ann Murphy Kennedy was living in the same neighbourhood with her adult children, Mary, Patrick, Thomas and John.

Meanwhile, back in Boston, Bridget Murphy Kennedy continued to prosper, living to witness her son, Patrick Joseph become a Massachusetts state congressman and senator, and the birth of her grandson, Joseph Kennedy, JFK's father. Bridget died of a cerebral haemorrhage in December 1888. According to her death record, she was 67 years old.[25] Her estate included $825 in stock and fixtures of her Border Street store, and a $1,000 mortgage against her daughter Johanna Kennedy Mahoney.[26] Catherine Murphy Roche died on 3 July 1896, at 57 Condor Street, Boston of 'old age and exhaustion'. It is not clear why she had returned to live in Boston. Her sister, Ann Murphy Kennedy died of bronchopneumonia in Salem on 17 July 1893.

The focus of my research now moved back to Ireland and the Murphy holding at Cloonagh. It is not known when Richard Murphy died but it was certainly before 1866 when we find that 'the widow Murphy of Cloonagh' paid two shillings and six pence for a dog licence for a red mastiff.[27] The 'widow Murphy' was, of course, Mary Barron Murphy, Bridget's mother, who must, by 1866, have been in her late 60s or early 70s at least.[28] Curious as to what had happened to the holding at Cloonagh after Mary's death, I searched the 1901 census for the townland. To my surprise, Catherine Murphy Roche's son, Martin Roche, who had remained in Ireland when the rest of his family had emigrated to the United States in the 1850s and 1860s, was now the tenant and the head of household at Cloonagh. He had not married but living with him was Johanna Murphy, described as his aunt and therefore the last known surviving sister of Bridget Murphy Kennedy. The dwelling at Cloonagh is described in the census as stone-built, hard-roofed and single-roomed, with five windows to the front, and three outhouses (a stable, cow house and barn). It had probably changed very little since Richard Murphy's day.[29]

As Martin Roche now owned the tenancy of the Cloonagh holding, I wondered if he had appeared at the New Ross sub-commission which was formed during the 1890s to examine rents on the Colclough estate and which was widely reported in local newspapers. An online search in the *New Ross Standard* found a report of Martin's evidence to the sub-commission in May 1896. It is worth quoting in full for the additional information it provides:

> James Murphy, Cloonagh, tenant. Area, sixteen acres no roods thirty-one perches; rent £8; valuation £10. Mr Colfer for the tenant. Martin Roche said he managed the farm for his uncle, James Murphy and deposed that the rent was raised three times. He had three-quarters of an acre of bog in Boley which was no use to him but he would not be satisfied to give it up. He reclaimed six acres and levelled sixty perches

of fences and put up sixty perches of new fences. He planted a good deal of trees, but the rats eat the half of them (laughter). Mr Flanagan valued at eighteen shillings. Landlord's valuation not produced.[30]

Obviously, James Murphy is another of Bridget's siblings and almost certainly the eldest of the family. He died, unmarried, at Cloonagh a few months later of senile decay, aged 85 years.[31] A browse through local newspapers for further information on James Murphy suggested that he had been involved with the land agitation movements in the 1870s and 1880s and that he had been a staunch supporter of Irish nationalist politician, Charles Stewart Parnell.

Martin Roche's aunt, Johanna Murphy died at Cloonagh in 1904 of senile decay and Martin died there in May 1907, also of senile decay. Surprisingly, Martin left a will, and the administration of his estate went to a Hugh Hennessey, a mercantile clerk. Martin's estate amounted to 172 pounds two shillings and six pence. In October 1907 the tenancy interest in Martin's farm at Cloonagh was put up for auction and was acquired by James Shannon of nearby Shannon's Mill for £215.[32] In the 1911 census, the house is vacant.

In late September 2019, I found my way to Cloonagh and, with the owners' permission, to the grove where the Barron and Murphy houses once stood. The remains of a lime kiln are visible at the entrance to a lane that leads up to the grove.[33] Although the lane is overgrown, it is still possible to see the low stone walls on either side of it. The Barron house has long since disappeared.[34] However, the remains of some of the Murphy buildings are still visible in the undergrowth, although it is impossible now to determine the type of building. The grove is full of trees of various types and, as I walked through them back to my car, I thought, Martin Roche would be pleased; the rats did not eat them all.

CHAPTER 2

'A HARMLESS REASSURANCE': JOSEPH KENNEDY, FDR AND THE 1938 ANGLO-IRISH AGREEMENTS

Michael Kennedy

I

On 25 April 1938, Ireland's Taoiseach and Minister for External Affairs Éamon de Valera and Britain's Prime Minister Neville Chamberlain were the primary signatories to a tripartite agreement between Ireland and Britain covering trade, finance and defence.[1] The trade agreement ended the 'economic war', a trade dispute between Britain and Ireland that had begun in the early 1930s. The finance agreement wrote off Irish debts owed to Britain in return for a £10 million lump sum payment from the Irish exchequer. The defence component returned to Ireland the three 'Treaty Ports', defended anchorages held by Britain at Cobh, Berehaven and Lough Swilly and it ended British rights under the 1921 Anglo-Irish Treaty to facilities in Ireland in wartime.

The defence agreement would be of critical importance to British–Irish relations during the Second World War, the looming context in which it was negotiated. The return of the ports saw the withdrawal of the remaining British military units from the state. Their departure allowed Ireland to later declare a meaningful form of neutrality during the Second World War and to facilitate its own defence. Since at least 1935 de Valera had stressed that

Ireland would be neutral in a future European war; now, with Ireland clear of foreign forces, this hitherto aspirational policy could be put into effect.[2] The 1938 agreements set the basis for an officially neutral, covertly co-operative Ireland on Britain's western flank in time of war.

The day the tripartite agreements were signed de Valera wrote to United States President Franklin D. Roosevelt, thanking him for affording help 'most opportunely at a critical moment in the progress of the negotiations'.[3] Historians have argued that Roosevelt, via the newly arrived United States Ambassador to Britain, Joseph P. Kennedy, influenced Chamberlain to bring the negotiations to a successful conclusion and that de Valera had reason to be grateful to the President.[4]

But could it really be so? In 1938 Britain was not greatly interested in Irish opinion. However, London was concerned about the impact British–Irish affairs had on views of Britain in the United States. De Valera hoped to persuade Chamberlain and British officials that the successful negotiation of an Anglo-Irish agreement would enhance Britain's standing in America. A few choice words of support from Washington might enable this outcome. Perhaps, given the choppy nature of Anglo-American relations in 1938 and the pro-Irish stance of United States Minister to Ireland John Cudahy, de Valera felt it would be judged opportune in Washington to intervene directly in Anglo-Irish affairs via the incoming American ambassador to the Court of St James. Yet would Washington really put support for Dublin in British–Irish relations before the Anglo-American 'Special Relationship'? What help was de Valera looking for, and what did he expect Roosevelt, and by extension Kennedy, could do for Ireland? Where in the 1938 agreements is Kennedy's intervention reflected? This essay examines the role of Joseph P. Kennedy and Franklin D. Roosevelt, in the 1938 Anglo-Irish agreements and it touches briefly, by way of conclusion, on where the episode fits into the triangle of British–Irish–American relations in the twentieth century.

II

The initial diplomatic choreography of Kennedy's journey to London is a revealing place to start this exploration. News broke in early December 1937 that Kennedy had been offered the London post.[5] Kennedy's closeness to Roosevelt was expected to make him one of the most influential members of the London diplomatic corps. Yet in Dublin there was initially an inexplicable lack of interest in the appointment of a prominent Irish-American Catholic as United States ambassador to the Court of St James. The appointment of such a diplomat who was also a supporter of Neville Chamberlain and a supporter of appeasement should have immediately appealed to Irish foreign policymakers. De Valera had a good working relationship with Chamberlain, he too supported appeasement. The Taoiseach had advocated at the League of Nations appeasement as a means of resolving differences between states before they went to war and would later openly support Chamberlain during the Munich crisis of September 1938.[6]

In reality Kennedy's interest in Ireland was limited. Despite fulsome speeches when it suited on his Irish background, he saw himself as American first and foremost and he did not want to get bracketed as tending solely to his own ethnic group.[7] He had 'declined to consider' the post of Minister to Dublin when offered it by Roosevelt in 1934. Having talked it over with his wife Rose they decided it 'wasn't of any particular interest'.[8]

With Kennedy planning to leave for London, de Valera finally displayed a growing realisation that Kennedy, Roosevelt and wider United States political opinion needed to be made aware of and engaged with ending the partition of Ireland. When United States Minister to Dublin John Cudahy met with de Valera on 14 January 1938 as the British–Irish negotiations were about to commence, the Taoiseach told him 'with great earnestness that he regarded the impending conference as of vital importance to the American people because of the great sympathetic interest in the United States for Ireland's cause, the inherent justice of that cause and because the peace of the world was involved'.[9] When Cudahy told de Valera that Kennedy would probably not be in London during the negotiations, the Taoiseach was 'visibly disappointed'.[10] De Valera, as Deirdre McMahon has put it, 'wanted, indeed expected, the American government to play its part in the forthcoming negotiations'.[11] The scene was being set in Irish official and political minds for an American démarche into Anglo-Irish relations.

The talks in London, which began in January 1938, were de Valera's first direct negotiations with the British government since coming to power in 1932. He saw them as a real opportunity to end the partition of Ireland. De Valera speculated that the settlement of partition would bring Britain the extra goodwill it wished for from the United States. The Taoiseach hoped for a deal on defence in return for an ending of partition. Chamberlain outflanked him by announcing that he would unconditionally return the ports to Ireland. Chamberlain was also willing to do a deal on the land annuities and on British–Irish financial relations.[12] However, there were limits to Chamberlain's appeasement of Ireland. Conscious of opinion within his own Conservative Party, that Northern Ireland Prime Minister Sir James Craig had just called a general election, and that the majority in Northern Ireland did not want a united Ireland, Chamberlain said there would be no deal on partition against the wishes of the majority of the people of Northern Ireland.

On 22 January 1938, the Secretary of the Department of External Affairs Joseph Walshe wrote to de Valera of the need to make the United States more concerned about seeking the end of partition.[13] Irish diplomats were now scheming that Kennedy's presence in London could be of value to British–Irish relations. De Valera instructed Ireland's Minister to Washington Michael MacWhite to brief Secretary of State Cordell Hull on the progress of the negotiations and to impress on him the potential of a successful outcome in the talks for improving Anglo-American relations. Dublin calculated that Hull would then put pressure on Britain to end partition in return for an agreement with Dublin. Walshe hypothesised that 'a word from Cordell Hull to the British Ambassador in Washington would have more weight than all the propaganda we can put together'.[14]

Dublin's timing was bad. MacWhite, who knew Roosevelt personally, was about to be recalled from the United States to become Ireland's first Minister to Italy. Posted to Washington since 1929, MacWhite understood American politics and was a popular envoy in official circles in the United States capital. He was replaced by his second-in-command Robert Brennan, a confidante of de Valera's, but a man who lacked MacWhite's diplomatic abilities, and who was absent from Washington during much of the London negotiations. Brennan did not present his credentials until October 1938. The Department of External Affairs demonstrated poor judgement in leaving the Irish legation in Washington effectively vacant when trying to court United States opinion on the matter of British–Irish relations. It was a stunning lapse in diplomatic strategy. It is one also which suggests that de Valera overestimated Ireland's influence in Washington and the Roosevelt White House.

Before MacWhite made his démarche James Farley, Chairman of the Democratic National Committee, had already requested Roosevelt to intervene in the London negotiations. Farley urged Roosevelt to act because it would impress Irish-American voters in the upcoming midterm elections in November 1938. His arguments were reinforced by Cudahy, who sent Roosevelt a confidential letter arguing for American intervention via a conversation between the President and Sir Ronald Lindsay, the British Ambassador in Washington. As the British–Irish talks in London were, in Cudahy's opinion, bound to fail, 'from a purely American viewpoint' he thought it 'important that you do this for if this opportunity of settling the Anglo-Irish hostility of seven centuries is lost no other such opportunity will be presented during this generation'.[15] Cudahy surmised that an Ireland friendly to Great Britain would mean the approval by a sizeable share of American public opinion of closer Anglo-American relations. The successful appeasement of Ireland might well also have implications for the future success of Chamberlain's similar initiatives in relation to other states, particularly Germany, over its territorial claims for Anschluss with Austria, which came to a head during the 1938 British–Irish talks, and later with Czechoslovakia over the Sudetenland.

De Valera really had only one thing on his mind at this early stage of the London talks: using the negotiations to end partition. Having lost his majority in the Dáil in the July 1937 general election he wished to use the negotiations to assuage public opinion in Ireland. Yet he was having little success with Chamberlain over ending partition. Faced with Chamberlain's flat rejection of any movement towards a united Ireland, de Valera decided to appeal further to American public opinion and directly to President Roosevelt. Interviewed by the *New York Times* and the International News Agency of America, he proposed an all-Ireland council as a precursor to unity. The results seemed good. Walshe wrote to de Valera that 'American opinion is playing a very important part in the negotiations.'[16] In London, Walshe also conveyed this to the Dominions Secretary Malcolm MacDonald in an attempt to kick-start British thinking in favour of ending the partition of Ireland.

Having completed his United States groundwork in the press and diplomatically via MacWhite, de Valera wrote personally to Roosevelt on 25 January explaining that the London negotiations were an opportunity 'for finally ending the quarrel of centuries between Ireland and Britain'.[17] Partition was the 'one remaining obstacle to be overcome', and, Britain, having partitioned Ireland, could end partition and bring about a united Ireland. De Valera further emphasised to Roosevelt that he had tried and failed to bring Britain around to this view.

De Valera contended that 'reconciliation would affect every country where the two races dwell together, knitting their national strength and presenting to the world a great block of democratic peoples interested in the preservation of Peace'. Knowing Roosevelt's interest in world peace he continued by asking 'whether you could not use your influence to get the British Government to realize what would be gained by reconciliation and to get them to move whilst there is time. In a short while, if the present negotiations fail, relations will be worsened.' De Valera thus sought United States influence not over the defence, trade and finance parts of the negotiations, but over ending the partition of Ireland.

De Valera's letter to Roosevelt was delivered by Frank Gallagher, de Valera's personal emissary, not by a representative from the Irish Legation in Washington as it would then have had to go through the thoroughly Anglophile State Department. De Valera told Cudahy during the negotiations that 'he did not repose great confidence in the American State Department, being under the impression that it was subject to a pro-Anglo tendency'.[18]

Roosevelt's reply to the Taoiseach on 22 February was choreographed to fit with Kennedy's departure for Britain by liner the following day. Roosevelt explained that he was 'greatly in sympathy with the thought of reconciliation, especially because any reconciliation would make itself felt in every part of the world. It would also strengthen democracy everywhere.'[19] But he said he could not officially, or through diplomatic channels, 'accomplish anything or even discuss the matter'. He was acting indirectly: 'I have taken the course of asking my friend, Mr Joseph P. Kennedy, who sails today for England to take up his post as ambassador, to convey a personal message from me to the prime minister, and to tell the prime minister how happy I should be if reconciliation could be brought about.' But what form of reconciliation did he mean, and between whom?

Arriving in Cobh on 1 March, Kennedy told journalists that as a neophyte diplomat he hoped that he would 'not make too many mistakes. In the past I have always been dealing with something with which I was familiar, but this is all completely new.'[20] When questioned about the negotiation of an Anglo-American trade pact, he parried the question by referring to the British–Irish negotiations and hoped that they would lead to closer friendship between the two countries.[21] This was not de Valera's hoped for reference to ending partition, but a direct reference to improved British–Irish relations. *The Irish Times* hoped that Kennedy's enthusiasm and 'friendly, if forceful, nature should do much to strengthen the bonds of Anglo-American friendship'.[22] That was the public side and it was deemed significant that Kennedy said after arriving in London that 'he began his new job on the same day as the Irish Ministers arrived from Dublin for the final stage of the Anglo-Irish talks'.[23] It was suggested that Kennedy wished to meet de Valera and would soon visit Ireland. A meeting in London could easily be arranged. It was noted by journalists that John Dulanty, Ireland's High Commissioner in London, had already made a courtesy call on Kennedy. In fact Dulanty had simply left his card and asked for a meeting to be arranged at an unspecified future date.

By mid-March 1938 the British–Irish negotiations had reached a critical stage. The two outstanding issues were the attitude of the British government towards Irish reunification and that of the Irish government towards trade concessions for Northern Ireland, which would improve access to the Irish market. Neither side was willing to give. It appeared the negotiations would collapse. Then, as Kennedy presented his credentials to King George VI on 8 March, the general prospects of a British–Irish agreement on trade, and possibly defence were suddenly deemed by *The Irish Times* to be 'better than they were last week'.[24] Defence had come to the fore and all talk of partition had been dropped. The press reported that de Valera and his ministers might remain in London. Perhaps there was a connection between Kennedy's arrival and progress in the negotiations?

On 14 March de Valera told Cudahy that when he left London two days earlier the negotiations had as good as collapsed.[25] Two days earlier was 12 March 1938, the day Nazi Germany occupied Austria. The time was right for a surgical diplomatic démarche by Roosevelt and Kennedy. On 15 March Dulanty met Kennedy at the American Embassy. Dulanty's subsequent report of the meeting to Walshe, which de Valera kept in his private papers, gives an insight into the limits of what Roosevelt and Kennedy would do to assist the British–Irish negotiations and honour de

Valera's request for assistance.[26] When talking to Dulanty, Kennedy effectively avoided the negotiations completely. He bluntly told Dulanty that 'he did not wish to ask questions' about the progress 'of the negotiations ... but he would like to be allowed to say how much he hoped that they might reach fruition.' However, 'speaking in the strictest confidence', and in terms to be communicated to de Valera only, he said Roosevelt viewed a British–Irish settlement as 'a matter of importance in regard to the question of Anglo-American relations'. Not British–Irish relations. Then there was the critical caveat. This was the President's opinion, but 'it could not be regarded as the opinion of the American Government since the subject had not been through or fully considered by the State Department'. The Americans were officially backing off. Nevertheless, Kennedy told Dulanty that he had himself spoken to Chamberlain, whom he called 'a good friend of Éire', 'acquainting him with President Roosevelt's opinion'. The United States government saw the negotiations in an Anglo-American light. They would not put Dublin before London and Roosevelt would not formally get involved in British–Irish relations, nor would he specifically exert influence over ending the partition of Ireland. Dulanty's report laid out clearly the limits of American intervention in British–Irish relations. Via Kennedy, Roosevelt would give little more, as John Bowman has written, than 'a harmless reassurance'.[27]

Nevertheless, three days later de Valera, having been in contact with his officials in London, was more hopeful of a settlement on trade and finance. Defence remained to be dealt with as did a proposed preferential trade regime for Northern Ireland that de Valera wanted removed. If Belfast got special treatment de Valera held that the 'negotiations would fail in their entirety'.[28] He told Cudahy that 'Partition remained undecided and had been dismissed from the agenda, but his position on this issue was just as unshakeable as ever. No significant reconciliation was possible with the partition of Ireland remaining an open wound and he was satisfied that sometime during his lifetime the partition issue must be resolved satisfactorily.'

Chamberlain told his Cabinet that Kennedy 'had spoken strongly to him of the valuable effect on opinion in America of an agreement with Éire'.[29] Had the Prime Minister listened? Britain wanted to improve its relationship with the United States. Perhaps Kennedy had achieved something after all? The argument then goes that after Kennedy's intervention the British duly dropped some of their trade demands, including a demand that de Valera give trade concessions to imports from Northern Ireland, handed over the three Treaty Ports, made financial concessions and concluded the three separate agreements on 22 April 1938 with the Irish government.[30] But much of this had already been decided. The difficult question of the trading relationship between Northern Ireland and Ireland was solved by discussions between Chamberlain and Craig on 11 April and the provision of financial assistance to Northern Ireland.[31] The final details of the defence agreement to return the ports were tidied up. The agreements were signed in London on 25 April.

Had Kennedy's involvement really done anything to alter the mood of the negotiations, or even their outcome? Chamberlain makes no mention of Kennedy's intervention in those of his letters to his family that have been published. However, one letter of 16 April 1938 to his sister Hilda does show Kennedy trying to set the mood to the negotiations by telling Chamberlain that de Valera had told Kennedy that Chamberlain was 'the only British minister he had met who made him feel that he could believe what I said'.[32] As de Valera and Chamberlain were already on good terms this chattering achieved little. The decision on returning the ports was taken in January and Chamberlain had already made up his mind on certain financial and trade concessions. The Northern Ireland trade question was solved within a United Kingdom context without outside assistance. Roosevelt's initiative via Kennedy achieved precious little. It was not a turning point in the negotiations and there was no British change of mind on partition as a result. There is no certainty that the new United States ambassador achieved anything, but then style and appearance mattered over substance to the former Hollywood investor Joe Kennedy.[33]

De Valera knew he had failed in his initiative to invoke United States influence over Britain in the 1938 talks. But he retained his composure. De Valera might need to appeal for American intervention in British–Irish affairs at a later date and he would certainly continue to court Kennedy who visited Ireland in June 1938 and was feted and awarded an honorary doctorate from the National University of Ireland.[34] On 22 April, the day the final texts of the 1938 Agreements were concluded, de Valera wrote again to Roosevelt.[35] On the surface de Valera appeared grateful for Roosevelt's personal intervention via Kennedy. The text is short but nuanced. In essence it is subtly critical of Roosevelt. The intimation is that the United States intervention in the negotiations achieved nothing. In a delicately phrased paragraph, de Valera praised Roosevelt: 'knowledge of the fact that you were interested came most opportunely at a critical moment in the progress of the negotiations'. So far so good; it was gratifying to know Roosevelt was 'interested' when the talks were almost at collapse. But de Valera then pointedly cast Chamberlain, not Roosevelt, as the key figure, continuing that 'were it not for Mr. Chamberlain personally the negotiations would have broken down at that time, and I am sure that the knowledge of your interest in the success of the negotiations had its due weight in determining his attitude'. Superficially positive yet damning with faint praise. The sentences could be read as one wished them. Can one really assume that they were universally positive? De Valera and Walshe were masters of the multiple meaning. Chamberlain was cast as the hero who saved the day. In a more fulsome letter to Malcolm MacDonald de Valera wrote of Chamberlain and MacDonald as 'the happy combination' making the negotiations successful.[36] Roosevelt was off centre stage in de Valera's mind and Kennedy was not the *deus ex machina* he thought he was.[37]

An agreement had been reached, Roosevelt would already know this from Cudahy, Kennedy and the international press when he got the letter. He would see the text in the ordinary way. There was no swiftly coded telegram of thanks to Washington to be delivered by emissaries from the Irish legation to the White House. There could not be as this was a private matter and there was no State Department involvement. Nor was Gallagher despatched again with a private message. De Valera's letter to Roosevelt was a polite acknowledgement that hid within it the Taoiseach's defeat and failure at playing the American card. There was general satisfaction in Dublin and London over the 1938 agreement, but, de Valera gloomily explained to Roosevelt, 'Unfortunately, however, the matter which most affects national sentiment – the ending of the partition of our country – finds no place in the agreement. A complete reconciliation, to the importance of which I referred in my previous letter, remains still for the future. All we can hope is that the present agreement will be a step towards it.'

The Taoiseach began to close by expressing his 'thanks for your kind interest, and for your assistance'. Aware of the problems facing the United States, he was 'deeply grateful that you could find time to give a thought to ours'.

A thought was what it had been; a thought by the United States not to get involved. It was hardly an action that, as Roosevelt later boasted, made him 'largely responsible' for the eventual 1938 Agreement.[38] In reality, Roosevelt had politely rebuffed de Valera. Kennedy had done what he was tasked to do and given lip service to his Irish constituency with the midterm elections coming up. He even made a courtesy call on de Valera on 22 April, the day the agreements were concluded and, in Kennedy's later words told the Taoiseach that the agreement was 'a remarkably fine job'.[39] But there were bigger and more important global matters at stake, particularly in central Europe, than Ireland for the United States Ambassador. London trumped Dublin in American eyes and America would stay out of Irish affairs.

De Valera hoped that United States involvement in Irish affairs would continue. In handwritten notes for a press briefing on 23 April he thanked the United States for its 'friendly interest' in seeing an end to Anglo-Irish antagonism, adding that it was 'an important factor in making this agreement possible'.[40] Looking to the future he hoped 'that interest will remain active until the full solution is reached' and Ireland was again united. No avenues would close.

III

Kennedy was looking globally and supported Chamberlain and appeasement. There was no way Kennedy was going to upset the British Prime Minister by siding with de Valera and calling for an end to partition and a united Ireland. America's policy of non-intervention in Irish affairs was set. This was the perennial problem that faced Irish diplomats engaging with the United States over Northern Ireland. Paraphrasing Ronan Fanning, the Anglo-American alliance, having become central to the conduct of American foreign policy since 1917, meant that no United States President was subsequently prepared to respond to Irish representations on ending partition in a manner that might seriously offend Britain.[41] Fanning gave three examples – the Sinn Féin delegation were refused access to the Paris peace conference in 1919, notwithstanding the obvious relevance to their case of President Woodrow Wilson's doctrine of self-determination. Subsequent requests for the recognition of the Irish Republic during the Anglo-Irish War also fell on deaf ears in Washington. Then the basis of what became the set

American position on partition emerged during the Boundary Commission negotiations of 1924 to 1925 when the American Ambassador in London was instructed to do nothing that might imply that his government would take sides in the border dispute.[42] Roosevelt had continued this when he explained to Cudahy in January 1938 that the United States would not intervene in the 1938 talks:

> a final solution of Anglo-Irish relations, and of the Irish internal problem, would be an immeasurable gain from every point of view, but I am not convinced that any intervention, no matter how indirect, on our part would be wise or for that matter accomplish the effect we had in mind. In the long run considerations of national defence may well lead England voluntarily to take the action … She is not blind to such considerations, but I feel it would be a healthier solution, even if a slower one, if her decision were reached voluntarily, and on the basis of her own self-interest, than as a result of representation from a third power.[43]

Kennedy sought to applaud Chamberlain's success with the 1938 Agreements. In late June while on a return visit to the United States he said the British Prime Minister was 'touched with genius' and he saw 'Britain's settlement of the Irish question … as the "outstanding achievement of British statesmanship in the last 300 years".'[44] This was wrong and a gross overstatement. But Kennedy's remarks placed the 1938 Agreement in a European context as seen through his continuation that 'Now Mr. Chamberlain can go ahead with his policy of dealing with the dictator nations with a reputation for fair dealing established, and no one can say to him … anything about cleaning up a situation in his own back yard.' The 1938 Agreement had, Kennedy continued, found 'Chamberlain firmly on the side of generosity at every phase of the negotiations, and Mr. de Valera was left with a high regard for the heads of the British Government.' The 1938 Agreement 'gave great hope for the peace of the world and was idealism in its highest form'. It had proved to the world Kennedy explained 'that when Mr. Chamberlain set out to make a "bargain" he "concluded a fair agreement"'.

The negotiations over the 1938 Anglo-Irish Agreement produced friction between Kennedy and Roosevelt. Both claimed credit for helping to bring agreement about.[45] Roosevelt's advisers spread the rumour that 'Kennedy got himself into a little trouble for posing' since he 'had set himself up as the mediator'.[46] They said that 'Kennedy had had absolutely nothing to do with [the negotiations].' The real catalyst they argued was Roosevelt's sympathetic recommendations and letters of encouragement to Chamberlain and de Valera. A 1974 biographer of Kennedy, David Koskoff, cites an interview where Malcolm MacDonald concluded that Kennedy had 'only marginal influence if any' on the negotiations.[47] Kennedy exaggerated the effect he had on the British position to make leading Irish-Americans like James Farley jealous. Perhaps he had his own possible candidature for the 1940 United States Presidential election in mind?

Joseph P. Kennedy ran rings around de Valera, Dulanty and Walshe. Irish diplomats and politicians would have to up their game when it came to the USA. It was not enough simply to write to the President to ask him to get involved. The special relationship with Britain was far too important for any American President to risk over Ireland. From 1922 to 1977 successive United States administrations resisted any Irish suggestions to intervene in Irish affairs and over partition. American national interest demanded that Britain rank higher than Ireland on any presidential agenda. The 1938 agreements showed that Irish diplomats and politicians would have to up their game when it came to dealing with Washington, the State Department and the White House. It was not enough to seek a meeting with the Secretary of State and to write to the President to ask him to get involved while engaging a friendly United States Minister to Ireland. Lobbying, pressure and a constant long-term diplomatic effort were needed. This would not come until the early 1970s. In 1938 Ireland lacked an effective diplomatic presence in Washington DC. The small Irish legation was more interested in pleasing Irish-American opinion, particularly Catholic opinion, than building relations with the White House, the State department and Capitol Hill. De Valera's letter to Roosevelt seeking his assistance overestimated his influence on the President of the United States and miscalculated American interest in Irish affairs.

If Joseph Kennedy's fleeting involvement in the negotiations for the 1938 Anglo-Irish Agreement tells us anything, it shows his consummate cunning, how he valued how he appeared to people over what he was, and his being all things to all people and emphasising his own role in affairs of state. He was an exemplary public relations man, particularly for himself and the historiography of his involvement in the 1938 Agreements shows this. Historians of Irish foreign policy, in particular Deirdre McMahon and John Bowman, have discounted his involvement. Some histories of the Kennedy family, such as that by Maier quoted in the early pages of this essay, are more willing to accept Joseph Kennedy's account of his role. However, more recent works, such as David Nasaw's *The Patriarch*, published in 2012, do not even mention a place for Kennedy in the events of January to April 1938.[48] Kennedy had little real interest in helping Ireland. He could not see the rationale for Irish unity. In a diary entry from March 1939 he noted a meeting with de Valera in Rome where the 'principal subject [was that] England should permit Northern Ireland to come in with Southern Ireland and if necessary let them all return their privileges. I never understood this'.[49]

There remains no compelling evidence to show that Kennedy's intervention had any impact on the 1938 negotiations. De Valera played the American card in hope rather than expectation. It had been an amateur performance, one that continued with the awarding of an honorary doctorate to Kennedy by de Valera as Chancellor of the National University of Ireland in Dublin in summer 1938 and which no doubt would have continued during de Valera's ultimately cancelled visit to the United States in 1939. Kennedy's involvement in the negotiation of the 1938 agreements showed that de Valera and the Department of External Affairs needed to act more strategically to engage the United States in British–Irish relations. It would take at least a generation and the outbreak of the Troubles for the Irish government to really begin to work to harness United States political opinion. When it did, it led to the 1977 Carter initiative, Ronald Reagan's influence on Margaret Thatcher leading to the 1985 Anglo-Irish Agreement and Bill Clinton's vital interventions to support the peace process and the Good Friday Agreement. This was in stark contrast to what had happened in 1938.

CHAPTER 3

ELECTING KENNEDY

Donnacha Ó Beacháin

Introduction

John Fitzgerald Kennedy's rise through national politics was meteoric, from winning a place in Congress in his late 20s and a Senate seat during his mid-30s to taking the presidency while still in his early 40s. These successes can be attributed in large part to JFK's father, Joseph Kennedy, a multi-billionaire in today's money. The Kennedy patriarch pursued with unrelenting zeal his ambition to have a son in the White House and JFK's path to power was paved with his father's largesse and influence. Most assessments of Kennedy's electoral performance confine themselves to the 1960 campaign when he became the youngest ever candidate and the first Catholic to win a United States presidential election. This appraisal, however, traces JFK's political career back to his campaigns for Congress and the Senate. As documented here, Joseph Kennedy's influence and fabulous riches underpinned all of JFK's elections, but despite Kennedy's profound wealth he managed to present himself as an outsider.

In his battles for seats in Congress and the Senate the family fortune enabled Kennedy, despite his conspicuous youth and lack of political experience, to overwhelm rivals in an avalanche of money and publicity. Kennedy's wealth also produced vital victories in the primaries that secured the Democratic Party presidential nomination. During Kennedy's presidential campaign in 1960, he had to deflect questions surrounding his religion, inexperience and health. Although JFK's financial advantage was less pronounced during this nationwide contest, Joe Kennedy spent millions on financing a huge campaign army and intervened at critical junctures to give his son the competitive edge. Kennedy's choice of Lyndon Johnson as vice-presidential running mate, his assured performance in the inaugural television debate, and his harnessing of the African American vote, combined with Richard Nixon's tactical errors, all contributed to the historic victory.

The burden of parental ambition

Already a multi-billionaire by the mid-1930s, Joseph Patrick Kennedy (JPK) 'bequeathed to his son [Jack] the habit of using wealth and connections to achieve success'.[1] While United States Ambassador to the United Kingdom, JPK transformed the 23-year-old Jack Kennedy's undergraduate thesis into a book entitled *Why England Slept*. The thesis had been a rushed job that required the help of no less than five paid assistants and had received the lowest honour grade possible.[2] Nevertheless, Kennedy Snr commissioned the services of his old friend, Arthur Krock, the Pulitzer-prize winning journalist, then Washington correspondent of the *New York Times*. Krock worked on the manuscript, making substantial revisions and refinements, before finding Kennedy a literary agent to ensure publication of the book and glowing reviews in major news outlets. JPK had approached the celebrated political philosopher Howard Laski to write an endorsement for the book, but the ambassador was rebuffed. Describing the work as 'very immature', Laski concluded that 'if it hadn't been written by the son of a very rich man, he wouldn't have found a publisher'.[3] Kennedy secured a suitably strong commendation from close family friend and media mogul Henry R. Luce who supplied the foreword to the book. The testimonial from someone as prominent as Luce, who published *Time* and *Life* magazines, boosted publicity. Moreover, JPK bulk ordered the book enabling it to get into a number of best-seller lists.[4] All this was with the longer-term view of establishing the new Kennedy generation in society and politics. As JPK told his son 'you would be surprised how a book that really makes the grade with high class people stands you in good stead for years to come'.[5] At an early age, JFK had been given a tutorial in how his life path would be paved. Recognition for the book in his name 'was secured through someone else's skills and connections, with the covert and insidious lesson that success would always be there as a natural consequence of money and power'.[6]

Joe Kennedy had harboured presidential ambitions of his own but by the time of his retirement from the Court of St James in 1940 these had been quashed 'thanks to his now-unfashionable isolationist sentiments (and oft-voiced anti-Semitism)'.[7] Following the death in military action of his eldest son, Joe Jnr, Jack became the object of JPK's intense ambitions. 'I can feel Pappy's eyes on the back of my neck,' Jack confided to his old Navy friend Paul Fay at Christmas 1944, 'It was like being drafted. My father wanted his elder son in politics. "Wanted" isn't the right word. He demanded it. You know my father.'[8]

Into Congress

The first thing to do was to locate a vacant winnable seat for his son. Failing that was to create one. As JFK came from distinguished Bostonian political stock, the Bay State capital was an obvious target. One grandfather, Patrick J. Kennedy, had represented Boston in both the Massachusetts House of Representatives and the state Senate, while the other grandfather, John F. 'Honey Fitz' Fitzgerald, had been mayor of the city and a United States congressman representing Massachusetts's eleventh congressional district. This constituency provided the optimal prospects for JFK. In addition to the Kennedy family history, the eleventh district also contained the predominately Irish wards of Brighton, Charlestown and Somerville and Jack's alma mater, Harvard, in Cambridge. Joseph Kennedy set out to create a vacancy. Although James Michael Curley represented the Massachusetts eleventh congressional district, the law was catching up with the flamboyant, corrupt party veteran. JPK saw an opportunity to make a mutually beneficial deal with Curley. In return for Curley vacating the seat, Kennedy handed over $100,000 ($1.3million in 2020) to pay off Curley's substantial debts and support his bid for mayor of Boston.[9] Coincidentally, JFK's grandfather, 'Honey Fitz', had been forced to step aside as Mayor of Boston three decades earlier when the same James Michael Curley threatened to publicise his marital infidelities.

Having induced Curley to vacate the constituency, JFK formally announced his intention to contest the seat in 1946. The sheer audacity of the move – the Kennedys had effectively left Boston years ago for New York and Florida – astonished some, like Tip O'Neill. 'Here was a kid', O'Neill recalled, 'who had never run for anything in his life … he had absolutely no political experience.'[10] JFK's opponents considered him a callow carpetbagger. Encountering resistance from local political organisations, the Kennedys built their own. To establish residency in the constituency, JFK was booked into a suite at the Bellevue hotel across from the State House.

Joe Kane, JPK's cousin who introduced JFK to politics in Boston, observed that 'Politics is like war, it takes three things to win – the first is money and the second is money and the third is money.'[11] Throughout JFK's political career his father would spend vast amounts of money to promote Jack's electoral prospects. Having paid a handsome sum to get Curley to vacate the seat, Joe Kennedy was not going to hold back on funds to push through his son's candidacy. As JFK made his bid for a congressional seat, Kennedy Snr boasted that 'We're going to sell Jack like soap flakes.'[12]

At this time, Kennedy was not the skilful, personable orator that he would later become. Campaign insiders remember him as a reluctant candidate competing against experienced and polished rivals. Speechwriter Joseph Healey recalled: 'We had to spend a great deal of time polishing something into a speech that we thought was fairly worthwhile and then, frankly, in our opinion he would not do it justice.'[13] Consequently, Jack relied heavily on his father's huge financial resources and army of experienced political advisers. As one author summarised the campaign:

> Unlike their opponents, the Kennedys employed an ad agency to handle press releases and advertising, keeping Jack's name in the papers and providing professionalism to the campaign. The Kennedy camp used a massive advertising blitz, putting the candidate's face in subways, on buses, and in other areas. Kennedy's opponents complained that although the young war hero and his family were being profiled in national magazines, other contenders were having a hard time receiving coverage in even the local papers due to Joseph Kennedy's influence.[14]

Even missing the deadline to submit his nomination papers – which should have dealt a fatal blow – did not derail his campaign but was remedied by phone calls to a 'well-placed accomplice' and an after-hours entry to the State House.[15]

Few issues emerged during the campaign to disrupt the handshaking and vote buying. Kennedy was described as a 'fighting conservative'[16] and few opportunities were missed to advertise Jack's status as a decorated United States navy veteran. This was a major asset in the immediate aftermath of the Second World War. Forty veterans would be elected to the House and eight more to the Senate in November 1946.[17] Shortly before Jack entered the election race, his father used his wealth and connections to get a new United States navy destroyer named the *Joseph Kennedy Jr*, thus linking the Kennedy name with wartime heroism.[18] The story of how Jack rescued survivors after his boat (PT109) sank made the front pages of the national newspapers, such as *The New York Times* and *The Boston Globe* (the headlines invariably referred to Jack as 'Kennedy's son').[19] Joe Kennedy arranged for an admiring account of his son's wartime record to be published in the hugely popular *Reader's Digest* and then had 100,000 copies reprinted as a brochure and circulated throughout the constituency.[20]

Kennedy's election motto modestly proclaimed that 'The New Generation Offers a Leader'; the projected image was that of a youthful veteran who understood the plight of the working man. Campaign literature featured a passage from Henry Luce's gushing introduction to *Why England Slept* in which he wrote: 'If John Kennedy is characteristic of the younger generation, and I believe he is, many of us would be happy to have the destinies of the Republic turned over to him at once.'[21]

JFK's major opponents had significant bases of support in their own regions but not necessarily throughout the constituency. The Kennedy team's campaign strategy was to come second in each neighbourhood where a rival was particularly strong and to garner a sufficient number of these second places to triumph district wide. Kennedy had three major rivals for the Democratic Party nomination. The most serious of these was Mike Neville, an experienced politician, formerly Speaker of the House of Representatives in Massachusetts and the mayor of Cambridge. Other heavyweight contenders included Charlestown's John Cotter who had worked as Curley's secretary and Joseph Russo, a member of Boston city council whose main appeal was that he was the only Italian-American running in the election.

The Kennedys tried to bribe Neville by offering him a job for life at the Kennedy Foundation with a $25,000 ($328,000 in 2020) annual stipend, two-and-a-half times a Congressman's salary.[22] Neville refused the carrot and quickly felt the stick. Kennedy Snr contacted his billionaire friend William Randolph Hearst and for the remaining two months of the election the Hearst-owned *Boston American* 'did not run a single ad, print a single Neville photo, or so much as mention the man's name.'[23] Reflecting on the campaign, Neville said 'The Kennedy strategy was to buy you out or blast you out.'[24] Neville had declined to be bought and so he was blasted.

John Cotter also claimed the Kennedys had descended on Boston to 'buy a seat in Congress'. He highlighted the disparity between the wealth of the Kennedys and that of their potential constituents, and stressed that while he had helped voters during the harsh winter Kennedy had been 'basking at Hialeah and the sun-baked sands of Palm Beach'.[25] Kennedy's resources dwarfed what was available to his rivals. In frustration, Joseph Russo took out an advertisement in the *East Boston Leader*:

Congress Seat For Sale
No Experience Necessary
Applicant Must Live In New York Or Florida
Only Millionaires Need Apply[26]

In retaliation, another Joe Russo, a 27-year-old anonymous janitor, was financially induced to put his name on the ballot to sow confusion and split the Italian vote for his more distinguished namesake.

Despite moving to Boston to direct operations and lavishly funding the whole campaign, Joe Kennedy remained in the shadows. He 'stayed away from headquarters and neighbourhood storefronts, didn't attend any "teas" or house parties or receptions, granted no interviews, gave no speeches, never even appeared in the same room or at the same rally or political forum with his son'.[27] Although Mark Dalton was the official campaign manager, he later conceded that 'The campaigns were run by Joseph P. Kennedy ... There never indeed was any campaign manager except Joseph P. Kennedy'.[28] 'You know,' remarked Tip O'Neill, 'you can be a candidate, you can have the issues, you can have the organisation, but money makes miracles, and money did miracles in that campaign. Why they even had six different mailings ... nobody had any mailings in that district.'[29] It is estimated that JPK spent something in the region of $300,000 ($3.93million in 2020) of his own money on Jack's campaign,[30] an unprecedented amount of money for a congressional race at the time, and more than the combined total of all nine opponents. 'With the money I spent,' he reflected, 'I could have elected my chauffeur.'[31]

Nothing could stop the Kennedy juggernaut. On 18 June 1946, Kennedy won the primary with 42 per cent of the vote of a 30 per cent turnout (i.e. 12 per cent of total party voters). The Kennedys had offered families in poor neighbourhoods $50 ($655 in 2020) to work at the polls on primary day.[32] JFK's 22,183 votes eclipsed the 11,341 for Neville, 6,671 for Cotter and 5,661 for the 'real' Russo (the 'faux' Russo managed to take over 12 per cent of the combined Russo total).

Boston continued to be the target of Joe Kennedy's philanthropy as largesse was showered on the constituency but always with substantial publicity. In mid-August, Joe Kennedy made a $600,000 ($7.86million in 2020) donation to the Catholic diocese of Boston via its Archbishop Richard Cushing (later, with Joe Kennedy's help, he was made a cardinal) and a further $250,000 ($3.28million in 2020) was spent on an altar named in Joe Jnr's memory.[33] Even the Association of Catholic Dentists received $10,000 ($130,000 in 2020). 'With each gift came a sole proviso: Son Jack got his picture in the newspaper handing over the cheque.'[34] JPK's friends at Henry Luce's media empire shoehorned a favourable profile of Jack into *Time* magazine.

In the general election, JFK soundly defeated the Republican candidate Lester Brown on 5 November 1946 by 69,093 votes (72.65 per cent) to 26,007 votes (27.35 per cent). Still in his twenties, JFK was now a *bona fide* member of the political elite in his own right, being duly elected as a member of the United States Congress. Comfortably ensconced in an unassailably safe seat, JFK cruised to easy re-election victories in 1948 (no opponent) and 1950 (82.28 per cent). As the Democratic incumbent, JFK could have represented Massachusetts's, eleventh district for decades, as his successor Tip O'Neill would do. However, Congressional life quickly bored him and it was clearly little more than a staging post *en route* to much greater things.

Into the Senate

When the Kennedys decided to put Jack in the Senate in 1952 there was no vacancy in Massachusetts. Instead, the Republican Party's Henry Cabot

Lodge, Jr an accomplished, three-term senator occupied the position. If Jack defeated Lodge, he would 'receive instant national fame as a giant killer'.[35] The election involved the representatives of well-established rival dynasties. To the older generations of Kennedys, a victory here would settle an old family score; Lodge's grandfather, Henry Cabot Lodge Snr, had defeated JFK's grandfather, 'Honey Fitz', in a tight Senate election race in 1916.[36] Being extremely wealthy and well-connected both men had much in common but 'the difference was in degrees. Lodge was handsomer, with more distinguished careers both in journalism and in government, and he had sacrificed far more to enter military service having resigned his Senate seat in 1944 to serve on active duty, but regaining it in 1946'.[37] But the Kennedys embarked on a more energetic campaign and were far more focused.

JFK did not produce a stellar record in Congress. As biographer Robert Dallek points out, 'Jack could hardly trumpet his six years in the House as a model of legislative achievement' and 'if he were asking voters to make him a senator because he had been an innovative legislator or a House leader, he would have been hard-pressed to make an effective case'.[38] Fortunately for JFK, Lodge's position as campaign manager for Eisenhower's presidential election bid meant he could not devote adequate time to defending his own Senate seat. Moreover, Lodge's backing of Eisenhower created a substantial body of disaffected influential conservative Republicans, particularly supporters of presidential aspirant Senator Robert Taft, already put off by Lodge's perceived liberalism. Kennedy's image as an avowed Cold War warrior and the more stridently hawkish and anti-Communist of the two candidates made the switch all the easier.

Under the tutelage of Joe Kennedy Snr and with 26-year-old Bobby Kennedy in charge of the day-to-day running of the campaign, key demographic groups were targeted as part of a sophisticated election strategy. In particular, the women's vote was assiduously courted through tea parties hosted by female members of the Kennedy clan, which attracted thousands of voters eager to meet the celebrity family members.[39] A 'Black Book' of 'Lodge's Dodges', was produced while another publication 'Said and Did From 1947–1951' maintained that Kennedy was more trustworthy on major issues of voter concern. Despite the energy invested in emphasising differences, the candidates were remarkably similar in terms of policy.

This was an election that would be decided on public perceptions of the personalities rather than the policies.[40]

One of the Kennedy campaign's achievements was ensuring that Joe McCarthy, the then very popular senator from Wisconsin, did not campaign for fellow-Republican, Cabot Lodge. With 750,000 Irish Catholics, Massachusetts 'was McCarthy country' and had the Wisconsin senator stumped for Lodge, 'he might have dealt a substantial, perhaps even fatal, blow to Jack Kennedy's challenge'.[41] Joe Kennedy asked McCarthy to stay out of the contest and he also made a contribution to McCarthy's re-election campaign fund.[42] He was pushing against an open door. McCarthy was a family friend, having holidayed with the Kennedys and had dated not one but two of Jack's sisters. Only one year before the election battle in Massachusetts, McCarthy had served as godfather to Bobby's first child, Kathleen.[43] Some thought Lodge too liberal and insufficiently supportive of McCarthy's endeavours to root out Communism. This resulted in papers like the *New Bedford Evening Standard* and the *Cape Cod Standard Times*, both owned by right-wing newspaperman Basil Brewer, backing Kennedy.

JFK was far more effective than Lodge in utilising the opportunities presented by the new medium of television. While Joe Kennedy arranged for his son to be coached in how to communicate on television, Lodge failed to connect with audiences. JPK exploited his contacts amongst television producers whom he had cultivated when producing Hollywood movies during the 1930s. He acquired the services of both Hollywood newsreel cameramen and the NBC network to help produce high-quality advertisements.[44] Batten, Barton, Durstine & Osborn (BBD&O), a nationally recognised television advertising agency, taught JFK 'how to communicate messages effectively on television with personal, intimate facial expressions and by looking directly into the cameras'.[45] Joe Kennedy's connections on BBD&O and NBC ensured that JFK appeared more frequently than Lodge. During the final month of campaigning, JFK appeared thirty-three times on CBS and ABC Boston affiliates, almost twice as many times as Lodge and was on air for a total of 480 minutes during the last month compared to just 260 minutes of television coverage for Lodge.[46] When the candidates debated on live television on 17 September, most analysts deemed Kennedy the most effective communicator with Lodge 'frequently coming across as uptight and often failing to look directly into the camera when speaking'.[47]

In an era of comparatively cheaply run elections, money mattered, and Joe Kennedy had millions of dollars to bolster his son's campaign. As one of the wealthiest men in the world Joe Kennedy was, as one author put it, 'in a position to use his money to influence the 1952 election … the 1952 campaign was extraordinary for how effectively the Kennedy family mobilized their wealth, experiences, resources, and influence to support JFK's run'.[48]

The campaign finance laws at the time were so lax as to constitute 'an invitation to break the rules'.[49] A candidate could only spend $20,000 ($193,000 in 2020) on the campaign and individuals were limited to $1,000 ($9,600 in 2020) contributions, there was no restriction on indirectly using party funds to support a candidate, nor was there any limit on the number of allied committees an individual could support. Thus the Kennedys established several committees, with generic titles such as the 'More Prosperous Massachusetts' committee that were used to funnel money into the election campaign. Individual members of the very large Kennedy family, including in-laws, were able to make multiple donations in this way and their contributions eclipsed Lodge's entire campaign fundraising efforts.[50] In terms of reported expenditure for every dollar the Lodge campaign spent, the Kennedys spent almost seven.[51]

Such was the infusion of resources that in each community the Kennedy campaign was able to establish a political organisation quite separate from the local Democratic Party organisation. Kennedy brochures were delivered to every single home in Massachusetts in 'an unprecedented effort to reach voters'.[52] A large reservoir of funds was created to pay for billboards and advertisements in the print media as well as radio and television and for extensive mailings. Joseph Kennedy was also able to make donations of thousands of dollars at a time dedicated to public or charitable purposes and this, according to the campaign finance laws, was not considered a political campaign expenditure given that JPK was not running for office. Nonetheless such donations undoubtedly benefitted JFK. In total, Kennedy Snr may have contributed several million dollars ($68 million in 2020) to his son's campaign[53] and this was topped up by contributions made by his circle of wealthy acquaintances.[54] As Dwight Eisenhower recalled: 'Cabot was simply overwhelmed by money.'[55]

No expenditure was more vital than the sum paid by Joe Kennedy to rescue the *Boston Post* from bankruptcy. The highly influential newspaper, which had more than 300,000 daily readers, was owned by Republican John Fox and was expected to back Lodge as the incumbent Republican senator. However, when Joe Kennedy extended $500,000 ($4.35 million in 2020) in loans to cash-strapped Fox the *Boston Post* abruptly endorsed Kennedy. Lodge estimated the endorsement cost him about 40,000 votes.[56] As Jack later put it, 'we had to buy that fucking paper or I'd have been licked'.[57]

Jack's narrow margin of victory over Lodge – 70,737 votes out of 2,353,231 cast, 51.5 per cent to 48.5 per cent – was all the more impressive given it bucked the national trend of victories for the Republican Party, which re-took the White House for the first time in twenty years and captured both houses of Congress. In Massachusetts, Eisenhower enjoyed a 208,800-vote advantage over Stevenson in the presidential election and incumbent Democrat Paul Dever lost the governorship to Republican Christian Herter by 14,000 votes.[58] It was Boston, which had voted for Lodge in 1946, that determined the outcome. Outside of Boston, Lodge won a greater share of the vote, gaining 48,656 over Kennedy (2.4 per cent). However, in Boston JFK enjoyed a two-to-one margin over Lodge, winning by 119,393 votes. This Senate race was a turning point in Massachusetts politics. Lodge's defeat signalled the beginning of the end of Yankee Republican dominance in the Bay State, ushering in a new era of Democratic Party hegemony. This trend was consolidated a decade later when JFK's youngest brother, Edward (Teddy) comprehensively defeated Henry Cabot Lodge's son, George, in a battle to represent Massachusetts, a result that also brought the Kennedy–Lodge election rivalry to end.[59]

Seeking the presidential nomination

The election catapulted Kennedy to national prominence and put him on the road to the White House. His legislative record remained unimpressive and JPK's advice about a good book doing wonders for one's reputation resurfaced at this time in the form of *Profiles in Courage*, a volume devoted to mini-biographies of former senators. In publishing the book, Kennedy hoped to inform the public of the kind of senatorial bravery he aspired to emulate. But while JFK kept an editorial eye on the book's evolution 'virtually all the research and writing were done by [Ted] Sorensen and Jules Davids'. Put simply, Kennedy 'did not write the book'.[60]

Joseph Kennedy again solicited the services of the indefatigable Arthur Krock in order to engineer the country's most prestigious literary honour, the Pulitzer Prize, for Jack. Krock lobbied hard to get the Pulitzer Prize Committee Board to overrule the decision of its own expert panel of judges, who had recommended the award go to a different book.[61] One of the most exotic explanations offered for this *volte-face* was that one usually inactive board member, Don Ferguson, had read the book aloud to his 12-year-old grandson who loved it. Apparently, the opinion of Ferguson's grandson swayed the other members of the board who decided to overrule their esteemed judges and give the prize to Kennedy.[62] As a result, 'the junior senator from Massachusetts was once again acclaimed as a distinguished author and intellectual. Perhaps most distressing, Kennedy appears to have accepted the description as appropriate.'[63] But the public recognition and political capital that JFK acquired as a result of the book were, in the words of one major biographer 'as deceptive as installing a Chevrolet engine in a Cadillac'.[64]

JFK received frequent jibes that the book had been ghostwritten, but the threat of a Kennedy-sponsored lawsuit usually secured silence or retractions.[65] The title and focus of the book also left him open to taunts that his congressional and senatorial record was anything but a profile in courage. 'Liberal critics of JFK and his increasingly apparent political ambition, such as Eleanor Roosevelt, charged that JFK's cautious, self-serving legislative behaviour and rhetoric regarding McCarthyism and civil rights contradicted the title and theme of *Profiles in Courage*.'[66]

When rumours circulated in 1956 that the Democratic nominee for President Adlai Stevenson was considering a Catholic as a running mate, Ted Sorensen, one of JFK's most trusted paid advisers, produced a memorandum entitled 'The Catholic Vote in 1952 and 1956,' which argued that having a Catholic like Jack Kennedy on the ticket would help defeat Eisenhower. The document pointed out that Catholics, who constituted about a quarter of the electorate, were more likely to vote than non-Catholics. The memo also pointed out that Catholics were highly concentrated in fourteen states with 261 electoral college votes. Franklin Roosevelt could not have won in 1940 without these key states, thirteen of which went Democratic. Eisenhower, however, had carried all fourteen of them in 1952 as the Catholic vote split evenly between the two major parties. To stem the flow of Catholic voters to the Republican Party, Sorensen argued that the Democrats needed to run Catholic candidates at the highest level.[67] The Kennedy camp ensured that Sorensen's memo was publicised and circulated widely amongst journalists.[68]

When Stevenson surprised delegates at the Democratic Party convention in 1956 by throwing the vice-presidential nomination to an open vote, Kennedy put his hat in the ring. His silence on the burning issue of civil rights had been rewarded with the bulk of Southern delegate votes[69] and JFK did well to come second. It was perhaps fortunate that he did not win on that occasion given that the Democratic Party was heading for a trouncing in the 1956 presidential election. Kennedy took a positive message away from the convention 'With only about four hours of work and a handful of supporters, I came within thirty-three-and-a-half votes of winning the vice-presidential nomination,' Kennedy told David Powers, his friend and personal assistant. 'If I work hard for four years, I ought to be able to pick up all the marbles.'[70]

Although his family resources and connections provided huge advantages in his quest for the presidency, the young senator presented himself as an underprivileged outsider. In an interview given to *Time* magazine on 18 November 1957, Kennedy said that 'Nobody is going to hand me the nomination. If I were governor of a large state, Protestant and fifty-five, I could sit back and let it come to me. But if I am going to get it, I'll have to work for it – and damn hard.'[71] Two weeks later, on 2 December 1957, JFK appeared on the cover of the same magazine, arguably the most influential in the United States at the time. In the same edition, JFK's wife, Jackie, defended her father-in-law 'against charges that he runs his children's careers'. 'You'd think he was a mastermind playing chess,' she said, 'when actually he's a nice old gentleman we see at Thanksgiving and Christmas.' For the front coverage of his son, Joe Kennedy gave Henry Luce, who owned *Time* magazine, $75,000 ($682,000 in 2020)[72] and felt he had got his money's worth. '*Time* did a great job for Jack,' Kennedy wrote to Luce, but he joked that he would sue the magazine for printing that he was a 'nice old gentleman'.[73] Although there was still two years to go to the presidential election, the Kennedy patriarch felt that he had created vital momentum for his son's candidacy. Following a meeting with the Director of the CIA, Allen Dulles, Joe Kennedy wrote to a confidante that Dulles was 'very aware of the fact that Jack may be the next President' and 'more than ever anxious to please'.[74]

At this critical juncture in JFK's quest for the presidency, his father remained one of the fifteen wealthiest men in America. Though generally irritated by jibes referring to his father's fortune, Jack took in good humour the skit put on by newsmen at the Gridiron Club dinner in 1958 that lampooned Joe Kennedy's lavish spending by portraying the Massachusetts senator as singing, 'Just Send the Bill to Daddy' (to the tune of *My Heart Belongs to Daddy*). In the speech that followed he claimed to have received a wire from his 'generous Daddy' saying: 'Dear Jack; Don't buy a single vote more than is necessary – I'll be damned if I'm going to pay for a landslide.'[75] Joking aside, JPK knew that to be considered a viable presidential candidate, a landslide senate re-election victory was exactly what was required.[76] And so it was that on 4 November 1958 JFK saw off the challenge of Republican opponent, Vincent J. Celeste, by a staggering 1,362,926 (73.20 per cent) to 488,318 (26.23 per cent). The winning margin of 874,608 votes was the largest ever in Massachusetts politics. The victory provided an opportunity for *Time* magazine to put Jack back on the front cover and to report that 'if the convention were held today, Kennedy would win on the first ballot, period'.[77]

JFK formally announced his candidacy on 2 January 1960. To convince the Democratic Party convention that he was the most credible candidate he competed in several primaries. His main adversary at this stage was a 48-year-old senator from Minnesota, Hubert Humphrey. Both Kennedy and Humphrey competed in the primaries because they believed they had no other route to being nominated. The primaries were less about winning delegate votes than proving their electability and making a favourable impression on party bosses. But as Teddy Roosevelt had discovered in 1912 and Estes Kefauver forty years later, victory in the primaries did not guarantee the Democratic Party nomination. The costs of contesting multiple primaries against a myriad of candidates were also prohibitive. Senate majority leader Lyndon Johnson and others preferred to keep their powder dry and limited financial resources intact until much closer to the convention. This proved to be a major miscalculation. Unencumbered by the pecuniary considerations that burdened regular candidates, JFK could contest anything and be assured of an army of talented advisers, battalions of foot soldiers and unlimited finances to advance. In terms of importance, two of the primaries eclipsed all others, those held in Wisconsin and West Virginia.

From the beginning, Humphrey and Kennedy had vastly different levels of resources available to conduct their campaigns. Nothing perhaps illustrated this more eloquently than their respective means of transport. Kennedy flew around Wisconsin in a private airplane. During the frozen winter, Humphrey travelled throughout the state in an old, slow and cold rented bus, where the Minnesota senator tried to rest and talk to journalists. According to his memoirs, the team 'rolled from town to town, all of us half freezing and uncomfortable'. Sometimes the bus would slide off the icy road or break down completely. When the bus arrived at its destination, Humphrey and his campaign team were, in the senator's words 'zombies, almost always late, rumpled, bleary-eyed'.[78] There they would pick up a newspaper in the morning only to see 'cheerful reports from all over the state of the Kennedy tentacles, like a friendly Irish octopus, ensnaring voters'.[79]

Kennedy refused to debate Humphrey in Wisconsin, citing a lack of policy differences between them, and his brother, Bobby, who directed his campaign put out a story that Jimmy Hoffa, the Teamsters boss reputed to be involved in organised crime, was backing Humphrey. The huge Kennedy family and in-laws (with the noticeable exception of Joe) were deployed throughout the state. As Humphrey put it: 'I felt like an independent merchant competing against a chain store: the Kennedys were everywhere.'[80] Despite the uneven distribution of campaign resources, the result was much closer than the Kennedys would have liked. Jack took 56 per cent of the vote and six of the ten districts. The *Washington Post* headline – 'Triumph for Kennedy Not Up to Expectations.' – summed up the feeling in the JFK camp. Many noted the importance of the Catholic turnout for JFK, which 'almost amounted to a bloc vote'.[81] As the mixed results came through, Eunice Kennedy noticed Jack's unhappy expression and asked him, 'What does it all mean?' He replied, 'It means that we've got to go to West Virginia in the morning and do it all over again'.[82]

In West Virginia, the Kennedy campaign team managed to adapt their tactics to incorporate the lessons learned during the Wisconsin primary. Firstly, they changed the way they managed election predictions. Whereas in Wisconsin they had talked up their chances, leading to deflation when the results did not match the projections, in West Virginia they did exactly the opposite. Less than a week before the primary, JFK said he would be lucky to get 40 per cent of the vote.[83] The Kennedy team also learned that on the issue of religion they had to take the initiative and frame the narrative in a way that boosted their prospects. On 13 April, JFK told voters: 'Nobody asked me if I was a Catholic when I joined the United States Navy and nobody asked my brother if he was a Catholic or a Protestant before he climbed into an American bomber plane to fly his last mission.'[84] As Catholics made up only 5 per cent of the population, winning West Virginia was vital as it would demonstrate that Kennedy's religion did not inhibit voters. Much to Humphrey's chagrin, Kennedy supporters suggested a victory for Humphrey, no matter what he himself might say on the stump, equated to a vote for bigotry. The influential columnist, Joe Alsop, for example, wrote that the majority of Humphrey's support was derived from 'people who were influenced by religious prejudice' and that 'if Sen. Humphrey wins ... he will owe his victory to Ku Klux Klan-minded voters'.[85] Now the burden of proof shifted to Protestants to demonstrate that they were not bigots. Voting for Kennedy was the only way to accomplish this.[86]

Many observers made the mistake of thinking religion would be the key issue for West Virginia voters but, instead, economic matters predominated. Humphrey became increasingly frustrated by the largesse that the Kennedy campaign could disseminate throughout the constituency. 'I can't afford to run through this state with a little black bag and a cheque book ... I can't buy an election ... I don't have any daddy who can pay the bills for me.'[87] These were much harsher criticisms than anything Richard Nixon would level during the presidential campaign later in the year.

West Virginia was impoverished and notoriously corrupt. It was customary to pay county bosses two to three dollars per vote. Humphrey spent no more than $30,000 ($260,000 in 2020) on the West Virginia primary. Kennedy was spending multiples of this figure on individual counties. In Logan County (won), Huntington (lost) and Charleston (won narrowly) alone, the Kennedys spent $350,000 ($3.023million in 2020) and there were fifty-five counties in West Virginia. So much money was sloshing about that when one minor operative requested '35' he was given $35,000 instead of the $3,500 actually requested.[88] We will never know for sure how much the Kennedys spent on the primary but realistic assessments are considered to be in the range of $1.5million ($13million in 2020) to

$2.5million ($21.6million in 2020).[89] On television advertising alone, which unlike many of the payments at local level is documented, for every dollar Humphrey spent, Kennedy spent seventeen.

Joe Kennedy and Cardinal Cushing of Boston – JFK's most consistent backer in the Catholic hierarchy – created a fund for making financial payments to Protestant (especially black) churches in order to secure support for Jack. Cardinal Cushing gave $950,000 in cash ($8,200,000 in 2020) from the diocese's Sunday collection plates and in return Kennedy wrote a tax-deductible cheque to the Catholic Church for $1million.[90] Both profited from this money-laundering scheme. Cushing made a profit of $50,000 ($432,000 in 2020) and Kennedy received a massive tax deduction and a huge sum of untraceable funds. Years later Cushing recalled: 'I keep reading these books by the young men around Jack Kennedy and how they claim credit for electing him. I'll tell you who elected John Kennedy. It was his father, Joe, and me, right in this room ... We decided which church and preacher would get two hundred dollars or one hundred dollars or five hundred dollars ... It's good for the church. It's good for the preacher, and it's good for the candidate.'[91]

Kennedy secured a decisive victory by 236,510 votes (61 per cent) to 152,187 votes (39 per cent). By convincing the media that JFK was the underdog in West Virginia, the victory seemed all the more complete, although in terms of votes per dollar spent the result was less impressive. The Kennedy campaign claimed victory in all ten primaries he had contested (though not all involved organised opposition) but none was as important as West Virginia. The state only gave him fifteen votes at the convention in Los Angeles, but its value was far greater. Although primaries only determined a minority of convention delegates, these victories, along with other inducements, could be used as leverage, when dealing with political bosses, 'favourite sons'[92] and uncommitted delegates at the convention.

JFK's rivals for the nomination mobilised too late and had obvious flaws. His closest challenger at the Democratic Party convention, Lyndon Baines Johnson (LBJ), made little effort to go into the states early and organise. Moreover, his support base in the segregationist south made him unacceptable to most northern Democrats. Given LBJ's seniority in the Senate, he underestimated JFK and when he finally made a last-ditch effort to mobilise, it was too late. In frustration, LBJ lashed out at Jack and Joe

Kennedy. Of Kennedy Snr, LBJ said: 'I wasn't any Chamberlain-umbrella policy man. I never thought Hitler was right'[93] while an LBJ campaign aide claimed that JFK had Addison's disease and would not be alive without cortisone.[94] Like Kefauver four years earlier, Kennedy had sought to use the primaries to make a claim on the nomination. However, Kennedy's strong regional base, his unlimited financial resources and the powerful campaign organisation it facilitated made him a far more formidable quantity than the maverick Tennessee senator. JFK secured victory on the first ballot defeating his nearest rival, Lyndon Johnson, by 806 votes (52.89 per cent) to 409 votes (26.84 per cent). On 13 July 1960, John Kennedy officially became the Democratic Party's nominee for President of the United States.

Choosing a running mate

With the nomination in hand, John F. Kennedy turned to the question of his running mate. Lyndon Johnson was the obvious choice and both he and Kennedy were pragmatic enough to see the larger picture. However, their respective campaign teams and allies had not been prepared. Having invested so much energy in discrediting each other, they now viewed the pact with disbelief. For them, this alliance was not initially considered a dream team but, rather, the stuff of nightmares. Bobby Kennedy was described as being in 'near despair' and he tried hard to undermine the agreement. Referring to the convention victory, Bobby said 'Yesterday was the best day of my life' before commenting on his brother's choice of LBJ as running mate, 'and today is the worst day of my life'.[95]

Bobby's fears proved ill-founded as Johnson was the ideal, indeed the only suitable, running mate if the election was to be won. Kennedy's geographical base made him a popular choice amongst voters in the north-east and industrial cities and he could present himself as an attractive candidate to labour, ethnic minorities and Catholics. Johnson appealed to every other section in the United States, particularly those in the south, and parts of the west and mid-west, as well as farmers and those worried that a Kennedy ticket might infringe on 'state rights', code in the south for the maintenance of racially based segregation. The ticket also appealed to different generations. Although JFK was less than nine years the junior of

LBJ, in term of image and temperament, they could have been father and son. As Donaldson put it: 'Whatever Johnson was, Kennedy was not; and whatever Kennedy was, Johnson was not. It was truly the perfect ticket.'[96]

Given the balanced appeal of the Democratic Party ticket, Richard Nixon needed a running mate that could inject vitality into his campaign and bring in a swing state or two. Had he chosen someone like Everett Dirksen or Hugh Scott, senators for Illinois and Pennsylvania respectively, they could have carried their respective vital states, each with a large number of electoral college votes. Senator Kenneth Keating of New York might not have been able to deliver his state, but as a Catholic he could have helped defuse the charge of religious bigotry. Instead Nixon chose Henry Cabot Lodge, the man Kennedy had ousted from the Senate eight years earlier. Convinced that an election fought on domestic issues would work against him, Nixon was determined to keep the focus on international affairs. 'If you ever let them [the Democrats] campaign only on domestic issues, they'll beat us,' he mused, 'our only hope is to keep it on foreign policy.'[97] At face value, Nixon's rationale had some merit, given the profound importance of the Cold War and Lodge's position as United States ambassador to the United Nations for the previous eight years. But despite his mastery of international affairs and regular high-profile television appearances, Lodge was not a dynamic figure and he adopted a leisurely approach to campaigning. Indeed, Lodge 'who was so laid-back that he got into his pyjamas after lunch for a nap every day … proved to be the most lethargic campaigner for national office of modern times'.[98]

The presidential campaign

JFK presented an inspiring narrative; the war veteran, the prize-winning author, handsome and charismatic but also intellectual, representing a new generation taking America forward to the new (if ill-defined) frontier. The great election story in 1960 did not revolve primarily around ideology, for there was little to separate the two men politically, campaign rhetoric aside. It was about the candidate or, more accurately, the image of the candidate. Despite being of approximately the same age as Nixon and suffering from chronic health problems, JFK monopolised the image of youth and vigour.[99] Although he was the son of a multi-billionaire and part of a major political dynasty, as a Catholic, Kennedy captured the mantle of victimised underdog against a rival who, despite being of underprivileged Quaker stock and having endured a very challenging career path, was depicted as being part of the establishment. And while being a serial womaniser, incapable of fidelity, Jack Kennedy capitalised on the image of being a family man with a young, glamorous and heavily pregnant wife who campaigned on his behalf in multiple languages. Most crucially, despite the fact that the United States had enjoyed a decade of modest prosperity under a hugely popular president, Kennedy made a successful pitch that it was time for change.

Nixon failed to capitalise on Eisenhower's popularity by making him a bigger part of the campaign. Instead, Eisenhower damaged the chances of his protégé by his lukewarm support during press conferences. Throughout the campaign, journalists repeatedly probed the president for examples of Nixon's stellar contribution to the administration. Eisenhower clearly found these persistent questions annoying, in part because they suggested that the five-star general was not fully in control of the ship of state. On one such occasion in August 1960, when asked if Nixon had initiated any important policies or ideas, the president responded 'If you give me a week, I might think of one. I don't remember.' One staff member described the blow as 'an emotional concussion' for the vice-president.[100] Eisenhower had not intended to inflict damage and, immediately after the press conference concluded, he phoned Nixon to apologise. But there was no public clarification from the president and his words would now be mercilessly exploited by the Kennedy campaign.[101]

Nixon's normally robust health also proved to be an unexpected problem. In August, just as the campaign was in full swing, he acquired a severe staphylococci infection, resulting in two weeks of hospitalisation. Thus, while Kennedy toured the country, Nixon was bed-bound. Many in the vice-president's campaign team advised him to abandon his pledge to visit all fifty states (including Alaska and Hawaii, newly admitted to the Union) but Nixon stubbornly persevered. He finally hit the campaign trail on 12 September, visiting nine states in three days only to be struck down with high fever on 15 September. Keeping his vow meant that during the penultimate week of the campaign, Nixon was campaigning in Alaska – which had just three votes in the electoral college – while Kennedy toured the heavily populated swing states of Illinois, New Jersey and New York.

Religion

Anti-Catholicism remained a potent force in America and religion was always going to be an issue in the election.[102] There had never been a Catholic president and previous efforts to elect one did not inspire confidence. In 1928, Al Smith, of Irish Catholic stock, who had grown up in the urban and liberal north-east had been overwhelmed by an avalanche of ill-disguised bigotry.[103] Kennedy declared that the presidential election of 1960 would 'not be a repeat of 1928'.[104]

While Nixon was in hospital, he received a political body blow from an ally, Norman Vincent Peale, who delivered a fiery warning against Catholicism on behalf of the ill-described National Conference of Citizens for Religious Freedom, an organisation composed exclusively of Protestant ministers.[105] These kinds of outbursts were of little value to Nixon and he quickly admonished Peale. As his biographer notes, 'rabid anti-papists were going to vote for him anyway' and the challenge was 'to prevent open-minded Protestants from stampeding to Kennedy to demonstrate to themselves that they weren't bigots and that they did not subscribe to the sort of nonsense that Peale had just endorsed'.[106]

Within days of Peale's attack, Kennedy made the tactically astute move of addressing the Greater Houston Ministerial Conference.[107] Though his audience was an assembly of Protestant ministers, his real target was the national electorate, not least in the swing state of Texas. Kennedy delivered a prepared speech, composed by Sorensen, covering the general themes of religious freedom and tolerance, the separation of church and state, and the potential influence (or lack thereof) of the Catholic Church on his presidency, if elected. JFK declared, 'Contrary to common newspaper usage, I am not the Catholic candidate for President. I am the Democratic Party's candidate for President who happens also to be a Catholic.' Kennedy instrumentalised the religion issue by laying down a gauntlet to American democracy and challenging voters to prove their lack of bigotry: 'if this election is decided on the basis that 40,000,000 Americans lost their chance of being President on the day they were baptised, then it is the whole nation that will be the loser in the eyes of Catholics and non-Catholics around the world, in the eyes of history, and in the eyes of our own people.'[108] The Kennedy campaign bought television time on twenty-two Texas stations to broadcast Kennedy's speech, printed tens of thousands of copies for distribution and produced three half-hour film versions of the speech, which were broadcast on around 200 occasions in forty states.[109] Despite pervasive anti-Catholicism in the United States, the Kennedy campaign team managed to influence the narrative in their favour so that it could be used to attract voters who wanted to express their opposition to religious bigotry.[110] After Houston, the Kennedy campaign had regained the initiative on this issue. JFK now progressed to what would be another triumph, his television debates with Richard Nixon.

Television debates

In 1960, presidential candidates were afforded the unprecedented opportunity to present their case to the nation via multiple live televised debates. Eisenhower advised Nixon not to participate. According to the president, 'debates merely tested reaction time, not administrative skill. And the vice president already enjoyed a much higher profile than his Democratic opponent. Why give Kennedy free exposure?'[111] To his disadvantage, Nixon underestimated both JFK and the powerful new medium of television. Kennedy appreciated how potentially seminal these debates would be in influencing the outcome of the election. Consequently, he was far better prepared than Nixon. In advance of the debate he grilled the producer Don Hewitt, to get a full understanding of the dynamics of the programme. As Hewitt recalled: 'Kennedy knew just how important it [would] be to his campaign, and he didn't want to leave anything to chance.' By contrast, Nixon, according to Hewitt, 'treated it as just another campaign appearance'.[112]

As is well documented, Kennedy won the battle of appearances. Nixon, who had campaigned earlier that day and was still recovering from illness appeared to many as haggard and pallid while the tanned, confident and relaxed Kennedy 'entered the studio looking like a young athlete come to receive his wreath of laurel'.[113] Both candidates pitched their tents in the political centre and what differences emerged were more of emphasis than of policy. Nixon addressed the panellists, the moderator, his opponent and the studio audience, but Kennedy was far more successful in addressing the television cameras and therefore the viewing public at home that would determine the election outcome.[114] The moderator of the debate Howard Smith said of Kennedy, 'He later told me he won the election that night.'[115] Nixon conceded in his memoirs that 'I paid too much attention to what I was going to say and too little to how I would look ... one bad camera angle on television can have more effect on the election outcome than a major mistake in writing a speech.'[116] Commenting on television debates in general, Nixon reflected that 'I doubt that they can ever serve a responsible role in defining the issues of a presidential campaign. Because of the nature of the medium, there will inevitably be a greater premium on showmanship than on statesmanship.'[117]

As many as seventy million people watched the first debate – nearly two thirds of the adult population and roughly the same number as would turn out to vote. The debate was also broadcast on radio to an audience of approximately fifteen million. In 1950, only 11 per cent of the forty million families in the United States owned a television, but by 1960 this figure had jumped to 88 per cent.[118] Nixon improved in the subsequent debates and in terms of appearance tried to remedy some of the mistakes made during the inaugural encounter. But the damage had already been done and there were far less people watching. Historians have hotly contested the extent to which these debates influenced the ultimate outcome of the election. The general consensus is that Kennedy benefitted far more than Nixon from the exchanges and according to one significant account, 'Almost certainly, the election would have gone a different way had there not been the debates that year.'[119]

The black vote

Before 1960, JFK's public support for civil rights had been tepid and his legislative record on the issue was similarly unimpressive. Consequently, his candidacy was not initially viewed with much enthusiasm amongst African Americans. His support for the jury trial amendment to the Civil Rights Act of 1957,[120] was widely viewed as a sop to segregationists, as were his close relationships with racists such as fellow party member, John Patterson, the Alabama governor who had been elected in 1958 with the support of the Ku Klux Klan. The liberal wing of the party was appalled by his choice of LBJ as running mate.

In order to appeal to black voters a civil rights section was established within the Kennedy campaign in April to present their candidate favourably on relevant issues and undermine the image of his opponent. 'Money was not a problem for black Democrats in 1960,' according to Gary Donaldson and 'Thanks to Joe Kennedy, big-city politicians with thousands of votes to offer had little difficulty obtaining cash, and neither did black preachers.'[121] As Louis Martin, the main black adviser to the Kennedy brothers, pointed out, 'Those [black] papers aren't going to do a damn thing for you unless you pay [them].'[122] Payments for politicians were also required. For example, Congressman Adam Clayton Powell Jr, the influential Harlem preacher who had supported Eisenhower in 1956, was discreetly given $50,000 ($432,000 in 2020) to deliver ten speeches supporting Kennedy on a pay-per-performance basis.[123] Powell delivered a core Kennedy message to African Americans that linked racial prejudice with anti-Catholicism and anti-Semitism, and advocated a coalition of Catholics, Jews and African Americans. In the urban centres of the north-east this was a vital bloc. 'All bigots will vote for Nixon,' Powell warned on cue, 'and all right-thinking Christians and Jews will vote for Kennedy rather than be found in the ranks of the Klan-minded.'[124] The public support of key black politicians and preachers was vital as many African Americans were Protestant and vulnerable to propaganda that cautioned against a Catholic in the White House.

The key turning point hinged on the events following the arrest and imprisonment of Martin Luther King Jr on a trumped-up probation violation charge. After considerable initial reluctance, the Kennedys were prevailed upon to intervene. A complicated series of manoeuvres followed involving intricate behind-the-scenes negotiations between the Kennedy campaign team and their party allies in the south, many of whom as ardent segregationists occupied the key political and legal positions. JFK made a two-minute phone call to King's wife, Coretta, then six months pregnant, to express concern and support. When asked later by the media why he had called her, Kennedy said that she was a friend of the family – an expedient fabrication given that he had never met Coretta King and never would. Bobby Kennedy had vehemently opposed any intervention, and was outraged when it was made, but quickly changed tack. In what has been described as 'a breach of legal ethics',[125] he telephoned the state judge to secure King's release.

The Kennedy intervention would pay handsome electoral dividends. On the night of his release from his Georgian prison cell Martin Luther King Jr delivered a sermon declaring that 'anti-Catholic bias and religious bigotry is as immoral, undemocratic and unchristian as racial bigotry'.[126] Ten days before election day, King's father, also a Protestant minister, told reporters that while he had planned to vote for Nixon because Kennedy was a Catholic he had now changed his mind. 'Because this man was willing to wipe the tears from my daughter-in-law's eyes,' he said, 'I've got a suitcase of votes, and I'm going to take them to Mr. Kennedy and dump them in his lap.' True to his word, King Sr mobilised his network of black ministers to generate a high vote for JFK.[127]

Realising they had achieved a major PR coup, the Kennedy campaign targeted the black media with advertisements highlighting the event. Two million blue-coloured pamphlets (quickly dubbed 'blue bombs') were distributed outside black churches[128] the Sunday before the election, half a million in Chicago alone. Written by senior Kennedy campaign figures, Harris Wofford and Louis Martin and headlined 'The Case of Martin Luther King Jr.' the pamphlet distinguished between 'No Comment Nixon' and 'A Candidate with a Heart, Senator Kennedy'. The leaflets were printed by the 'Freedom Crusade Committee', a non-existent organisation invented to camouflage their association with the Democratic National Committee, though the payment to the printers was made via a personal cheque from Joe Kennedy.[129] In one black radio advertisement civil rights leader and Baptist minister Ralph Abernathy said it was 'time for all of us to take off our Nixon buttons' as Kennedy 'did something great and wonderful when he personally called Mrs Coretta King and helped free Dr Martin Luther King Jr'.[130] Maintaining that it was not just King on trial but America itself, Abernathy said 'Since Mr Nixon has been silent through all this, I am going to return his silence when I go into the voting booth.'[131]

Victory

Although the popular vote was extremely close (34,220,984 to 34,108,157, 49.72 per cent to 49.55 per cent, a margin of just 112,827 votes or 0.16 per cent), it all came down to a few vital states where the majorities were wafer-thin. Historians frequently emphasise that the margin was much more impressive in the crucial electoral college, where Kennedy triumphed by 303 to 219. However, had slightly more than 11,000 Kennedy voters switched to Nixon in New Jersey and 4,500 in Illinois, the election would have gone the other way. This was the first election in which the winning candidate received a majority of the electoral votes despite the second-placed candidate carrying a majority of the states.[132] Allegations of voter fraud proliferated but Nixon ultimately decided not to push for a recount, which he felt would damage the presidency and, indeed, United States democracy.[133]

The result demonstrated the wisdom of Kennedy's choice of running mate, Lyndon Johnson. LBJ delivered the vital swing state of Texas with only 46,000 votes to spare; almost half of Kennedy's national majority came from Texas.[134] The Texan had proved to be 'the most influential vice-presidential candidate of the twentieth century'.[135] Nixon's choice of running mate, on the other hand, had only compounded his problems. Henry Cabot Lodge added nothing to the ticket; he 'probably did not move a thousand votes one way or another, in an electorate of nearly seventy million'.[136]

The Democratic Party walked the delicate tightrope with Kennedy appealing to blacks in the north and LBJ assuaging the fears of southern whites. Nixon was outspent, outmanoeuvred and outwitted on civil rights. This bore heavily on the election outcome. Southern white voters stayed with the Democratic Party in 1960 but black voters in the south – although more suspicious of Kennedy's Catholicism than their counterparts in the north-east – shifted in substantial numbers from the Republicans for whom they had traditionally voted.

The African American vote proved decisive in this election, as Martin Luther King Jr had predicted. Three years earlier, King had written to Nixon that 'the Negro vote is the balance of power in so many important swing states that one almost has to have the Negro vote to win a presidential election'.[137] The 1960 election confirmed this analysis. An estimated 80 per cent of African Americans voted for Kennedy and this was the difference between victory and defeat. In Illinois, which Nixon lost by 8,000 votes, an estimated 250,000 blacks voted for JFK. In Missouri, 100,000 black Kennedy voters pushed the Democratic Party candidate over the line by 35,000 votes. Similarly, in South Carolina, the black vote for Kennedy was much larger than his margin of victory. As one Nixon biographer surmised, 'it is hard to resist the conclusion that for the want of a phone call, an election was lost'.[138]

During the presidential campaign, as in all of JFK's previous election-related endeavours, Joseph Kennedy studiously avoided public appearances, even interviews.[139] He did not need to make formal addresses as his money spoke for him. During the first organisational summit meeting for the 1960 campaign, held in Palm Beach on 1 April 1959, Kennedy Sr told the inner circle, which included Jack and Bobby: 'We've come this far, we're not going to let money stand in our way, whatever it takes, even if it requires every dime I have.'[140] The Kennedy patriarch was an integral part of the campaign to elect JFK, spending in the process at least $10million ($86million in 2020) on the 1960 presidential bid. For many, Kennedy's candidature aroused fears not so much about separation of church and state, but of father and son. As Harry Truman put it: 'It's not the Pope I fear, it's the Pop.'[141]

On 20 January 1961, JFK, was inaugurated President of the United States of America. To this day he remains the youngest-ever elected president and the first Catholic. It had been the first presidential election where both major candidates were less than 50 years of age and born in the twentieth century. Eisenhower was old enough to be the father of either candidate (he was only two years younger than Joseph Kennedy). Irrespective of who emerged victorious, an inter-generational shift in presidential power was inevitable. After the inauguration Nixon told a Kennedy aide that he regretted he had not said some of the things Kennedy had in his inaugural address. Intrigued, the aide asked Nixon which part of the address he was referring to. Was it, for example, that part where Kennedy said, 'Ask not what your country can do for you, but what you can do for your country?' 'No,' said Nixon, 'the part that starts, "I do solemnly swear."'[142]

CHAPTER 4

'GO TALK TO SENATOR RUSSELL': JOHN F. KENNEDY AND RICHARD B. RUSSELL, JR

Howard Keeley

Introduction: Russell anent Kennedy's civil rights legacy

In early January 1961, Vice-President-elect Lyndon B. Johnson delivered an instance of the in-your-face 'Johnson treatment' to Richard Brevard Russell, Jr (1897–1971), the senior United States senator from Georgia. Johnson posed a rhetorical question to Russell, referring to him in the third person: '[W]hat good will it do me if Dick Russell – the best friend I've got in the whole world – gets up and snots and fusses and embarrasses me and the president and the president's brother ...?'[1] The issue at hand was president-elect Kennedy's desire to nominate Robert F. ('Bobby') Kennedy for the position of attorney general. As the Senate's foremost southern Democrat, born a little over three decades after Lee's surrender at Appomattox, Russell feared the erosion of white ascendancy in the south by means of prospective, Jack Kennedy-propelled civil rights legislation – potentially sweeping legislation that, if passed, Bobby Kennedy as AG would enforce.

The co-author of the Southern Manifesto of 1956, a response to Supreme Court-mandated school desegregation,[2] Russell had, by the time of Kennedy's ascent to the presidency, established himself as chief among the bloc of conservative, segregationist southern senators opposed to civil rights bills, whether their focus be lynching, voter-disenfranchisement, or shared accommodations (from the public bus to the privately owned lunch counter). In advancing this agendum, Russell's vast, detailed knowledge of parliamentary rules and precedents rendered him an adept deployer of such strategies as the filibuster.[3] However, on 10 June 1964, for the first time in its history – too late for Kennedy to witness – the Senate managed successfully to invoke cloture to end the filibustering of a civil rights bill.

Having survived sixty days of debate, that Russell-engineered filibuster was outmanoeuvred, using strategies learned from Russell, by the Democratic whip, Hubert Humphrey (Minnesota), who, at President Johnson's insistence, had secured vital co-operation from the Republican Minority Leader, Everett Dirksen (Illinois).[4] Thus, in spite of Russell, Johnson achieved what, addressing a joint Congressional session two days after Kennedy's funeral, he had deemed a memorial superior to any 'oration or eulogy' in honour of '[t]he greatest leader of our time [Kennedy]', namely, 'passage of the civil rights bill for which he fought so long'.[5] This vision on Johnson's part should be juxtaposed with a remark Russell made to Orville Freeman – the former Democratic Governor of Minnesota and Kennedy's (and Johnson's) Secretary of Agriculture – on 24 November 1963, two days after the assassination: 'We could have beaten Kennedy on civil rights, but we can't [beat] Lyndon.'[6]

Beyond the first-order matter of civil rights, it is instructive to contemplate some additional roles that Russell – Johnson's 'best friend'; his 'trusted and wise counsellor'[7] – played in the political career of John Fitzgerald Kennedy. Russell's power and influence were exceptional, a result, in part, of his chairmanship of the Senate Armed Services Committee from 1951 to 1953 and again from 1955 to 1969. The former period coincided with most of the Korean War, while the latter began in the first year of the almost nineteen-and-a-half-year-long Vietnam War. Russell's association with Armed Services caused President Kennedy to request him to 'place the Presidential wreath at the Tomb of the Unknowns in Arlington' on Memorial Day 1961, a gesture reported in the *New York Times* and acknowledged by Russell in a note to Kennedy: 'This is an honour that I highly prize. I do not think that my forebears who wore the Confederate Gray would object to my participating in a programme of this nature.'[8]

Russell's thirty-eight-year Senate career also included stints chairing other critical committees and subcommittees, and he died while President pro tempore of the United States Senate, the third office in the line of presidential succession.[9] Of note is the reputation Russell developed for running committees in a bipartisan fashion, a means of nurturing the professional relationships and friendships whose legacy includes the ninety-nine-to-one Senate vote that, in 1972, renamed the Old Senate Office Building on Capitol Hill in Russell's honour.[10]

Although Russell spearheaded a southern boycott of the August 1964 Democratic National Convention to criticise President Johnson's signing, a month earlier, of the landmark 1964 Civil Rights Act, he had, in 1948, declined to join the new, explicitly segregationist States' Rights Democratic Party (or Dixiecrats), whose leading members' separation from the mainstream Democratic Party proved short-lived. Furthermore, never was his rhetoric of the firebrand, race-baiting type rehearsed on the Senate floor by Theodore Bilbo (Louisiana), nicknamed the 'Bilboic plague', who, during the successful effort – supported by Russell – to filibuster the Costigan–Walker anti-lynching bill of 1938, warned that should the legislation pass, the 'daughters of Dixie' would suffer rape and other 'crimes' intolerable to 'red-blooded Anglo-Saxon White Southern men'.[11]

In an important speech to over 1,000 people in Rome, Georgia, thirteen days after Johnson signed the 1964 Act, Russell insisted that he '[did] not like these statutes', but he also declared that as the eleven titles constituting the act were 'now on the books', all 'good citizens' had a 'duty ... to learn to live with them for as long as they are there' and 'avoid all violence' during the implementation period, which he knew would be 'marked by tension and unrest'.[12] Via a personal note, dated 23 July 1964, President Johnson responded to the lack of demagoguery in Russell's Rome 'statement': 'Your call for compliance with the law of the land is, of course, in keeping with your personal code and I am confident it will have a great impact. It was the right and courageous thing to do.'[13]

Russell anent Kennedy's 1960 presidential campaign

Johnson's bond with Russell, slightly less than eleven years his senior, was a defining dimension of his political life, and it should be acknowledged as a factor in Kennedy's success in the 1960 presidential election. Once Kennedy secured the nomination – by gaining over 52.8 per cent of the first-round vote at the Democratic National Convention in Los Angeles on 13 July 1960 – he, to the consternation of labour leaders, among others, offered the vice-presidential slot to Johnson, the runner-up in the ballot, with over 26.8 per cent of the vote.

Norman Mailer's November 1960 *Esquire* magazine essay about the gathering described Kennedy as being 'unlike any politician who had ever run for President', and it attributed 'how Kennedy got to where he is' to 'money ... votes in primaries ... and, most of all ... a jewel of a political machine'.[14] Recognising the multiple constituencies that convened in Los Angeles, Mailer labelled Johnson's core supporters 'the Texas-twanging steel-stringing geetarists of Bubber Lyndon', and – of note, given the later acrimony between Johnson and Bobby Kennedy – he compared the nominee's brother, orchestrator of his political machine, to a footballer prepared to deliver 'a bony king-hell knee in the crotch'.[15]

Diagnosing his Yankee and Catholic identities as strikes against him in the south, a region where he had garnered no nominating votes, JFK determined that LBJ would be necessary to secure southern states in the general election; however, his calculus did not extend to Dick Russell.

Russell's desire had been for Johnson, his protégé, to head the Democratic Party's 1960 presidential ticket, perhaps contemplating such an outcome as recompense for his own disappointments in that arena. In 1948 and again in 1952, the Georgian had made it onto the presidential nominating ballot at the party's conventions, but his support for Jim Crow[16] sank him, notwithstanding his New Deal track record of helping modernise the south's infrastructure and economy.[17] (The Rome speech, discussed above, was delivered to the Coosa Valley Area Planning and Development Commission, founded in 1961.)

Once the Kennedy–Johnson pairing emerged, Russell expressed incredulity that Johnson would forsake leadership of the Senate for the vice-presidency. Nevertheless, he endorsed the ticket, albeit without any intention of hitting the campaign trail. Gilbert A. Fife avers that while Russell labelled the 1960 Democratic platform 'reprehensible' as regards race and 'socialistic' in many other respects, he deemed Kennedy a 'very capable young man' and judged his Catholicism irrelevant as a political consideration.[18]

Running unopposed for his Senate seat in the autumn of 1960, Russell repeated a pattern he had evolved of avoiding the white heat of presidential contests by travelling in Europe, primarily to inspect United States military installations. Back in his home town of Winder, Georgia, on 30 October, after three weeks away, Russell began fielding telephone entreaties from Johnson to come to the campaign's aid in the critical battleground of Texas. After some hesitation, Russell decided to help, and his activity intensified in response to an incident on 4 November 1960, at the Adolphus Hotel, Dallas, in which Johnson had to extract his wife, Lady Bird, from a group of rowdy, abusive Republicans. Lady Bird once characterised Russell as 'the archetype and bellwether of the South',[19] and he held her in affectionate esteem. Fully acceptable to Texas's socially and economically conservative Democrats, Russell 'stumped the state, speaking highly of Johnson and agreeing to accept Kennedy as "the lesser of two evils"'[20] – that is, preferable to Nixon. Gary A. Donaldson reflects, '[S]everal of Johnson's aides believed that Russell's last-minute contribution played a key role in the [Texas] victory,' won by just 50.52 per cent of the popular vote on election day, 9 November.[21]

On the following morning, the front page of the *New York Times* characterised Kennedy's national margin of victory as 'astonishing'. There is much consensus that the edge was 112,827 votes out of over 68.8 million cast, the closest margin (0.17 per cent) since 1916. In the Electoral College, the Kennedy ticket received 303 votes; the Nixon ticket, 219; and a segregationist ticket headed by Senator Harry F. Byrd, Sr of Virginia, fifteen. (With Senator Strom Thurmond of South Carolina as his vice-presidential choice, Byrd had not run a campaign, and his Electoral College tally came primarily from all of Mississippi's eight votes and six of Alabama's eleven.) It is plausible that word of the active, if belated campaigning by Russell, 'the Southern generalissimo',[22] in Texas helped influence Georgia, Louisiana and South Carolina also to elect the Democratic presidential ticket, an outcome none of the three would repeat until Georgia native Jimmy Carter's run in 1976.[23]

Although, in the end, Kennedy–Johnson carried Georgia handily, considerable pressure from within and without the state was, after polling day, visited upon Georgia's twelve Electoral College members to act independently and support Byrd–Thurmond, an action that, if successful, would almost certainly have forced the presidential decision into the House of Representatives. Georgia's Governor, Ernest Vandiver (married to Russell's niece, Betty Russell), favoured independent electors, a stance distasteful to Russell. Analysing the controversy, Patrick Novotny maintains, 'Russell became the most influential Democratic leader to challenge [Georgia's] unpledged electors ... warning that unpledged electors would ... "reduce whatever amount of influence" Georgia might have with the election of Kennedy.'[24] Novotny concludes that Russell's admonitory intervention and the more general 'support of Kennedy' by Russell and Georgia's junior senator, Herman Talmadge, constituted the 'most important' reasons for 'the failure' of the 1960 'unpledged-electors movement' in Georgia.[25] Thus, a case can be advanced that, without Russell's participation in Texas and Georgia, Kennedy might have missed taking the presidential oath of office in 1961.

Russell anent Kennedy's national security policies

Race and Russia, the two principal realities that would face the incoming president, received cogent rehearsal in Norman Mailer's November 1960 *Esquire* essay, 'Superman Comes to the Supermarket,' invoked above. Taking as benchmarks Sputnik 1 (4 October 1957) and the 'Little Rock Nine' (25 September 1957), Mailer argued, 'The national Ego was in shock: the Russians were now in some ways our technological superiors, and we had an internal problem of subject populations equal conceivably in its difficulty to the Soviet and its satellites.'[26] While Russell's anachronistic views on racial segregation were unshakable, his national-security and anti-Communist résumés could – and did – provide the basis for co-operation with the Kennedy administration, which, especially in its early days, was keenly cognisant of the electoral benefit the south had provided and, thus, had an added incentive to engage with Russell, beyond his seasoned sagacity and his raw power to deliver Senate votes. In assembling the president's cabinet, Kennedy and his team solicited Russell's counsel 'constantly',[27] not least respecting a Georgian, Dean Rusk, under consideration for the top foreign policy post, Secretary of State. Russell expressed reservations, but Rusk got the job.[28]

Cold War affairs quickly challenged Kennedy and Rusk, with the failed Bay of Pigs invasion of Cuba by a brigade of CIA-supported Cuban exiles, on 17–20 April 1961, constituting an early fiasco. In a 1971 interview, Rusk claimed 'no recollection' of a three-page memo, reputedly about the invasion, sent by Russell to Kennedy and Johnson on 21 April.[29] Predictably, the Bay of Pigs received attention during the 4 June 1961 Vienna summit between Kennedy and the Soviet leader, Nikita Khrushchev; however, that meeting's prickliest issue was the Soviet Union's threat to cede to East Germany the land-access routes to Berlin, whose western zone the Americans, British and French oversaw. In mid-August, the Berlin question intensified, as the East Germans began construction of a barbed-wire barricade, soon to be followed by the infamous wall, to prevent further emigration from East to West Berlin.

In his memoir, *As I Saw It*, developed with his son and first published in 1990, Rusk speculated that the Soviet Union's dissatisfaction over the West's continuing presence in Berlin 'may have been a precipitating factor' in its decision to establish in Cuba the ballistic missile complex photographed by an American U-2 reconnaissance aircraft on 14 October 1962.[30] Within six days, Kennedy and a specially assembled sixteen-person inner circle – ExComm, which did not include Russell (or any other member of Congress)[31] – made the determination to respond, at least in the first place, by imposing a naval quarantine on Cuba.

Per Rusk's memoir, it was only on 20 October, two hours before he intended to appear on television to inform the American people about the Cuba-based missiles, that Kennedy 'called about thirty congressional leaders', Russell among them, 'to the White House for their first briefing' on the subject.[32] Asked, in the 1971 interview, to comment on the claim that Russell had earlier knowledge of ExComm and its deliberations, Rusk responded (perhaps coyly) that 'it's possible' that either Defence Secretary Robert McNamara or Johnson 'was in touch with Senator Russell'. Given the briefing's timing, Kennedy had little intention of heeding any advice the lawmakers might proffer. Senator J. William Fulbright, the Foreign Relations Committee chair, joined Russell in strongly advocating an immediate military strike on Cuba, a course of action already considered and rejected by ExComm; however, neither man was ever to use a public forum to question Kennedy's decision.[33]

As regards the dominant Communist powers, Russia and China, Russell's national-security philosophy, while always broad-based, privileged overwhelming deterrents, such as the Strategic Air Command's capacity to deliver atomic destruction anywhere. Almost invariably, Russell was sceptical about new domestic initiatives and hostile towards foreign-aid programmes, believing that their costs effectively robbed the bank for investments in next-generation weapons technology, a domain rendered urgent by Sputnik 1 and 2. Most of Kennedy's New Frontier initiatives struck Russell as ideologically and fiscally extreme, but the 'Georgia Giant' was cheered by the young president's promise to significantly boost defence spending – rhetoric validated by concrete proposals as early as February 1961.

The year's emerging Berlin crisis motivated Congress to approve still further military-related expenditures, especially on long-range bombers, a course of action wholeheartedly sanctioned by both Robert McNamara as Kennedy's (then 45-year-old) Defence Secretary and Russell as Chairman of the Senate Armed Services Committee. Fairly quickly, the two men became reasonably close, with McNamara delivering the keynote at an Atlanta dinner on 11 November 1961, produced, in part, as a tribute to Russell. However, one national-security matter on which Russell diverged from McNamara and the president was the Limited Nuclear Test Ban Treaty, an agreed text for which was signed, in Moscow, by the United States, the Soviet Union, and the United Kingdom on 5 August 1963. Vigorous campaigning by the White House helped persuade eighty senators, but not Russell, to ratify it. Aware of the emerging Chinese and Israeli programmes, Kennedy sought to prevent nuclear proliferation, but Russell aligned with the military's Joint Chiefs, who, apart from being sceptical of the proposed inspection-for-verification regime, reckoned that restrictions on United States testing would prevent the nation from gaining or maintaining nuclear superiority.[34]

Tragically, forty-six days after signing the ratified treaty into law, Kennedy succumbed to an assassin's bullet. Had the President served a full term or two, one can but conjecture about the evolution of his relationship with Russell, whose 'warm friend' he, by January 1963, considered himself to be.[35]

One area of speculative interest is America's Vietnam policy. On 2 October 1963, the White House announced that a report recently submitted by McNamara and the Joint Chiefs' Chairman, General Maxwell D. Taylor, provided a timeline for the gradual withdrawal of the 15,000 American troops deployed in South Vietnam. As President, Johnson would reverse that policy, but since April 1954, when the French found themselves beleaguered in Vietnam, Russell had been wary of – and often vociferously resistant to – American intervention there.[36]

Conclusion

Jack Kennedy's engagement with Dick Russell was far broader and more nuanced than this essay can acknowledge. While turbulence within the nuclear scene abroad and the racial one at home precipitated many of their interactions, direct and indirect, other matters also connected the two men. A coda to the relationship was Russell's service on the commission of inquiry into Kennedy's assassination. Russell participated reluctantly, not least because he held the Chairman, Chief Justice Earl Warren, 'in contempt' for his court's civil rights record.[37]

Of undoubted advantage to Kennedy as President was Russell's availability to counsel him about agricultural programmes and legislation. At his core, Russell was a constituency politician, committed to advancing his beloved Georgia, where the farm remained the dominant economic engine. While Russell facilitated 'New South' industrial projects, much of his policy expertise resided with agriculture, by choice as much as necessary. Via multiple actions, he enabled the increasingly scientific, big-business, and international character of the agri-food system;[38] however, he also lamented the decline of the family farm and sought protections for it. Russell drew his Capitol Hill interns from Georgian members of a youth organisation, 4-H, largely associated with farm life. Although buffeted by mid-western interests, Russell endorsed Kennedy's attempts to tighten federal grain-production controls. In addition to arguing that the storage of surplus grain cost Washington too much money, the Georgian resented the grain sector's enjoyment of a federal regulatory regime not accorded to such key southern crops as cotton and peanuts.[39]

Despite the profound gap between the two on race, Kennedy esteemed Russell for the generosity – and the respect – that he exhibited when the younger man, the President, asked the older, a Lion of the Senate, for guidance.[40] He esteemed him, too, for his thoroughness and integrity during their exchanges, whether the matter was the field of battle, the peanut field, or another site of human endeavour. In a 2009 interview, Charles Campbell,

Russell's last Chief of Staff, recalled that when Edward M. ('Ted') Kennedy entered the Senate, having won his brother Jack's former seat in a November 1962 special election, he 'went to President Kennedy' to inquire, 'What can I do to get off on a good foot and to do the things ... necessary to be effective and be a good senator?' Campbell concluded his anecdote by quoting the President's advice to the future Lion: 'Go talk to Senator Russell.'[41]

CHAPTER 5

SCREENING KENNEDY IN IRELAND

Harvey O'Brien

Though the assassination of President John F. Kennedy in November 1963 would come to define a global epoch, the four days the President spent on Irish soil between 26 and 29 June that same year, were arguably more meaningful to Ireland and the Irish.[1] The President's visit was widely seen in Ireland as one of the defining moments of Hibernian modernity. Commenting at a public address at the John Fitzgerald Kennedy Presidential Library in 1998, thirty-five years after the visit, Irish President Mary McAleese said 'None of us will ever forget the impact of his visit to Ireland at a time of dramatic change and challenge in our own country.' Kennedy's visit endorsed and cemented an image of twentieth-century Ireland corresponding with Kennedy's own persona: combining youthful vigour with a strong sense of tradition. As David Lubin concludes in his meditation on the image of JFK in post-war American culture, 'Pictures of JFK remain compelling to us today only because the story they tell is not his alone but also ours.'[2] This is equally true of his relationship with Ireland, and exactly so in the case of the films made from his visit to Ireland, both in what they show and what they consciously occlude.

Kennedy's visit was a major diplomatic event in the still relatively young Irish state, a politically resonant assertion of the international standing of a state free of direct British rule for just over forty years and a fully declared republic for less than fifteen. This public spectacle and media event was also seen as a homecoming for the Irish diaspora, symbolic of the longed-for return of so many friends and family lost to emigration. Furthermore, paradoxically, Kennedy himself was seen as a symbol of the success of that diaspora – the Irish boy made good all the way to the White House. If he could do it, why not the son or daughter who had left in tears and poverty five, fifteen or fifty years before?

Between 17 March 2006 and 15 September 2007 an exhibition ran at the John F. Kennedy Presidential Library and Museum in Boston entitled *A Journey Home – John F. Kennedy and Ireland*. It is still archived online. The theme of the exhibition was the historical connections between the Kennedy family and Ireland, exhibiting historical documents and objects tracing Kennedy lineage back to the Norman conquest. It was also intended to demonstrate the immense and genuine affection which President Kennedy held for Ireland and the Irish. The press release for the exhibition quoted the President's speech in Limerick on 29 June 1963 where he said 'This is not the land of my birth but it is the land for which I hold the greatest affection.' Though there is no doubt that Kennedy did have a soft spot for Ireland insofar as is expressed in comments of this kind, the fact is that the President owed a great deal of his political success to Irish American voters and politicians in the United States, and, quite apart from any spontaneous gestures of love and affection he felt inclined to make, Kennedy's visit to Ireland was important in cementing his ties to Irish America as much as to Ireland itself. That said, White House aide Kenny O'Donnell was reportedly against the trip on the grounds that 'You've got all the Irish votes in this country that you'll ever get.'[3] As presidential assistant Dave Powers, who accompanied the President on his journey to Ireland, commented in the film *John F. Kennedy in the Island of Dreams* (1993): 'You could say that the Irish elected him President, and he was going home to thank their cousins.'[4] In reality, however, the visit represented a far deeper significance.

The visit

President Kennedy's visit to Ireland was part of his European tour of 1963. Just before he came to Ireland, he visited West Germany, and in Berlin, at the Berlin Wall, the very day he travelled to Ireland, he delivered one of the best remembered quotes of his international political career. In the ideologically and recently logistically besieged city of West Berlin, surrounded by the seemingly implacable forces of international Communism, President Kennedy remarked: 'Two thousand years ago the proudest boast was "*civis Romanus sum*." Today, in the world of freedom, the proudest boast is "*Ich bin ein Berliner*."' Nothing Kennedy said in Ireland resonated so loudly or so greatly, nor has it endured so long, but this is not to say that he said nothing of consequence, or that his trip to Ireland served no political purpose, even though, writing in 1965, Arthur Schlesinger would refer to it in his book *A Thousand Days* as '… a blissful interlude of homecoming, at once sentimental and ironic'.[5]

In a memo to President John F. Kennedy dated 22 May 1963 from Special Assistant for National Security Affairs McGeorge Bundy, the matter of 'Why are we Going to Europe?' (also the title of the memo) was addressed.[6] On one level, the memo stated, the trip was a response to the many invitations received. Invitations of this kind are rarely spontaneous and, in the case of Ireland, exploratory negotiations had taken place some time before. In 1961, United States air carriers had complained about the restrictions on access to Irish airports for the lucrative and expanding tourist trade. By July 1962, the new economic policies of T.K. Whitaker and Seán Lemass had begun to bear fruit in terms of reversing the protectionist trends of the preceding decades, and that month saw the ground-breaking ceremony at the new American Embassy in Ballsbridge, Dublin. During that same year, Irish Minister for Foreign Affairs Frank Aiken was approached by a representative of President Kennedy's office on the possibility of a visit to Ireland by Kennedy as part of his planned European tour. Aiken informed the representative that such a visit would be received positively, and so an official invitation was issued by Irish President Eamon de Valera shortly afterwards, which was immediately accepted.

In December 1962, the United States Secretary of State Dean Rusk visited Ireland on a stopover and met with President de Valera. At a press conference on 18 December Rusk praised de Valera, saying 'It is given to few men to be a legend in their own lifetime as the father of their country,' which is all very right and proper and friendly from the point of view of international diplomacy. However, though this is not the appropriate place to explore the matter more fully, the shadow of Seán Ó Faoláin must fall here with his famous observation that de Valera was not so much a great man as a great Irishman. J.J. Lee softens the blow of this comment in his assessment that 'O'Faolain's criticism is less a reflection on de Valera than on Ireland. De Valera is entitled to be judged by the only standards with which he could reasonably be expected to be familiar. By those standards he has an indubitable claim to greatness.'[7]

That seeming aside is relevant because part of the symbolism of the Kennedy visit in endorsing the achievements of Ireland in the modern world was, in Ireland at least, in linking a politician of world stature with one of national stature who, on a local level, seemed even greater. It is rather extraordinary from a rhetorical point of view alone that at Kennedy's greeting at Dublin airport by de Valera the President of Ireland said to the President of the United States: 'We are proud of you.'

Kennedy's visit was not cynically contrived to be a disingenuous and artificial boosting of Ireland's ego, but it was a self-conscious appeal to Ireland to step up and join the great powers of the Western World in a military alliance against the Eastern Bloc. The second point of reference in the McGeorge Bundy memo of 22 May 1963 was as follows:

> ... more broadly, this is your first chance to visit Europe in almost two years. In those two years great things have happened – the threat to Berlin has been successfully resisted; a great crisis in Cuba has been surmounted; progress has well begun in the movement for freer trade; and while important issues have arisen within the Atlantic alliance, the alliance itself and the American commitment to it are in fact stronger than ever. In this situation it is important to meet and talk with major European leaders and to represent the people of the United States to all the peoples of Europe. So it is our hope that by this trip itself, and by what you say there, you will be able to emphasise the enduring commitment of the United States to peace and progress through the Atlantic partnership.[8]

The 'Atlantic alliance' and 'partnership' of which Bundy is speaking is, naturally, NATO. And though President Kennedy never spoke openly of NATO during his visit to Ireland, his speech at the Dáil is fairly unambiguous in its encouragement of Ireland and the Irish to play an active role in the fight against Communism.

Speaking first of all in general historical terms and quoting speeches by Irish and American political figures from centuries past, President Kennedy outlined the history of Ireland's fight for freedom not so much in terms of a national struggle for liberty, but an international one for the cause of freedom itself. He spoke of the Irish Brigade at the Battle of Fredericksburg in 1862 (and made a mistake in the detail, picked up by more than one observer at the time), and commended more recent efforts by Irish peacekeeping forces in the Congo and the Gaza Strip. He praised Ireland's censure of the repression of the Hungarian revolution and Ireland's ongoing role as an active member of the United Nations. But although it must have seemed to the parliamentarians assembled in the Dáil[9] that day that this represented the end of history and a firm pat on the back for a job well done, it was, evidently as Kennedy saw it, only the beginning. In his speech, he remarked:

> I am glad, therefore, that Ireland is moving in the mainstream of current world events. For I sincerely believe that your future is as promising as your past is proud, and that your destiny lies not as a peaceful island in a sea of troubles, but as a maker and shaper of world peace.
>
> For self-determination can no longer mean isolation; and the achievement of national independence today means withdrawal from the old status only to return to the world scene with a new one. New nations can build with their former governing powers the same kind of fruitful relationship that Ireland has established with Great Britain – a relationship founded on equality and mutual interests. And no nation, large or small, can be indifferent to the fate of others, near or far. Modern economics, weaponry and communications have made us all realise more than ever that we are one human family and this one planet is our home.
>
> ... The central issue of freedom, however, is between those who believe in self-determination and those in the East who would impose on others the harsh and oppressive Communist system; and here your nation wisely rejects the role of a go-between or a mediator. Ireland pursues an independent course in foreign policy, but it is not neutral between liberty and tyranny and never will be.

For knowing the meaning of foreign domination, Ireland is the example and inspiration to those enduring endless years of oppression.[10]

Kennedy knew his audience. The points at which applause occurs are not recorded in the written transcript of his address, but they were captured by the television cameras of Telefís Éireann. Interestingly and significantly, of the various film and television compilations of the Kennedy visit which exist or were in general circulation, only the Telefís Éireann broadcast features the full Dáil speech. Most films do not reference it at all. It is as if the hard sell of Kennedy's politics was of no interest then or now, and yet, evidently, this was by definition the most important part of his trip – speaking directly to the Irish Parliament – in fact a special session in which both houses were assembled together for the first time for the occasion.

Early on in his address, Kennedy spoke of the religious links between the Christian West and Ireland itself in opposing Communism: 'The supreme reality of our time is our indivisibility as children of God,' he said.[11] Kennedy was a canny politician, and there were no accidents in his speech to the Dáil (his errors on Fredericksburg excepted). Kennedy was making a sincere and direct attempt to highlight Ireland's importance to the military and ideological strategy of the Western alliance. Those airports to which access was so slowly granted to commercial operators and which are still to this day central to political issues regarding the status of Ireland's neutrality, were and are an important logistical element of any potential military operations directed east of the United States. Inspections of Soviet aircraft landing in Shannon in the early 1960s were already a serious potential compromise of Irish neutrality, but arguably justifiable in terms of homeland security much as they served the purpose of assisting United States interests by monitoring Soviet traffic from Europe to Cuba.

As early as 1952 Kennedy was directly addressing the question of Ireland's military status, as demonstrated in a note to Congressman John E. Fogarty of Rhode Island, sent obviously as part of Kennedy's bid for the Senate:

Ireland is an indispensable link in the chain of European defence. Under the present circumstances, with a divided military setup, it is easy to forsee the tremendous difficulties that would be encountered in an attempt to co-ordinate the defence of Ireland. To eliminate that weakness and to bolster the defence of the free world, Ireland should be treated as a military unit.[12]

Here Kennedy is not only addressing the central importance of Ireland in military terms, he is also responding to issues of partition. A united Ireland, he is suggesting, is in the best interests of European defence. Again here we see a linking of the local and the global in political terms which invite a romantic nationalistic interpretation, but which can also be read in broader political terms within ongoing ideological discourses of American foreign policy in general. And yet, as James Robert Carroll points out in his 2003 book on the Kennedy visit, partition was one subject that did not arise in any of the speeches or press coverage surrounding the event.[13] The meeting between Taoiseach Seán Lemass and President Kennedy on 27 June was not followed by a press conference and notes of the meeting remained classified largely because, Carroll reports, based on observations by former White House Assistant Press Secretary Malcolm Kilduff, neither Lemass nor Kennedy wanted the issue of partition to come up. Though in 1952 Kennedy may have yearned for a united Ireland, or at least claimed to, he was pragmatic enough to recognise that keeping the Republic aligned with the interests of NATO, however tacitly, was a more valuable immediate political objective.

Lemass, for his part, was most likely very happy to pursue the agenda of Ireland's place on the global stage rather than its internal domestic affairs, an attitude which corresponded with his prevailing economic and ideological policies of the period. In fact, Lemass's return visit to the Unted States in October 1963 was to serve as a very real economic platform from which the Taoiseach appealed successfully for American investment in Ireland in the form both of business deals, establishing operations for American companies at the industrial estate in Shannon, and the establishment of the Irish-American Foundation, a tax-exempt body intended to promote exchange of personnel and ideas between the two countries.

Screening the visit

In spite of all of the above, Kennedy's visit to Ireland is still to this day seen more in terms of a sentimental journey to the green and misty isle of his distant ancestral past: a quaint and irrelevant sideshow in the great political performance that was Kennedy's trip to Europe, especially falling as it did right after West Germany and just before Great Britain where 'real business' was being done. This has been thoroughly and repeatedly reinforced by the films that have emerged out of the visit, both those filmed at the time and those that followed.

The most complete of them all is the aforementioned Telefís Éireann piece, entitled, in its daily broadcast form, *President Kennedy in Ireland June 26–29, 1963* (1963), but also compiled into a single piece called *Welcome Mr. President.* Telefís Éireann's coverage essentially represented the official state visual record of the event and this film comes with a commentary written by Barry Baker and spoken by Pádraig Ó Raghallaigh which offers particular and explicit interpretations of events. Early on, as the presidential motorcade proceeds down O'Connell Street in a scene featured many times since in subsequent representations of the event, we are told 'The two Presidents rode together, one born in America, one sentenced to death for his part in the Easter Week rising the year before the other was born, both now heads of state that are very different in size, wealth and power, but both alike and equal in liberty.'[14] We may laugh now at the semantics of it, but this comment unproblematically represents the official reading of the situation, a reading not wholly originating within Ireland itself. It recalls Dean Rusk's statement of December 1962 and it reinforces the important political point that de Valera stood for liberty and for Ireland, and that, even by dint of his birth, gave further credence to the sense of historical connection between the United States and Ireland from an American–Irish perspective, not merely an Irish–American one. President Kennedy remarked on this in his speech in the Dáil, quipping that if de Valera had not left Brooklyn, he might be standing where Kennedy was standing now, and that if Kennedy's great grandparents had not left Ireland, he himself might be sitting with the others in the Dáil.

The Columban Fathers Present President Kennedy in Ireland (1963) is a film of comparable length to the Telefís Éireann film, but is far more superficial and openly editorial. This film takes as its initial point of reference a quote by W.B. Yeats: 'Soldier, scholar, statesman, he, as 'twere all life's epitome, what made us dream, That he could comb grey hair.' It was relatively commonplace in Irish documentary at that time to use Yeats this way, a point I remark on in my book *The Real Ireland* (2004), but it is, in many ways, as significant a juxtaposition as linking de Valera and Kennedy in the Telefís Éireann film to link Yeats and Kennedy in this way, however clumsily: fitting Yeats's description to Kennedy as if the connection between the two men was organic by dint of the ancestral umbilical cord between the Anglo-Irish poet and the Irish-American politician.[15] The film which follows strongly emphasises the ideological connections between the United States and Ireland which were so much the cornerstone of the trip. If anything, it plays to the American side of the story more strongly than the Irish, almost as if demonstrating its gratitude for the visit, and though it uses Kennedy's quote that 'In Ireland I think you see something of what is so great about the United States. And I must say in the United States, through millions of your sons and daughters and cousins, 25 million in fact, you see something of what is great about Ireland', the film's voice-over goes on to present Kennedy's visit as if it were the coming of a God among men: 'the man whose fame encircles the earth has come among them', it says. Though the fact is indisputable, the sentiment is biblical to say the least, unsurprising given that the producers were a religious missionary organisation. Furthermore the film comments that Kennedy is 'president of the greatest nation on earth' and concludes, following a rendition of *When Irish Eyes are Smiling* with the comment 'He went as he came, like a whisper in the dawn; but Ireland and her people were richer for the visit of John Fitzgerald Kennedy.' This jaw-droppingly condescending film was screened on BBC Northern Ireland in 1995 during United States President Bill Clinton's visit to Ireland, and was followed by a political panel discussion on Clinton's role in the peace process. How frightening that such a representation should serve an unproblematic role as historical preface in a contemporary political debate?

In a similar vein, and even more peculiar is *Kennedy's Ireland* (1968) also later known as *O'Kennedy's Ireland*, an American-produced but Irish-filmed overview of Irish history and culture which, arguably slightly ironically,[16] filtered its 'view' of Ireland through the story of the Kennedys. It also ingeniously manages to combine samples from Kennedy's speeches and outtakes from other films to provide its overview of Ireland and Irish culture, making such bizarre feints as citing President Kennedy's concern for education and the arts in general as being a Celtic trait and therefore exemplified in Ireland by the Book of Kells — cue footage of the book itself. Another interesting sidenote in the film is the representation of Irish

Travellers as 'a classic example of the traditional Irish love of personal liberty' – a curious generalisation combining and compressing two strands of cultural and political identity under the banner of one harmonious, democratising aphorism – essentially erasing decades of ongoing struggle between settled and travelling communities around issues of ethnicity.[17]

The point here again is that in all of these cases, the official reading of the Kennedy visit serves as the jump-off point for what, in two cases, descends into mawkish piffle. Only the Telefís Éireann coverage features the Dáil speech, as noted, and even then this serves as part of the 'public record' of the event rather than being posited in terms of a particular presentation of a political reading of what was said. If anything, the politics of it are de-emphasised by the unedited coverage, which becomes like so much wallpaper. However, as discussed earlier, noting the points at which applause occurs does tell you something about the disconnect between what Kennedy was saying and what those in the Dáil were hearing.

Further testament to the failure of the President's political mission is to be found in the fact that when Taoiseach Seán Lemass in turn visited Kennedy in the United States in October, 1963, a National Security File memo providing 'Talking Points' for President Kennedy specifically states that he might wish to avoid discussing the 'Irish position on military commitment to the West'. In effect, Kennedy was being told not to mention the most substantive issue he had raised during his trip. The rationale provided was that Lemass would be quizzed about this back in Ireland on his return, and it was suggested that he did not want to be put under that particular pressure. This did not however, as noted, prevent Lemass from securing the vital business deals upon which the new 'special relationship' between Ireland and the United States would be based, and though partition was again an unacknowledged spectre, tacit 'blind eye'-style military co-operation between Ireland and the United States continued, and still does.

But what about the American reaction then? How was JFK's trip to Ireland viewed in the United States? Well, as in Ireland, the visit was largely seen by American commentators as a sentimental journey to the old country. Kennedy did nothing to disabuse them of that notion, nor, in fact, was it untrue. The fact that Kennedy had a political mission does not *ipso facto* preclude the possibility that there was a human side to his interest in Ireland. That was nowhere more evident than in the strange tale of *WHS1 Reel 2*

(1963), Army Signal Corps photographer Cecil Stoughton's official record of the President's visit, recorded from within his inner circle.

Stoughton, insofar as possible, tried to replicate the event as it might have been seen from Kennedy's own point of view. Not entirely, of course. It would have been impractical to have a camera over his shoulder all of the time, but Stoughton was specifically instructed by Kennedy to try to capture more footage of what he was seeing rather than simply footage of him. Stoughton therefore had superior access to Kennedy and all of the visit sites than any other media practitioner, and the result was a fascinating home-movie style insight into the physical details of the Kennedy visit. *WHS1 Reel 2* ranges from small things like a close-up of the cake bearing the President's profile prepared by Mrs Ryan in Wexford for the so-called 'intimate family party' held there, or a pronounced close-up of Kennedy's foot tapping to the beat of Irish music at a dance exhibition in Cork, to bigger things, including an overdub of cheering crowds and wildtrack Irish music to create a sense of being in the moment even though the film was shot silently.

Most interesting of all is that this film, which was only one reel of the overall European tour film, was among Kennedy's favourite entertainments at the White House: so much so, apparently, that his family tried to hide it at one point to stop him watching it over and over.[18]

On a more public level, the sense that the President's pleasure was being indulged is strongly emphasised by two contemporaneous television news reports, CBS News Extra's *JFK Goes Home* (1963) and NBC News's Special Report *The President's Journey* (1963). Some of the footage from *WHS1 Reel 2* makes it into these reports, as do many sound bites regarding Kennedy's affection for Ireland and the Irish. Of the two, the NBC report is by far the more pointed, quoting the Dáil speech and further using scenes of the President at the ceremony at Arbour Hill Cemetery, honouring Irish military dead, to reference the military significance of Ireland in European terms. However, the panel discussion which follows the report tends to dismiss the Irish visit as 'a raising of the President's stock' and does not debate Irish issues in themselves. The presence nonetheless of the question of the military agenda attests to at least the availability of that reading to contemporary American media commentators.

The CBS report, by contrast, is horrifically condescending, featuring well-known Irish broadcaster Micheál O'Hehir vainly attempting to report from Ireland in between CBS voice-overs which undercut his journalism with 'helpful' observations such as 'The biggest thing about Dunganstown is its name' and 'There normally isn't a lot to do in New Ross, and a lot of people doing it. Why, there hasn't even been a fire in years' over footage of a bored-looking horse standing outside the local fire station. The CBS broadcast corresponds with a well-worn tradition of representing Ireland in documentary film dating back to James A. Fitzpatrick, whose travelogues were a staple part of the cinema-going experience from the 1930s.

Fitzpatrick's film *Glimpses of Erin* (1934) established a template for American-produced documentaries about Ireland which, in general terms, envision the country as a kind of counterpoint to the United States, symbolic proof, if you will, of the modernity of America through representing the primitivism of other places.[19] It is interesting how completely opposite this reportage stands relative to the perception of the Kennedy visit within Ireland, let alone the genuine political motives behind it, or even to the NBC report. The depiction of Kennedy's 'home' as a backward, comical, picaresque Irish peasant village reinforces the sense that Kennedy's visit to Ireland could be nothing but a pleasure trip and that Ireland could serve no valuable political function on the global stage, and arguably tars Kennedy himself with the same indolent brush, suggesting his 'Irishness' might represent an undesirable ancestral atavism.

All of the above films originate roughly within the timeframe of the Kennedy visit, all bar one within his lifetime. Two later films raise the question of perspective gained with time. In *Mother of the Kennedys* (1973) Rose Fitzgerald Kennedy was interviewed by Fr Peter Lemass as part of the *Radharc* television series. Radharc Films was an independent production company and their long-running magazine programme examined all aspects of then contemporary Irish life, usually with a religious inflection. The fact that it was produced by religious personnel meant that *Radharc* were rarely refused access to whatever it was they wanted to film. It was in just such a context that Rose Kennedy granted an interview to Fr Lemass in 1973, a very rare event. Mrs Kennedy accepted the interview on the basis that she would not be quizzed on names, dates, places or any other historical or political kinds of issues. She spoke instead about her faith, her belief in family, and her praying for grace and resignation upon the death of her two most famous sons. The programme was a fascinating insight into the

Kennedy clan though, and featured interviews with Teddy and Jean Kennedy among others, who added even more perspective on their mother's life. The programme was first broadcast in 1973 on the night of the tenth anniversary of JFK's death, and was repeated on RTÉ in 1995 three weeks after Rose Kennedy's own death at the age of 105. In this alone we again begin to see the deep currents of history and culture running from Kennedy and from his visit to Ireland, resonating here across time and theme. Though marking his death as a broadcast, the film is not about him, but it is, in the way of these things, about his 'Irishness', namely – his Catholic mother.

The final film I would like to draw attention to in this essay was also produced to mark the anniversary of the President's death, but twenty years later again. *John F. Kennedy in the Island of Dreams* (1993) was a reflective, almost meditative overview of the Kennedy visit, filmed in a slightly abstract style using slow dissolves and soporific music to induce the sense of dream and fantasy, not so much to undercut the subject as to render it 'poetic'. Interestingly, though the programme had a sense of perspective on Ireland in the 1960s because of the historical distance from it and was therefore able to put Kennedy in the context of the changes taking place in Ireland at that time, changes of the kind referred to by President McAleese in 1998 (such as the slow waning of nationalism on the national agenda, the economic transformation, the gradual emergence of youth culture and the slow turning of the head towards America that was culturally pervasive at the time anyway), it still did not explore the hard political edge of the visit and its meaning. The question of the military agenda and the economic basis of the increased sense of connection between Ireland and America were not raised in the film, although it did attempt to introduce an aspect of critical history by producing interviews with dissenting voices, such as Máirín de Burca, who recalled fleeing to the Aran Islands to avoid the hype, and featured interesting de-romanticising details such as the story of a secret serviceman pulling a gun on an Irish journalist during the trip. However, a sense of warmth and nostalgia eventually overwhelms whatever critical investigation there is. Made at a time when the 'Celtic Tiger' was emerging and Ireland seemed to be developing a keener sense of scepticism about its own past, the 'poetic' and 'dreamlike' qualities in the film prevail over its ability to contextualise Kennedy in terms of the New Ireland, producing instead yet another restatement of the myth of the visit, the myth that continues to permeate the historical re-presentation of those days in the summer of 1963.

What is clear from the body of films that emerged from the Kennedy visit was that the geopolitical realpolitik was essentially ignored by the media and wilfully downplayed or merely diplomatically occluded by those with instrumental power in Ireland at the time. The Irish State clearly desired international diplomatic and political recognition, and sought to claim Kennedy's ethnic identity as a symbolic alignment with the centre of political power, but it nonetheless politely eschewed overt military commitment. However, it did not decline friendly diplomatic relations, aircraft landings (military or not), or transatlantic economic investment, and the details of these were hammered out over the course of the arrangements for and during the aftermath of the visit. None of this featured in the filmed representations of the visit, so it should come as little surprise then that the legend of the visit should continue to drift free of the details and assume the mantle of myth. Symbolically, the Kennedy visit was extremely significant, and achieved precisely what it was intended to portray. As the non-fiction record fell back upon its simplest of functions – recording – it rendered a fair and accurate picture of what transpired, at least in public.

CHAPTER 6

FROM SHANNON TO DALLAS: THE FINAL TWENTY-ONE WEEKS OF JFK'S PRESIDENCY

Brian Murphy

Introduction

The distance from Shannon Airport to Dallas, Texas, is 7,045 kilometres. It took the thirty-fifth President of the United States 146 days to make this journey, although he took a rather circuitous route. On 29 June 1963, John Kennedy spent his last ever day on Irish soil. Prior to departing, Kennedy famously said 'this is not the land of my birth but it is the land for which I hold the greatest affection and I certainly will come back in the Springtime'.[1] That pledge was not honoured because of an assassin's bullet in Dealey Plaza, Dallas, on 22 November 1963. Kennedy's time in Ireland has been described as the happiest of his presidency,[2] but from the moment he departed on Air Force One he rode a political and emotional rollercoaster. Between leaving Shannon and arriving in Texas, Kennedy experienced some of the most tumultuous and defining days of his presidency.

In this short twenty-one week period, Kennedy triumphantly concluded an important test ban treaty. He significantly advanced détente with the Soviet Union. He put out peace-feelers towards Cuba and China. His administration was complicit in a coup in Vietnam while, at the same time, Kennedy was, paradoxically, planning to downscale American involvement in South East Asia. He endured the huge personal bereavement of losing a child. He made incremental progress on the burning issue of civil rights legislation. He also began, to all intents and purposes, campaigning for his re-election in 1964.

Kennedy's visit to England

Kennedy got the biggest laugh of his Irish visit when he started to say that Limerick was his final stop before going on to England and then Italy. Instead, he caught himself, and said, 'From here I go to – another country – and then Italy.'[3] Kennedy had told his close adviser, Kenny O'Donnell, that his visit to Ireland was 'a pleasure trip'.[4] In contrast, Kennedy's visit to England involved significant political business, but before this could be conducted, the President availed of the opportunity to discharge a family debt of honour.

Minutes after the President's plane left Shannon Airport, the White House announced that Kennedy would visit a family grave in Derbyshire and Air Force One made a hitherto unpublicised stop at Waddington RAF base, where the President transferred by helicopter to the Chatsworth Estate in the Peak District.[5] There Kennedy paid his first and only visit to his younger sister Kathleen's grave. She had died in a plane crash in France in 1948 and had been buried on the estate of her late husband, an English aristocrat and heir apparent of the tenth Duke of Devonshire.[6]

From Chatsworth, Kennedy travelled to Birch Grove, the country residence of the British Prime Minister, Harold Macmillan, for talks with his closest European ally on forthcoming negotiations on a nuclear atmospheric test ban treaty. After twelve hours of talks, Kennedy and Macmillan agreed to 'push urgently' for a treaty with the Soviet Union and much of the discussion between the leaders was 'concerned with firming up Allied strategy for the talks'. However, the United States President failed to persuade the British Prime Minister to support the concept of a Multilateral Force, an American project for the creation of a multi-nation nuclear force of Polaris-armed surface vessels.[7]

Kennedy also used his United Kingdom visit to secure British support on an issue of concern in the United States's geopolitical sphere of influence.

Kennedy's administration was urging Macmillan to suspend the constitution in British Guiana, a self-governing British colony on South America's North Atlantic coast, and 'to impose direct rule in the riot-torn country'.[8] British Guiana's left-wing Prime Minister, Cheddi Jagan, was pushing for full independence and the United States was strongly opposed to such a course, while Jagan remained in power. Dean Rusk, the United States Secretary of State, who accompanied Kennedy in his talks with Macmillan, had made it 'clear' that the Kennedy administration viewed Jagan as 'cast from the same mould as Prime Minister Fidel Castro of Cuba and that the Guianese leftist's assumption of control would heighten American difficulties with Cuba'. At Birch Grove, Prime Minister Macmillan assured Kennedy that 'independence was not contemplated now'. One possible British solution that Kennedy and Rusk found acceptable was the introduction of proportional representation for voting in British Guiana.[9]

Italy, the Vatican and NATO

Kennedy's next stop was Italy, where he rested at Villa Serbelloni, a Rockefeller Foundation-owned property, at a northern beach resort on Lake Como.[10] The President's visit coincided with the coronation of Pope Paul VI, but after consulting with Cardinal Cushing from Boston, Kennedy did not attend the ceremonies. 'Stay away from Rome until after the coronation,' the Cardinal advised. 'It's the biggest day of the man's life and you don't want to take the play away from him.'[11] President Kennedy waited until two days after the coronation before he went to the Vatican to meet with the new pope. This meeting was, in fact, a renewing of acquaintanceships because Paul VI had first met the President and other members of the Kennedy family at the coronation of Pope Pius XII in 1939. On that occasion, Ted Kennedy had received his First Communion from Pius XII.[12]

Journalists who accompanied President Kennedy's delegation to the Vatican reported that 'Kennedy appeared clearly moved by the [private] audience with the Pope.'[13] In the days prior to the President's meeting with Paul VI, there was heightened newspaper speculation as to whether Kennedy would kiss the Pope's ring, which is the custom for Roman Catholics when received by the Pontiff. Kennedy, however, had no intention of doing so because 'he was visiting Paul as a head of state, not as a Catholic'. Kennedy sarcastically remarked to Kenny O'Donnell that 'Norman Vincent Peale would love that ... And it would get me a lot of votes in South Carolina.'[14] Kennedy was determined not to give ammunition to those who believed that a Catholic president would be subservient to Rome. According to Shaun Casey, the author of *The Making of a Catholic President*, 'the argument was, when push came to shove, a president who was Roman Catholic would ultimately be more loyal to the Vatican because the fate of his eternal soul was at stake'.[15] Kennedy had narrowly prevailed in a presidential election in 1960 that had nasty sectarian overtones with some Protestant critics of the Democratic Party candidate openly questioning whether Kennedy's religious faith would allow him to make national decisions independently of his church. According to Anderson Yanoso's study, *The Irish and the American Presidency*, by the time Kennedy began seriously planning to run for president,

> his Irish-Catholic background remained a potentially troubling issue. In particular, Kennedy's religion became a frequent friction point, just as it had for Al Smith in 1928. To be sure by 1960 voters had become far more tolerant than the electorate of 1928. Yet even so, a May 1959 *Time* magazine poll revealed that 'one of every four respondents wouldn't vote for a presidential candidate who was Catholic ...' a concern still felt by many Americans in 1960 [was] an Irish-Catholic president could not separate church and state, and ultimately his allegiance would be to the Catholic Church's hierarchy, not to the Constitution. Most of the attacks on Kennedy during the 1960 campaign focused on his Catholic religious faith, not his Irish ethnicity.[16]

Because Kennedy made it to the White House, a neat narrative has developed that his brilliant speech to a group of Protestant ministers, on 12 September 1960, at the Greater Houston Ministerial Association 'played a major role in defusing the Catholic issue, which enabled Kennedy to win a narrow victory over the Republican nominee Richard Nixon'.[17] In fact, the Catholic issue was still very much alive with many Protestant voters, as America voted on 8 November 1960. Research conducted by the Centre for Political Studies at the University of Michigan shows that 'Kennedy did very poorly with church-attending Protestants. He only carried 25 per cent of the Baptist vote, 31 per cent of Methodists, 24 per cent of northern evangelicals, 30 per cent of southern evangelicals and 0 per cent of Pentecostals.' Another estimate suggested that 4.5 million Protestants who had voted for Adlai Stevenson in 1956 switched to Nixon in 1960.[18]

Kennedy understood electoral numbers and he also recognised that his Catholicism had nearly caused his defeat in 1960. Had he been prepared to kiss the Pope's ring in July 1963, sixteen months out from another presidential election, Kennedy would have been re-opening the tinder box of the Catholic issue and providing fodder to those who would inevitably want to make religion a factor in the 1964 election. Nearly three years into his presidency, Kennedy's religion was still contentious. Photographs or reports of the President of the United States of America kneeling to kiss the Pope's ring, which is considered to be an expression of fidelity to the Catholic Church, would certainly have been viewed as inappropriate and/ or offensive by many Americans. In 1963, the United States did not even have formal diplomatic relations with the Vatican. *Time* magazine noted that just two years later, in 1965, when Pope Paul VI planned a trip to New York to address the United Nations, Lyndon Johnson's administration struggled with the protocol around receiving the Pope in America because, firstly, the United States did not have formal diplomatic links with the Vatican and, secondly, because 'many Americans believed' that to establish such relations 'would violate the separation of church and state and could give the Holy See undue influence'.[19] In a climate where anti-Catholic prejudice was a sad reality of public life in 1960s America, the new pope seems to have recognised the invidious position Kennedy would be placed in if he observed Catholic tradition when greeting him. The initial engagement between the President and Pontiff in the Vatican took place 'at the threshold of the papal library' and Paul VI moved quickly to initiate a handshake as the form of greeting:

> the moment came, amid the crush of photographers and members of the press: the pope and president shook hands. Obviously pleased and delighted, Paul VI, the new pope, resplendent in his red mozzetta and stole, offered his hand to the president of the United States, dressed in an everyday blue business suit and tie. President John F. Kennedy, realising the import of this moment, gave a slight nod of his head in

the pontiff's direction and they both shook hands, solemnly.[20]

Leaving no room for misinterpretation, mischievous or otherwise, 'Vatican sources' briefed members of the media, who were not present at this initial greeting, that 'Kennedy and the Pope shook hands when they met.' At the same time, 'a US Embassy official' told the media that 'Kennedy did not kiss Pope Paul's ring, as Roman Catholics normally do when received by the Pope.'[21] Kennedy was only the third serving United States president to meet a pope. One syndicate journalist went to the trouble of pointing out that the audience of 'the first Catholic President' with Pope Paul VI lasted '13 minutes longer than President Eisenhower's audience with Pope John XXIII in December 1959'. Any imputation in this statement was negated by the Pope, who, after Kennedy's departure, received American journalists accompanying the President on his European trip and told them: 'You know what we discussed: Above all the peace in the world.'[22]

On 1 July 1960, Kennedy was guest of honour at a dinner in the Quirinale Palace hosted by the President of Italy, Antonio Segni and attended by a range of Italian politicians, including Prime Minister Giovanni Leone. Kennedy made a point of engaging with Italian Communist leaders and 'exchanged cool and correct greetings with Communist Party chief Palmiro Togliatti. He also talked privately for more than ten minutes with Pietro Nenni, leader of the Marxist Socialist Party.'[23]

President Kennedy's main political set piece in Italy took place in Naples. At a speech at NATO Headquarters, Kennedy assured his Western Allies that 'our negotiations for an end to nuclear tests and our opposition to nuclear dispersal are fully consistent with our attention to defence – these are all complementary parts of a single strategy for peace'.[24]

Test ban treaty negotiations

Formal negotiations on a nuclear test ban treaty got underway in Moscow on 15 July, 1963. Kennedy appointed Averell Harriman, an elder statesman of the Democratic Party, a former Governor of New York and a former American Ambassador to the Soviet Union, as his lead negotiator.[25] However, a core team, based in the White House, including President Kennedy, Dean Rusk and Bob McNamara, the Secretary for Defence, were in daily and often intense communication with Harriman.

On 25 July 1963, a treaty was agreed between the United States, the Soviet Union and the United Kingdom which was designed to work towards 'the speediest possible achievement' of disarmament and to guard against nuclear fallout.[26] Specifically, the treaty outlawed nuclear testing in the atmosphere, outer space and underwater. John Kennedy considered this agreement his administration's greatest achievement,[27] but he knew he faced another battle to convince the United States Senate of its merits.

Constitutionally Kennedy needed a two-thirds majority of the Senate, sixty-seven votes, to ensure the treaty's ratification. The President however was gravely concerned that the treaty could be scuttled by Republican senators, many of whom were sceptical of any rapprochement with the Soviet Union and who also did not believe that Soviet Premier Nikita Khrushchev could be trusted. Privately Kennedy mused that this outcome would be a catastrophe equivalent to America's failure to ratify the League of Nations following the First World War .[28]

Kennedy's forceful side

The President was not averse to using strong-arm tactics to deliver his favoured outcome. In 1961, Sherman Adams, who had been the White House Chief of Staff during the presidency of Kennedy's predecessor, Dwight Eisenhower, was facing an impending indictment of serious tax fraud.[29] Eisenhower was concerned that if Adams was convicted he might commit suicide and he indirectly intervened on his old political retainer's behalf with President Kennedy.[30] Eisenhower asked Everett Dirksen, the Republican Senate Minority Leader, to approach Kennedy with a view to the President quietly getting the Justice Department to drop Adams's indictment. Dirksen promised Kennedy that if he did so he would have a political 'blank cheque' in his account from both himself and Eisenhower.[31]

On 12 August 1963, Kennedy chose to call in these political favours in order to assist the ratification of the Limited Test Ban Treaty. At a meeting in the White House, after reminding Dirksen that both he and Eisenhower owed him one, Kennedy said: 'Ev, I want you to reverse yourself and come out for the treaty. I also want Ike's public endorsement of the treaty before the Senate votes. We'll call it square on the other matter.' In reply, Dirksen said 'Mr President, you're a hell of a horse trader. But I'll honour my commitment, and I'm sure that General Eisenhower will.'[32] Three days later, on 16 August, the *New York Times* reported that former President Eisenhower was now in favour of the Test Ban Treaty. Dirksen subsequently followed suit. Following a further meeting with Kennedy, he publicly endorsed the treaty on 9 September 1963.[33]

The endorsements of two of the most popular and influential figures in the Republican Party undoubtedly impacted positively on the safe passage of the Limited Test Ban Treaty. On 10 September, Kennedy sent a letter to the Senate giving his 'unqualified and unequivocal assurances' that United States security would be protected under the Test Ban Treaty. In this intervention, Kennedy particularly assured the Senate that if Cuba should be used 'either directly or indirectly to circumvent or nullify this treaty, the United States will take all necessary action in response'. According to the Washington correspondent of United Press International, this assurance was issued by President Kennedy 'apparently in answer to criticism by Sen. Barry Goldwater, R-Ariz., that the treaty signing be deferred until Russia removed troops from Cuba'.[34]

Goldwater's criticism and Kennedy's swift rebuttal went beyond policy differences and into the realm of electoral politics, as both politicians believed they would ultimately face-off against each other in the 1964 Presidential Election. Throughout 1963, there was mounting media speculation that Goldwater would seek the Republican nomination and the Arizona senator did little to dampen this. Grassroots Grand Old Party support for a Goldwater presidential run was reflected by a crowd of '8,000 screaming, flag-waving enthusiasts,' drawn from across the United States, who attended a 'Draft Goldwater for President Independence Day Rally' in Washington's National Armory on 4 July 1963.[35]

On 24 September, the Senate comprehensively ratified the treaty by eighty votes to nineteen.[36] The treaty was subsequently signed by 102 nations. On 7 October, the historically-minded Kennedy formally signed the Limited Test Ban Treaty, on behalf of the United States, during a specially staged ceremony in the White House's Treaty Room on the same table which President William McKinley had signed the peace protocols that concluded the Spanish–American War in 1898.[37]

A race for peace

The Test Ban Treaty was just one of a series of measures that Kennedy pursued in the Autumn of 1963 as part of a wider peace strategy. Kennedy had entered into office as a dedicated Cold War warrior, but the Cuban Missile crisis in October 1962, in which the world had come to the brink of nuclear annihilation, had deeply affected him. He had come to the stark realisation that both the United States and the Soviet Union had, in his own words, a 'mutual interest in avoiding mutual destruction'.[38]

Rather than an arms race, by 1963 Kennedy was engaged in a race for peace. Though he personally abhorred Communism, Kennedy confronted hawkish attitudes and argued that peaceful co-existence between East and West was not just possible, but essential to the survival of mankind. In an extraordinary speech to the United Nations General Assembly on 20 September, Kennedy made a direct appeal to the USSR to work with the United States in pursuit of a sustainable peace. The President said: 'I would say to the leaders of the Soviet Union, and to their people, that if either of our countries is to be fully secure, we need a much better weapon than the H-Bomb – a weapon better than ballistic missiles or nuclear submarines – and that better weapon is peaceful co-operation.'[39]

Kennedy's actions in this period show that this was not mere rhetoric. On 26 August, he had told the Soviet Ambassador, Anatoly Dobrynin, that he hoped the Test Ban Treaty could be followed by United States–Soviet agreements on civil aviation and the prohibition of weapons being introduced into outer space.[40]

Grain for the Soviet Union

A more tangible expression of unprecedented goodwill occurred in early October when President Kennedy agreed to sell surplus American wheat to the Soviet Union. Russia was undergoing severe grain shortages, as a result of a combination of drought and inefficient agricultural programmes.

Though Kennedy knew that the wheat sale would help America's balance of payments and would bring considerable income to United States farmers and shippers, it also exposed him to strong domestic criticism. Lending Khrushchev a helping hand was especially unpopular with Polish-Americans, a key electoral demographic group. Richard Nixon, who had stood against Kennedy in 1960, called the deal 'a major foreign policy mistake'. Within his own administration, Vice President Lyndon Johnson was privately deeply critical of Kennedy's decision.[41] The President, however, was undeterred. He believed that this gesture to Khrushchev would help to underpin a lasting peace.

Co-existing with Castro's Cuba

In September 1963, Kennedy authorised a back-channel of communications with Fidel Castro's Cuba, via William Attwood, a key official of Adlai Stevenson, the United States Ambassador to the United Nations. Attwood had been two years behind Kennedy in Choate, an elite Connecticut boarding school, and knew the President well enough to 'craft a memorandum that would catch his attention'. In this document, he argued that rapprochement with Castro was worth looking into as a 'course of action which, if successful, could remove the Cuban issue from the 1964 campaign'.[42] With the encouragement of the President, Robert Kennedy, Averell Harriman and McGeorge Bundy, the United States National Security Adviser, Attwood began making discreet overtures to the Cuban Ambassador to the United Nations, Carlos Lechuga. This back-channel fed into Kennedy's desire for a normalisation in relations with Cuba. Bundy told Attwood that the President favoured 'pushing towards an opening towards Cuba' that could remove Castro from 'the Soviet fold and perhaps wiping out the Bay of Pigs and maybe getting back to normal'.[43] Attwood's overtures led to Castro secretly agreeing to meet Attwood in Havana. In an interview recorded in spring 1964, Robert Kennedy said that he and President Kennedy had 'always discussed' as 'a possibility' making a deal with Castro or learning how to live with him. Robert Kennedy also confirmed that President Kennedy had given the 'go-ahead' for Attwood to visit Cuba, 'see Castro and see what could be done'.[44] On 31 October, Attwood received word that Castro 'would very much like to talk to the U.S. official anytime and appreciated the importance of discretion to all concerned.' He was 'willing to send a plane to Mexico to pick up the official and fly him to a private airport ... where Castro would talk to him alone ... In this way there would be no risk of identification at Havana Airport.'[45]

A Greek intermediary had told Attwood that 'Castro would welcome a normalisation of relations with the United States if he could do so without losing too much face.'[46] The planned timeframe for Attwood's secret visit to Cuba was December 1963 or January 1964. At the same time, the Kennedy administration was conscious of the risks of being perceived to be soft on Communism entering into an election year. Commenting on the basis for Attwood's proposed engagement with Castro, Robert Kennedy observed that 'we had certain things that were required: the end of the military presence of the Russians and the Communists, the cut-off of ties with the Communists by Cuba, and the end of the exportation of the revolution. In return for those basic points, and perhaps more, there would be normalisation of the relationship.'[47] Dallek's assessment of how palatable these requirements would actually have been to the Cuban regime is mixed: 'It was conceivable that Castro could expel the Soviet military and even call a halt to subversion in the hemisphere. But ending his ties with the communists seemed highly unlikely, even if it was conceivable that he could mute his connections to the Soviet bloc.'[48] Nevertheless, the proposed engagement was a real step forward for the cause of peace, as the Kennedy administration were now, for the first time, actively considering the basis for co-existing with Castro's Cuba.

The President's eagerness to arrive at an accommodation with Cuba is evident from the fact that, alongside the Attwood initiative, Kennedy himself also personally opened a second back-channel to Castro. On 24 October 1963, Kennedy met with Jean Daniel, a socialist and noted French journalist, who that November was travelling to Havana. Kennedy told Daniel, who he knew would report the conversation back to Castro, that the United States could peacefully co-exist with Cuba and would end the economic blockade if Castro's regime stopped attempting to export communism to other countries in the region.[49] In his memoir, published in 2006, Castro wistfully recalled Kennedy's assassination as a lost opportunity for United

States–Cuban relations. Castro noted:

> He made mistakes, I repeat, but he was an intelligent man, sometimes brilliant, brave and it's my opinion – I've said this before – that if Kennedy had survived, it's possible that relations between Cuba and the United States would have improved ... The day he was killed I was talking to a French journalist, Jean Daniel, whom Kennedy had sent to me with a message, to talk to me. So communications were being established, and that might have favoured an improvement in our relations ... when [Kennedy] was taken from the stage he had enough authority in his country to impose an improvement in relations with Cuba. And that was palpably demonstrated in the conversations I had with that French journalist, Jean Daniel, who was with me – bringing me very important words from Kennedy.[50]

In his meeting with Daniel, President Kennedy made it clear that he wanted to meet him again on his return from Cuba. Daniel recognised that Kennedy had effectively co-opted him into being an 'unofficial envoy', which became the title of one of a series of enlightening articles he wrote on his intermediary work between Castro and Kennedy.[51] Initially, Daniel had difficulty in gaining access to Castro, but when he did meet the Cuban leader on the night of 19 November and recounted the content of his recent discussion with the United States President, the French journalist had Castro's undivided attention: 'Fidel listened with devouring and passionate interest: he pulled at his beard, yanked his parachutist's beret down over his eyes, adjusted his maqui tunic, all the while making me the target of a thousand malicious sparks cast by his deep-sunk, lively eyes.'[52]

As he later admitted in a 1984 interview with Ted Szule, Castro was under no doubt that Daniel's presence was an olive branch from President Kennedy: 'This unquestionably was a message from Kennedy ... a message in the sense of inquiring how we felt holding a dialogue with the U.S. – with him – and reflecting his concern and readiness to find some channel of contact, of dialogue to overcome the great tension that had existed.'[53] In Daniel's initial discussion with Castro, which took place in his Havana hotel room and lasted for six hours, stretching into the early hours of 20 November, the Cuban leader emphasised to Daniel that he would be prepared to enter into discussions to see if a new understanding could be brokered with the United States.

> 'I believe Kennedy is sincere,' Fidel declared. 'I also believe that today the expression of this sincerity could have political significance ... I also think he is a realist: he is now registering that it is impossible to simply wave a wand and cause us, and the explosive situation throughout Latin America, to disappear ... I believe the United States is too important a country not to have an influence on world peace. I cannot help hoping, therefore, that a leader will come to the fore in North America (why not Kennedy, there are things in his favour!), who will be willing to brave unpopularity, fight the trusts, tell the truth and most important, let the various nations act as they see fit. I ask nothing: neither dollars, nor assistance, nor diplomats, nor bankers, nor military men – nothing but peace, and to be accepted as we are! We are socialists, the United States is a capitalist nation, the Latin American countries will choose what they want ...' In conclusion, Fidel Castro said to me: 'Since you are going to see Kennedy again, be an emissary of peace, despite everything. I want to make myself clear: I don't want anything, I don't expect anything, and as a revolutionary the present situation does not displease me. But as a man and as a statesman, it is my duty to indicate what the bases [sic] for understanding could be.' All this was said two days before President Kennedy's death.[54]

In the same conversation, while critical of past United States policy towards Cuba, Castro stressed his respect for Kennedy's abilities and underlined his belief that they could work productively together towards building peace. He also displayed flashes of good humour.

> During this nocturnal discussion, Castro had delivered himself of a relentless indictment of United States policy ... He was speaking, he said, from the viewpoint of the interests of peace in both the American continents. To achieve this goal, a leader would have to arise in the United States capable of understanding the explosive realities of Latin America and of meeting them halfway. Then, suddenly, he had taken

a less hostile tack: 'Kennedy could still be this man. He still has the possibility of becoming, in the eyes of history, the greatest President of the United States, the leader who may at last understand that there can be coexistence between capitalists and socialists, even in the Americas. He would then be an even greater President than Lincoln. I know, for example, that for Khrushchev, Kennedy is a man you can talk with. I have gotten this impression from all my conversations with Khrushchev. Other leaders have assured me that to attain this goal, we must first await his re-election. Personally, I consider him responsible for everything, but I will say this: he has come to understand many things over the past few months; and then too, in the last analysis, I'm convinced that anyone else would be worse.' Then Fidel had added with a broad and boyish grin: 'If you see him again, you can tell him that I'm willing to declare Goldwater my friend if that will guarantee Kennedy's re-election!'[55]

Castro was so taken by the opportunity provided by Daniel's presence in Cuba – and the direct line of contact that this created to President Kennedy – that he deferred all other Government business to personally drive the French journalist to his summer villa in Varadero, eighty miles east of Havana, for further discussions. These talks were abruptly interrupted 'around 1.30 in the afternoon, Cuban time' on 22 November 1963.

Fidel picked up the phone and I heard him say: '*Como? Un atentado?*' ('What's that? An attempted assassination?') ... He came back, sat down, and repeated three times the words: '*Es una mala noticia.*' ('This is bad news.') He remained silent for a moment, awaiting another call with further news ... The second call came through: it was hoped they would be able to announce that the United States President was still alive, that there was hope of saving him. Fidel Castro's immediate reaction was: 'If they can, he is already re-elected.' He pronounced these words with satisfaction ... Now it was nearly 2 o'clock and we got up from the table and settled ourselves in front of a radio ... finally the fatal announcement: President Kennedy is dead. Then Fidel stood up and said to me: 'Everything is changed. Everything is going to change. The United States occupies such a position in world affairs that the death of a President of that country affects millions of people in every corner of the globe. The cold war, relations with Russia, Latin America, Cuba, the Negro question ... all will have to be rethought.'[56]

For Castro, there would remain a lingering regret that the timing of Kennedy reaching out to him, via Daniel, 'coincided exactly with the moment of his death'. Twenty-one years on from Kennedy's death, Castro still maintained that 'for Cuba, and for the relations between the US and Cuba, the death of Kennedy was really a great blow, an adverse factor'.[57]

If the secret peace feelers that President Kennedy was extending towards Castro in the final weeks of his life had been revealed at this time, there would have been consternation within the sizeable Cuban community in Florida, one of the southern states Kennedy was prioritising for his 1964 re-election campaign. Kennedy was prepared to risk this to put in place the foundations for a new direction on Cuba in his second term, at which point he would no longer have to worry about facing the American electorate again.

Second term plans for peace

In the meantime, Kennedy had to walk a fine line between securing re-election and deepening his peace strategy. He knew that he would have greater room for manoeuvre in his second term and he confided in his friend, David Ormsby-Gore, the British Ambassador to Washington, that if he was re-elected he intended to visit Moscow as a step towards further improving United States–Soviet relations.[58]

Kennedy also intended to explore détente with China in his second term. In November 1963, he was directly involved in the preparation of a speech that the Assistant Secretary of State for Far Eastern Affairs, Roger Hilsman, would be delivering on United States–Sino relations. It was Kennedy's intention that this speech would, in his own words, 'open the door a little bit'.[59] In his 1967 book, *To Move a Nation: The Politics of Foreign Policy in the Administration of John F. Kennedy*, Hilsman contended that Kennedy turned 'a small corner' in policy towards China by explicitly abandoning the Dulles assumption that Chinese Communism was a passing phase, whose passing America should hasten by isolation.[60] Kennedy's press secretary, Pierre Salinger, also claimed that Kennedy had intended to use his second term 'to bridge the gap' between Washington and Beijing.[61] In a 1971 interview with the BBC, Salinger rejected claims that President Kennedy had neglected to educate the American public on the need for relations with China and said:

> Every American president from 1946 to 1970 can be convicted of that same charge. The immense popularity of President Eisenhower could very well have been used to lead the American people to understand that we have to have relations with communist China. While I am not a great admirer of the Nixon administration, the one thing they have done which has been very sensible was to try to move American public opinion in the direction of understanding and accepting a relationship with China. President Kennedy was elected with a very small margin. He looked on the presidency as an eight-year occupation and I think he would have been re-elected in 1964 without any trouble whatever. And he always had China marked as a part of policy for the second four years of his administration. If he had lived he would have moved forward to relations with China during those four years.[62]

Tito, Lemass and bereavement

Kennedy had already begun the process of preparing the United States public for this unprecedented engagement with the Communist world. On 17 October 1963, Josip Tito, the President of Yugoslavia, became the first Communist head of government to be received at the White House. President Eisenhower had previously invited Tito, but he then rescinded the invitation following protests from Congress.[63] Tito arrived at the White House by helicopter and, in greeting him, Kennedy told the assembled media it was a good thing that countries with differences in political philosophies should try to know the policies of each other 'to lessen the danger of war'.[64] Kennedy was, however, clearly conscious that Tito's visit was going to be the subject of some domestic criticism and he did his best not to be seen as being overly friendly to the Communist dictator. The *New York Daily News* reported:

> The official welcome included most of the usual trimmings – 21-gun salute, colour guard trumpet calls and a White House luncheon. But Kennedy, with an eye cocked on his political critics, kept everything

in extra low-key. In fact, when he greeted the 71-year-old marshal on the White House lawn he seemed downright uncomfortable. He avoided being photographed shaking Tito's hand.[65]

Kennedy's talks with Tito were productive. The Yugoslav leader reiterated his country's support for the Test Ban Treaty and described it as 'a significant initial step in lessening international tension'. A joint statement from both leaders said the basis for war could be reduced and world peace assured if all nations contributed their 'determined effort and support'. The statement also said that both leaders looked forward to the development of improved relations in the 'expansion of normal trade, economic contacts and cultural and scientific exchanges'.[66] As a further gesture of goodwill, Kennedy also promised to send surplus army barracks, which would house some 10,000 victims of the Skopje earthquake.[67] On departing the White House, Tito described Kennedy as 'a good partner for discussion' and revealed that he had invited the United States President to Yugoslavia. The White House was 'non-committal' about whether Kennedy would take such a trip.[68]

Though Kennedy saw diplomatic engagement with the Communist world as a means to break down barriers in pursuit of peace, his approach was a gradualist one, at least until he could secure re-election. Kennedy was an electoral realist and he knew that extending olive branches to Communist leaders had to be carefully managed for fear of generating suspicion and alienating voters. Even as Kennedy conferred with Tito, a picket of about 100 Serbian-Americans and Croatian-Americans paraded near the White House with placards protesting: 'Murderer', 'Red Pig' and 'JFK don't shake hands with killer.'[69] Tito's visit had also led to criticism from both the President's political friends and foes in Congress. Democratic senator Thomas Dodd of Connecticut described Tito's reception at the White House as 'a terrible mistake'. Senator Barry Goldwater, who was closely marking all of Kennedy's political manoeuvrings, said it was 'a shame' that the President of the United States would 'play host' to 'a tyrant'.[70]

Tito's visit had almost immediately followed on from a less contentious and more light-hearted state visit. Two days previously, the Irish Taoiseach, Seán Lemass, had been the guest of honour at a state dinner which concluded with a private late night party in the President's White House quarters. Gene

Kelly, the celebrated Hollywood star, performed for the guests and Dorothy Tubridy, an Irish friend of the Kennedy family, sang the *Boys of Wexford*. After noticing how much this song had moved the President, his sister, Eunice Kennedy-Shriver, with Lemass's help, sourced a recording of it to give to him at Christmas.[71] It was a present that John Kennedy would never receive.

In the final autumn of his life, as Kennedy publicly strove to underpin world peace, he was privately mourning the death of his newborn son. Patrick Bouvier Kennedy was born on 7 August 1963. He died two days later at Boston Children's Hospital of Hyaline Membrane disease, a respiratory distress syndrome.[72] The White House press secretary broke the news to journalists, though some had guessed at the tragedy even before Pierre Salinger had begun his briefing: 'When Press Secretary Salinger met newsmen a short time later his sombre face told the news. "Patrick Kennedy died at 4.04 a.m.," he said. "The struggle of the baby boy to keep breathing was too much for his heart."'[73] Patrick Kennedy, named after the President's great-grandfather who had left New Ross during the Great Famine, was the first child born to an incumbent United States president in almost seventy years.[74] The birth of the Kennedy baby had been the subject of much anticipation and comment in the United States media and Patrick's premature death was the cause of genuine national and international mourning. Though President Kennedy requested that his son's passing be respected as a private family matter, the Kennedy family's despair and every morsel of information regarding the baby's death was considered front-page news and syndicated around the world:

> When the president arrived, Friday morning he wore his grief on his face. His eyes were red and swollen as he strode from the helicopter to the hospital room where his 34-year-old wife is recuperating from the caesarean birth. He was spared the anguish of telling his wife that the infant had died despite the combined efforts of some of the nation's finest pediatricians, who used a rare treatment in an effort to save his life. Dr John W. Walsh, the first lady's obstetrician, gave her the sorrowful news when she awoke Friday morning. She then was given a mild sedative and slept until her husband arrived. When Kennedy

emerged from the hospital, he cast his eyes downward and bit his lip. The entire area was deathly still outside the hospital and no one spoke ... Later, he helicoptered to the summer White House at Squaw Island to see his 5-year-old daughter, Caroline, and 2-year-old son John Jr., apparently to tell them gently the brother they had looked forward to was dead.[75]

Vietnam

Vietnam also loomed large in Kennedy's consciousness in this period. From mid-August 1963, Kennedy had prevaricated on whether his administration should support a coup against the South Vietnamese president, Ngo Dinh Diem.[76] Diem had increasingly fallen under the sinister influence of Madame Nhu, the wife of his younger brother. Diem's government was engaged in a campaign of persecution against South Vietnamese Buddhists.

In protest at this repression, in June 1963, a Buddhist monk, Thich Quang Duc, had burnt himself to death in Saigon. Photographs of Quang Duc's death received huge coverage in newspapers and Kennedy remarked that 'no news picture in history has generated so much emotion around the world as that one'.[77] Further immolations followed and continued media coverage of these incidents horrified millions across the globe, including Kennedy. Madame Nhu made matters worse by referring to the immolations as 'barbeques' and offering matches and fuel for further immolations.[78] On 1 November, having received assurances from the United States Ambassador Henry Cabot Lodge that the United States would not intervene, the South Vietnamese Generals ousted Diem in a *coup d'état*.

Whatever about effecting regime change in Vietnam, Kennedy was determined to ensure that the United States did not become enmeshed in South East Asia. On 2 October Kennedy asked his Defence Secretary, Bob McNamara, to announce the immediate withdrawal of 1,000 soldiers and to pledge that all American forces would leave Vietnam by the end of 1965.[79] This commitment was reversed in the immediate aftermath of John Kennedy's death.

During President Lyndon Johnson's administration, the United States pursued a policy of military escalation in Vietnam, which was publicly criticised by some of Kennedy's former close aides, including Hilsman and Salinger. Hilsman resigned from Johnson's administration in February 1964 after 'fighting a losing battle against what he considered a disastrous American strategy in Vietnam'. After only a few weeks of the Johnson presidency, Hilsman concluded that 'from both the people he turned to for advice on Vietnam and his own approach to the problem, it seemed clear that his natural instinct was towards attempting a military solution to the question of Vietnam'.[80]

Hilsman's 1967 book argues that Kennedy was determined to pursue a political approach to Vietnam with only a limited military commitment, whereby guerrilla aggression would be countered within a counter-guerrilla framework. He maintained that Kennedy 'preferred to treat the problem of Vietnam as something other than war and to avoid getting American prestige so involved that the United States could not accept a negotiated settlement along the lines of the Geneva accords in Laos – when and if the Vietnamese desired it'.[81] In an interview with CBS News anchorman Walter Cronkite on 2 September 1963 in Hyannis Port, Kennedy had emphasised that there would be no Americanisation of the war on his watch: 'In the final analysis, it is their war. They are the ones who have to win it or lose it. We can help them, we can give them equipment, we can send our men out there as advisers, but they have to win it, the people of Vietnam, against the Communists.'[82] Hilsman stressed that this was not a throwaway remark from Kennedy and that, although the thirty-fifth president believed the United States should advise and assist, 'President Kennedy made abundantly clear to me on more than one occasion that what he most wanted to avoid was turning Vietnam into an American war. He was sceptical of a policy of escalation and of the effectiveness of an air attack on North Vietnam.'[83]

In the final months of his life, Kennedy believed that if Communism could not be defeated in Vietnam, he needed to give himself enough leeway to be able to enter negotiations for a settlement without fatal consequences to America's position in the rest of Asia, a factor that would be complicated if American troops had become immersed in the conflict and United States military pride was dented. By the autumn of 1963, Kennedy had arrived at a fixed position in his own mind that he would never commit combat troops to Vietnam, a position that Hilsman has affirmed in a significant but unheralded speech at Corning Community College, New York, in March 1968. A local newspaper reported:

Wearing a PT-109 tie clip of the type given by President Kennedy to many of his close associates, Hilsman told the group that Kennedy had never envisioned the Vietnam War as 'our' war. At the time of the Kennedy assassination, there was only 15,000 American 'advisers' in Vietnam, Hilsman said. President Kennedy always thought of it as 'their war – win or lose,' Hilsman said. 'And if they lost, Kennedy would have gone to Geneva with the hope of getting the best possible settlement'.[84]

In his 1971 BBC interview, Salinger also emphasised that Kennedy's commitment to Vietnam was a limited military one. Contrasting Kennedy's approach to that of President Johnson, Salinger maintained that President Kennedy never intended a major escalation in Vietnam and contended that only the South Vietnamese could solve their problems with the Communist North. Salinger did concede that, over his time in office, President Kennedy had increased America's strength in South Vietnam from a military mission of 800 men to 16,000, but he emphasised that their role was 'passive' and

'there were only 12 Americans killed in that time … Now there's a great leap from that belief to putting a half million men in Vietnam as President Johnson did and creating a land war in Asia,' he went on. 'President Kennedy never had the idea that Vietnam was a bottomless, endless commitment so far as the United States was concerned. The month before he was killed [in fact, it was two months beforehand] he stated that in the final analysis the only people who could win that war or lose that war were the South Vietnamese themselves.' Salinger accused the military leaders of influencing the White House into the huge escalation of manpower.[85]

Civil rights

On 28 August, Kennedy stood at the third-floor window of the White House solarium with Preston Bruce, the White House doorman, and watched a crowd of over a quarter of a million people march to the Lincoln Memorial.[86] Gripping the windowsill, Kennedy turned to the African American staff member and said: 'Oh, Bruce, I wish I were out there with them.'[87] The rally organised by the Civil Rights Movement was the largest ever mass protest in American history. After Martin Luther King had delivered his iconic 'I have a dream' speech, Kennedy had a robust encounter with leaders of the Civil Rights Movement in the Oval Office. The civil rights leaders wanted Kennedy to expand the scope of his civil rights bill to include a Fair Employment Practices Commission, which would prevent racial discrimination in hiring. The President however doubted that an expanded bill, including this fair employment measure, would attract significant support to pass through Congress.[88]

Kennedy was fully committed to the civil rights agenda, but he took a piecemeal, pragmatic approach. A Gallup Poll on 12 October 1963 showed that Kennedy's approval rating had dropped from 50 to 35 per cent after he had submitted his civil rights bill. A Harris Poll in the *Washington Post* on 14 October suggested that Kennedy would lose up to half of the southern States he had won in 1960.[89] The President's visit to Texas was about shoring up southern support. With an eye on the 1964 election, Kennedy was already in campaign mode.

Safety concerns and final days

He had visited Tampa, Florida, on 18 November 1963. On this trip, Floyd Boring, a secret service agent who had previously foiled an attempt on President Harry Truman's life, expressed concerns to Kennedy that by travelling by open-top motorcade the President was endangering his own safety.[90] Kennedy replied: 'Floyd, this is a political trip. If I don't mingle with the people, I couldn't get elected as a dog catcher.' Kenny O'Donnell later told the Warren Commission, Kennedy's journey through Dallas was planned to give the President maximum public exposure.[91]

At 12.30 p.m. on 22 November 1963, John F. Kennedy's open-top motorcade turned left onto Elm Street in Dallas. Seconds later shots rang out which would change the course of history. It was just 146 days since John Kennedy had said goodbye at Shannon.

CHAPTER 7

JUDGING KENNEDY

Felix M. Larkin

The inscription on the plaque alongside the stark memorial to President Kennedy in Dallas, Texas – the city where he was assassinated – begins with these words: 'The joy and excitement of John Fitzgerald Kennedy's life belonged to all men. So did the pain and sorrow of his death.'

These are good and valid sentiments, which those of us of a certain age who remember the horror of his assassination would certainly endorse. The impact of that event was such that those who were alive on that fateful day – 22 November 1963 – can recall exactly where we were and what we were doing when we heard about the assassination. With the passage of time, however, Kennedy is gradually ceasing to be part of living memory – and he becomes instead part of history. Today, nobody under the age of 60 will have a living memory of him. So now is perhaps an appropriate moment to begin to ask in a serious way just how good a president was he? It is a difficult question to answer, for the tragedy of his early death and the later romanticisation of his short period in office as 'Camelot on the Potomac' inevitably colour our judgement. There are only a few good books – disinterested studies – among the plethora that have been written about him and his administration, my own favourites being Robert Dallek's biography published in 2003 and Richard Reeves's study of Kennedy as president published ten years earlier. I will rely heavily on those two works in this essay – and on a more recent book by the economist Jeffrey Sachs on JFK's quest for peace in 1963, which led to the first nuclear weapons test ban treaty.[1]

Let me say straightaway that I don't think John F. Kennedy would like this essay – not because of any criticism that I might make of him, but because he distrusted the very act of judging his predecessors in office. Ranking the presidents, and separating the truly great and the truly bad from the rest, is a game that historians play compulsively – but Kennedy disapproved. He was once quoted as saying that, in his view, 'No one has the right to grade a president ... who has not sat in his chair, examined the mail and information that came across his desk and learned why he made [his] decisions.'[2] He had a point: Kennedy himself had written history – his book *Profiles in Courage* won the Pulitzer Prize in 1957 – and he knew first-hand that historians never have enough information to fully understand the past. Nevertheless, we must try to do so.

In judging Kennedy, the first consideration is that he was a transformative president, someone who changed the character of the United States presidency. That is one of the criteria which historians tend to use in assessing the significance or otherwise of individual presidents. As Reeves points out: 'The timing was right ... Kennedy came to power at the end of an old era or the beginning of a new [one].'[3] He was the first president born in the twentieth century, the first Roman Catholic, the first of the men who actually did the fighting on the ground in the Second World War to become president and the first president to master the medium of television and use it effectively – and he was the youngest man ever elected president. All these factors make him at least a notable president. Furthermore, he was the first president to be 'self-selecting' – by which I mean that he claimed the nomination through winning primaries, rather than being the choice of the party bosses. Norman Mailer wrote shortly after the 1960 Democratic Party convention which had nominated Kennedy for president that 'Kennedy is ... not in the old political focus,'[4] and Reeves explains this as follows:

> ... the most important thing about Kennedy was not a great political decision, though he made some, but his own political ambition. He did not wait his turn. He directly challenged the institution he wanted to control, the political system. After him, no one else wanted to wait either, and few institutions were rigid enough or flexible enough to survive impatient ambition-driven challenges. He believed (and proved) that the only qualification for the most powerful job in the world was wanting it.[5]

Also relevant to any assessment are his skills in oratory and his undoubted charisma. David McCullough, the distinguished American historian, has said: 'If we could put presidential power in a pot and boil it all down, a big part of what we would find at the bottom would be language, the use of language, the potency of words.'[6] The greatest presidents are thus remembered as much for their rhetoric – their memorable phrases – as for their deeds, and Kennedy's best speeches stand comparison with those of any president before or after him. He keenly understood the power of oratory in forging political leadership. As Sachs has observed:

> Kennedy was, of course, no stranger to the power of oratory. He had studied it since his youth, relished it, championed it and aspired to greatness in it. His lifelong role model, in this arena as in so many others, was Churchill, whose incomparable rhetoric had helped save a civilization ... Kennedy had been present for the speeches in the British House of Commons when war was declared in 1939, and [he] had been deeply affected by them, particularly by Churchill's words. Kennedy noted in April 1963 that Churchill 'mobilised the English language and sent it into battle.'[7]

Kennedy's inaugural address is generally reckoned to be one of the best six, the others being Jefferson's first, Lincoln's two, Franklin Roosevelt's first and Reagan's first. Kennedy himself greatly admired Jefferson's first inaugural address and was of the opinion that it was better than his own.[8]

Probably the greatest, and certainly the most famous, speech by any American president was Lincoln's Gettysburg address – delivered on 19 November 1863, 100 years, almost to the day, before Kennedy's assassination. Lincoln may well have been a better orator than Kennedy, at least on paper – but he did not have Kennedy's charisma, which was legendary. Charisma is always difficult to deconstruct, but Kennedy's granddaughter, Tatiana Schlossberg, came close to identifying the essence of his charisma when speaking in the National Library of Ireland at the opening of the 'JFK Homecoming' exhibition there in 2013. She referred to her family's 'Irish heritage', which she jokingly defined as 'our good looks, our humour, our intelligence and of course our humility'.[9] Those were essential elements in JFK's charisma – good looks, humour, intelligence and a measure of self-deprecation. The historian Nigel Hamilton speaks about JFK's 'shy charisma',[10] and I think that paradoxical phrase just about hits the nail on the head. There was also a sexual frisson. The distinguished American journalist, Murray Kempton, captured that particular aspect in this description of Kennedy on the campaign trail:

> John F. Kennedy treated southern Ohio yesterday as Don Giovanni used to treat Seville. His progress, as ever, was an epic in the history of the sexual instinct of the American female. Outside Dayton, a woman of advanced years but intact instinct sat with her dog. Kennedy passed; she waved; he waved back ... Jack Kennedy is starting to enjoy these moments, and he is starting to enjoy them as a man of taste. He turns back now and goes on waving; the lingering hand gestures and the eye follows; its object is always a quietly pretty girl and the hand says that, if he did not have miles to go and promises to keep, he would like to walk with her where the Mad river meets the Stillwater.[11]

The combination of his rhetoric and charisma enabled Kennedy to capture the imagination and idealism of the American people as few other presidents have done. His vision of the 'New Frontier' was a potent variation on the theme of endless possibility that is at the heart of the American dream, the dream so poignantly captured by Scott Fitzgerald in *The Great Gatsby*:

> ... the last and greatest of all human dreams; for a transitory enchanted moment man must have held his breath in the presence of this continent, compelled into an aesthetic contemplation he neither understood nor desired, face to face for the last time in history with something commensurate to his capacity for wonder.[12]

For much of America's history, the frontier was the focus of that 'capacity for wonder' – a place where men and women could shape their own destinies and realise their very highest ambitions. This was the heritage that Kennedy's 'New Frontier' evoked, and the goals that he set under this banner – especially the target of putting a man on the moon by the end of the 1960s – re-awakened and challenged a nation which had become lethargic and complacent in the years of prosperity after the Second World War. The American people responded in full measure. The JFK presidency was the last time Americans had confidence in their political system and trust in their politicians. When he died, a generation lost hope that politics could effect real change and improve the condition of humanity. The succeeding presidencies of Lyndon Johnson and then Nixon were profoundly disillusioning. Despite some substantial achievements, both were undermined by deplorable policy failures and errors of judgement – and, in Nixon's case, also by malfeasance. For many, the disillusionment was complete when Robert Kennedy, the President's brother, was also assassinated while seeking the presidency in 1968. As JFK's legendary speechwriter and close associate, Theodore Sorensen, remarked, 'the assassination of President Kennedy represented an incalculable loss of the future'.[13]

The impact of Kennedy's death invites comparison with the impact of the assassination of Grand Duke Franz Ferdinand and his wife in Sarajevo on 28 June 1914, the event that led to the outbreak of the First World War. The best contemporary account of how Europe went to war in 1914 – Christopher Clark's wonderful book, *The Sleepwalkers* – makes that comparison explicitly. Clark writes: 'The Sarajevo murders, like the murder of President John F. Kennedy in Dallas in 1963, were an event whose hot light captured the people and places of a moment and burned them into memory. People recalled exactly where they were and whom they were with when the news reached them.'[14]

The difference was, of course, that the Sarajevo assassinations caused a world war – and this, in turn, defined most of the twentieth century. Kennedy's assassination, thankfully, did not alter the course of history – notwithstanding its impact on a generation left to mourn a lost leader and his unfulfilled promise. Franz Ferdinand was not mourned as a lost leader in the same way. Clark records that he was uncharismatic and irritable, no crowd-pleaser, and there was no outpouring of collective grief when he was killed.[15]

For us in Ireland, a better parallel is perhaps the death of the great nineteenth-century constitutional nationalist leader, Charles Stewart Parnell. Though he was not the victim of an assassin, the shadow that Parnell's death cast, memorably captured in the writings of James Joyce and W.B. Yeats, had an effect similar to that of Kennedy's death – albeit on a narrower canvas.

There are many striking correspondences in the lives of these two remarkable men:

- both were young leaders who died prematurely – Parnell at 45, Kennedy at 46;
- whereas Kennedy had Irish ancestors, Parnell had an American mother;
- Kennedy was a Catholic leader in a predominantly Protestant country, while Parnell was a Protestant leader in a predominantly Catholic country;
- Parnell made a triumphant visit to the United States in 1880, and Kennedy famously came to Ireland in June 1963;
- the sense of possibility in Kennedy's vision of the 'New Frontier' chimes with Parnell's assertion that 'no man has the right to fix the boundary to the march of a nation;'[16] and
- both Parnell and Kennedy have become part of the mythologies, as well as part of the history, of their respective countries.

Parnell and Kennedy are indeed good examples of the 'lost leader' syndrome, great men cut down in their prime whose reputations are more enduring than those of their contemporaries who lived on to make a more substantial contribution to their country's fortunes. As Stephen Collins, the *Irish Times* journalist, has suggested, lost leaders are remembered with such fascination and admiration precisely because they 'have not had to govern for long, if at all, and so don't get sucked into the messy compromises that are the inevitable fate of long-serving politicians entrusted with the thankless task of government'.[17]

There is some evidence that Parnell may have influenced Kennedy's style and mode of operation as a political leader. Dallek records that Kennedy 'was conversant with Irish leader Charles [Stewart] Parnell's counsel: "Get the advice of everybody whose advice is worth having – they are very few – and then do what you think best yourself."'[18] Moreover, Kennedy referred to Parnell in his speech to the joint session of the Dáil and Seanad during his visit to Ireland in 1963. He first mentioned the fact that he had in his office – the Oval Office – the sword of Commodore John Barry, the founder of the American navy, who was born in county Wexford. He then went on to note:

Yesterday [27 June 1963] was the 117th anniversary of the birth
of Charles Stewart Parnell, whose grandfather fought under Barry
and whose mother was born in America, and who, at the age of 34,
was invited to address the American Congress on the cause of Irish
freedom. 'I have seen since I have been in this country', he said, 'so
many tokens of the good wishes of the American people towards
Ireland'. And today, eighty-three years later, I can say to you that I
have seen in this country so many tokens of good wishes of the Irish
people towards America.[19]

Parnell's grandfather and namesake was Admiral Charles Stewart, commander
of the USS *Constitution* during the War of 1812, and Kennedy had on his
desk in the Oval Office two bookends with brass replicas of cannons on
the USS *Constitution* and on the walls flanking the fireplace in the office
were pictures of the famous naval engagement between the *Constitution* and
the British frigate *Guerriere*. A model of the *Constitution* was displayed on
the mantelpiece above the fireplace, and when Kennedy met Khrushchev in
Vienna in June 1961, he presented the Soviet leader with another model of
the ship – perhaps as a gentle reminder of the power of the United States
Navy.[20] The USS *Constitution* (nicknamed 'Old Ironsides') is now a tourist
attraction in Boston Harbour, like the *Dunbrody* in New Ross. Admiral
Charles Stewart's magnificent desk is among the exhibits in Avondale House,
the ancestral home of the Parnells in County Wicklow.

The artefacts in Kennedy's office relating to the *USS Constitution* testified
to his love of the sea and his own wartime service in the navy. His wartime
service, coupled with the fact that his father had been American ambassador
in Britain in the critical period from 1938 to 1940, led to an intense interest
in foreign policy, evident from his earliest days as a politician. His most
substantial achievements as president were in the field of foreign policy.
Notwithstanding failures at the Bay of Pigs and in Vietnam, he rose to the
challenge of Soviet pressure both in Berlin and during the Cuban missile
crisis – and the Soviets backed down, defeats from which arguably they
never recovered. It was a turning point, the beginning of the end of the
Cold War. There then followed the Partial Nuclear Test Ban Treaty, covering
tests in the atmosphere, in outer space and under water. It is hard for us
– or at least for those under 60 – to recapture today the very real fear of

nuclear Armageddon that the world had in the late 1950s and early 1960s. JFK defused that threat, and left the world a safer place. It is his greatest legacy, and ensures an honoured place for him in history. An editorial in the *Guardian* newspaper in November 2013, marking the fiftieth anniversary of the assassination, summed it up well: 'Kennedy faced the spectre of nuclear war and played his part in saving us from evil on a scale we cannot even now wholly fathom.'[21]

As regards the Cuban missile crisis, Sachs does not exaggerate when he claims that 'we owe our very lives to John Kennedy's grace under pressure in October 1962'.[22] The phrase 'grace under pressure' is Ernest Hemingway's, and Kennedy appropriated it as a definition of courage in his book *Profiles in Courage*.[23] Kennedy's achievements in foreign policy won the admiration of probably the most distinguished United States diplomat of the post-Second World War era, George Kennan – the architect of the 'containment' strategy that defined United States policy towards the Soviet Union until its collapse. In private correspondence with the President in October 1963, just one month before JFK's assassination, Kennan wrote:

> I am full of admiration, both as a historian and as a person with diplomatic experience, for the manner in which you have addressed yourself to the problems of foreign policy with which I am familiar. I don't think we have seen a better standard of statesmanship in the White House in the present century.[24]

Kennedy's achievements on the domestic front were, however, less spectacular. He was a politician of the centre – famously describing himself as an 'idealist without illusions'.[25] Reeves qualifies that, arguing that JFK 'had little ideology beyond anti-Communism and faith in active, pragmatic government ... What he had was an attitude, a way of taking on the world, substituting intelligence for ideas or idealism.'[26] Kennedy's greatest difficulty was building a political consensus with the United States Congress. Legislative gridlock prevented every one of Kennedy's major domestic initiatives from becoming law, and this led the journalist and savant, Walter Lippmann, to write a month before Kennedy's assassination that there was 'reason to wonder whether the Congressional system as it now operates is not a grave danger to the Republic'.[27] Because of his rhetoric and charisma, Kennedy was, however, able to reach out beyond Congress to the people of the United States to garner support for his policies and so pressurise the Congress to act on his proposals – though we cannot know whether this effort would eventually have yielded more fruit than it had done before his premature death. Most historians agree that he at least deserves credit for what might have been.

Kennedy is often criticised for the delay in acting on his commitment to advance civil rights for black Americans. In his inaugural address, he had spoken of 'those human rights to which this nation has always been committed and to which we are committed today *at home* and around the world [my italics]'.[28] This was a difficult issue for him, for he was constrained by the incredibly narrow electoral mandate he had received in 1960 and the fact that he had been dependent on the votes of segregationist southern states in the Electoral College for his victory. Nevertheless, in June 1963, he took decisive action – spurred on by a crisis over the admission of black students to the University of Alabama. He made a memorable speech and followed up his rhetoric with draft legislation sent to the Congress for approval. This became the Civil Rights Act of 1964, signed into law by his successor, Lyndon Johnson. Kennedy thus passes the test of leadership that Lippmann prescribed in 1945 on the occasion of Franklin Roosevelt's death: 'The final test of a leader is that he leaves behind him in other men the conviction and the will to carry on. The genius of a good leader is to leave behind him a situation which common sense, without the grace of genius, can deal with successfully.'[29]

It is open to question whether the Civil Rights Act would have been passed by Congress but for JFK's assassination. President Johnson skilfully harnessed the emotions unleashed by the assassination to force the legislation through Congress,[30] but it would not have happened without Kennedy's initiative. The result was the most radical social reform in the United States since the early days of Roosevelt's 'New Deal' and the last such advance until Obamacare.

That civil rights speech in June 1963 has been described in the *New York Times* as Kennedy's 'finest moment'.[31] Pushing the cause of civil rights was an act of great political courage which matches those instances of courage which Kennedy had fêted in his book *Profiles in Courage*. Kennedy knew that he would thereby alienate the support of the southern states – the former states of the Confederacy, hitherto solidly Democratic in politics – and so jeopardise his chances of re-election in 1964. The southern states have largely voted for Republican candidates for the presidency and for Congress ever since.

We must conclude, therefore, that Kennedy's record as president is a positive one. He was a significant president – a president of consequence – who made a difference for the better and who might have been among the greatest of the presidents but for the brevity of his time in office. This is reflected in the polls that American historians and other experts in related disciplines periodically carry out to rank their presidents. As already noted, ranking the presidents is a game that United States historians play compulsively.[32] Kennedy's place in the rankings has now settled just inside the top ten – number eight, in fact, in the most recent C-SPAN Presidential Historians Survey, published in 2017. He is clearly not among the very greatest – only Washington, Lincoln and Franklin Roosevelt are so regarded. In Dallek's pithy formulation, their historic roles were respectively to 'launch, preserve and rescue the ship of state'.[33] Theodore Roosevelt, Eisenhower, Truman and Jefferson are the next highest in the C-SPAN poll, and then comes Kennedy – followed by Reagan and Lyndon Johnson, to complete the top ten.[34]

That Eisenhower gets a higher ranking than Kennedy is a surprising reversal of fortune since – as Kennedy's immediate predecessor – he was most unfavourably compared with Kennedy during the period of the JFK presidency. Kennedy himself defined his 1960 presidential campaign as an effort 'to start the United States moving again' after eight years of stagnation under Eisenhower.[35] John Shaw argues that that campaign was essentially 'a confrontation between Kennedy and the Eisenhower administration'.[36] I think Kennedy was a better president than Eisenhower and support for that opinion can be found in a poll in which a representative sample of over 2,000 adults in the United States – not professional academics – were asked to evaluate the presidents from Eisenhower to Clinton on a scale of 0 to 10. Kennedy scored the highest at 7.6. He was followed by Reagan at 6.9, Eisenhower at 6.8 and Clinton at 6.7; none of the other presidents scored above 5.[37]

Kennedy's ranking among the presidents should be seen against the background that all the presidents rated more highly, with the exception of Lincoln, served for at least two terms or very close to two terms – and even Lincoln was elected for a second term, though assassinated in the first weeks after his second inauguration. In contrast, Kennedy was president for just two years and ten months – barely a thousand days. When put in that perspective, his ranking represents a very strong endorsement of his presidency. Inevitably, it leads us to wonder what greater achievements might have been his had he lived to serve a full two terms in office. We shall never know the answer to that, but we do know that he is remembered as few presidents are remembered – even some of those more highly rated and with greater accomplishments. A factor in this, setting him apart from other presidents, is undoubtedly his early and violent death. He is one who 'shall not grow old, as we who are left grow old'[38] – he did not suffer the indignity of a gnarled old age, like his brother Teddy – and the manner of JFK's death still has the capacity to shock. Our remembrance of him may, however, also tell us something about the contemporary world – since, in his own words spoken at Amherst College just a few weeks before his assassination, 'a nation reveals itself not only by the men it produces but also by the men it honours, the men it remembers'.[39] We hunger for the kind of enlightened leadership that Kennedy offered. As the American historian Alan Brinkley has stated, Kennedy 'remains a powerful symbol of a lost moment, of a soaring idealism and hopefulness that subsequent generations still try to recover'.[40] In a similar vein, Dallek writes:

> Some presidents hold an endless fascination for Americans: Washington, Lincoln, the two Roosevelts, and more recently John F. Kennedy and Ronald Reagan. The public's interest has a lot to do with its craving for heroes or, probably more important, its wish to understand and revel in what constitutes effective leadership. In a nation that often feels adrift in an uncertain world, where domestic and foreign crises repeatedly endanger the country's well-being, great presidents are a comfort – a sort of salve for the national psyche.[41]

Some may say, having regard especially to the '#MeToo' movement today, that Kennedy's serial womanising diminishes his record. The full scale of that only became known to the public at large long after his death – and certainly it reflects badly on him as a human being, though it is not strictly relevant to his standing as a leader or as president. A daughter of his great friend, the English peer Lord Harlech, has said that her father, while acknowledging Kennedy's faults, viewed them as insignificant when weighed against his potential for good – and it is hard not to agree with that.[42] As Roy Jenkins, the British politician once wrote:

> No one with any sense of history or realism can pretend that sexual purity has been the outstanding characteristic of great political leaders … So there is no room for mounting high moral horses about sexual peccadilloes. Indeed, it would be more plausible to argue that the energy and charisma which are necessary for successful leadership (and sadly lacking today) are mostly accompanied by an unusual sexual drive which has rarely contained itself within monogamous bounds.[43]

At a time when the press exercised greater discretion than they do now in divulging the secrets of the private lives of politicians, it was never likely that Kennedy's sexual behaviour would compromise his ability to discharge the duties of his office – as happened when President Clinton's dalliance with Monica Lewinsky hit the headlines, and arguably Clinton's initial denial of that relationship did more harm than the fact of the relationship. Like Nixon and Watergate, it was the attempted cover-up that caused problems for Clinton. Within informed circles, Kennedy's womanising was the subject of much gossip during his lifetime – and a blind eye was turned to it. It may even have been grudgingly admired by some, or treated as a source of mild amusement. For example, the London-based publisher Rupert Hart-Davis, on a visit to the United States in the early days of the Kennedy presidency in 1961, wrote to his old Eton schoolmaster, George Lyttelton, as follows: 'Apparently President Kennedy is a great one for the girls, and during the election his opponents said that if he got to the White House they only hoped he would do for fornication what Eisenhower did for golf.'[44]

Kennedy may have disapproved of judging the presidents, but he knew that what he called 'the high court of history' would nevertheless eventually sit in judgement upon his period in office.[45] Nobody gets the last word in history – the record is always open to revision – but my own view is that, for a long time to come, the verdict on Kennedy will continue to be that rendered by Dallek in the eloquent concluding passage of his Kennedy biography, a passage that contains echoes of some famous words uttered by JFK's most illustrious predecessor, Abraham Lincoln. It is as follows:

> The sudden end to Kennedy's life and presidency has left us with tantalising 'might have beens'. Yet even setting these aside and acknowledging some missed opportunities and false steps, it must be acknowledged that the Kennedy thousand days spoke to the country's better angels, inspired visions of a less divisive nation and world, and demonstrated that America was still the last best hope of mankind.[46]

CHAPTER 8

JOHN F. KENNEDY'S PRESIDENCY AND THE IRISH–UNITED STATES RELATIONSHIP

Mary Daly

John F. Kennedy's brief presidency and his visit to Ireland in 1963 offer a framework for examining the relationship between Ireland, the United States and Irish-America at a critical period in the history of independent Ireland. The early 1960s was a time of transitions in Ireland; the disappearance of the founding generation of political leaders; a re-orientation of economic policy and policy towards Northern Ireland, and efforts to engage more fully in international relations, both at the United Nations, and as an aspiring member of the European Economic Community. Eamon de Valera, the dominant political leader since independence, had left active politics in 1959 to assume the role of President of Ireland. Although Seán Lemass, his successor was also a veteran of the 1916 Rising and the struggle for independence, he expressed a different political and economic philosophy, highlighting the importance of economic development as a national aspiration.

Ireland was emerging from the isolation that characterised the years immediately after the Second World War. Joining the United Nations in 1955 helped the state play a greater role in international affairs. Government policy towards partition and Northern Ireland was abandoning the rather tedious formulaic resolutions in favour of a united Ireland – a campaign that showed little interest in changing the minds of Ulster unionists – towards building closer pragmatic relationships with Northern Ireland and its business community. The domestic economic agenda was shifting from a failed policy of self-sufficiency, and a belief in the central position of agriculture and rural society, towards free trade, and the encouragement of foreign investment. In 1961 Lemass announced that Ireland would apply for membership of the EEC. Although the 1961 census recorded the lowest population ever – the legacy of a grim decade of mass emigration – a more upbeat attitude towards Ireland's economic prospects, because of the 1958 Programme for Economic Expansion, led to a belief that the era of net emigration was coming to an end. Mass migration from Ireland to the United States ceased during the depression of the 1930s. Most post-war emigrants went to Britain. Although the rate of emigration during the 1950s was higher than at any time since the 1880s, Ireland never filled its annual United States emigration quota of 17,853, and emigration only reached 50 per cent of that quota in 1957 and 1958 when Britain was in recession.[1] In official circles the Irish-American community was seen as ageing, losing cohesion, and no longer of interest to the Irish government, other than as a market for tourism and products such as Waterford glass, Belleek china and knitted or tweed garments.

In this essay, I want to examine John F. Kennedy's presidency and his visit to Ireland in 1963 in the context of four related themes: the transitions in Irish-America, and Irish relations with Irish-America; Ireland's new economic agenda; partition, Irish-America and Irish–US relations, and closely linked to this, the significance of Ireland's stance at the United Nations. I will begin with a brief look at the Irish response to Kennedy's election in November 1960.

At the time of John F. Kennedy's presidential election campaign most of Ireland was living in the pre-television age. Those living close to the border with Northern Ireland or along the east coast could watch the election campaign on British television, but these were a minority. There were 20,000 televisions in Ireland in 1958 and by 1960 it is estimated that approximately 30 per cent of households, people living along the east coast or near the border, could watch British television stations.[2] But a majority of the Irish people were unable to watch the Democratic and Republican Conventions, the landmark Kennedy–Nixon debate, or the drama of the election count. (Living close to the border with Northern Ireland in a home with a television,

I still remember being fascinated by the showbiz nature of the Democratic primary – it made a more lasting impression than other aspects of the campaign.) This was also the era of brief, rather dry and factual radio news bulletins, so radio did not compensate for the absence of television coverage.

On 2 November, six days before the election, Thomas J. Kiernan, the Irish ambassador to the United States drafted a long report on the campaign, which is quite revealing. Much of his report related to the respective attitudes of Kennedy and Nixon towards the Cold War – which is not of direct relevance to this essay. Kiernan placed more emphasis on the fact that Kennedy was a Catholic than on his Irish heritage. Kennedy was, and until very recently remained, the only Catholic to be elected president of the United States, and his Catholicism was undoubtedly a major issue in the campaign – specifically the argument that his decisions on foreign policy would be influenced by the Vatican. Kiernan reported on the many sectarian attacks on Kennedy in church sermons. He speculated that this might result in 'a landslide Catholic vote in favour of Kennedy'.

He was extremely dismissive, however, about the significance of Kennedy's Irish ancestry. 'Nixon's wife is of Irish origin. Kennedy it is well known is of Irish origin. Neither candidate is interested in the least in Ireland. In regard to the Irish vote, there is no such thing. In general, those who are rich vote Republican, the majority, who are pulling the devil by the tail vote Democrat.' He suggested that many Irish-American Republican voters would support Kennedy, 'as a result mainly of the bitter Protestant attacks'. A supplementary commentary by Kiernan's colleague in Washington, concentrated on the religious aspect (and on some foreign policy issues), but said nothing about Kennedy's Irish ancestry.[3] This dispatch is telling; it reflects the low value that Irish government officials (and probably politicians) attached in 1960 to Irish-America as a vehicle for enhancing Ireland's international profile. This was possibly a reaction to the failure of the anti-partition campaign of the 1950s, which involved Irish-American politicians, including Senator John F. Kennedy, proposing resolutions in favour of a united Ireland on Capitol Hill, which had no practical effect. The other noteworthy feature is the strong emphasis on Catholicism as a proxy for Irishness. It is true that Catholic schools and parish churches staffed by priests and nuns of Irish birth or descent played a critical role in sustaining Irish culture and an identity with Ireland in the United States. In 1957 Jack Conway, Irish consul-general in New York, claimed that, for Irish Americans, Catholicism was more important than Irishness. He described the New York St Patrick's Day parade as 'a demonstration of Catholic presence with some Irish overtones'.[4] The association of Irishness with Catholicism and Catholic institutions was a reflection of the continuing immigration into the United States of Irish-born priests and nuns and the tacit encouragement by the American Catholic Church of ethnically based parishes – Hispanic, Polish, Italian or Irish – in the major cities. The other key Irish-American organisations were the county associations and the Ancient Order of Hibernians. None of these entities received significant support from the Irish government. At this time there was no network of cultural institutions or academic programmes that would promote a knowledge of Ireland and an affinity with modern Ireland, though in the 1930s Eoin MacNeill – scholar and founder of the Irish Volunteers – had tried to persuade de Valera to support the establishment of a network of Irish libraries in major American cities.

The presidential election on 8 November 1960 coincided with news of the massacre of ten Irish troops serving the United Nations at Niemba in the Congo – the first deaths of Irish troops on a UN peacekeeping mission. Ireland's reaction to the Niemba massacre overshadowed news of Kennedy's election. Nevertheless national and local newspapers were more alert than the Washington Embassy to the significance of the election of the descendent of Irish emigrants as President of the United States, though they also presented Irish-America as synonymous with Catholicism. The *Irish Independent* reported 'country-wide jubilation' at the election of the 'great-grandson of a County Wexford exile' as President of the United States. It noted, however, that plans in New Ross to celebrate Kennedy's election were cancelled because of the Niemba massacre.[5] The *Evening Herald* claimed that Kennedy's election was a historic occasion: he was 'the first Catholic, first Irishman to enter the White House', a comment that discounted the many former United States Presidents of Scots/Irish ancestry. The *Cork Examiner* reported that news of Kennedy's election was received 'with gratification ... hailed as a victory for Irish blood and the old faith, while others saw it as the culmination of the battle for recognition of this land which took part in the great diaspora of our race after the Famine. Their fight has been a hard one but eventually, they gained admission to the councils of their adopted country only to be denied the supreme honour' – of becoming

President of the United States. They saw Kennedy's election as a 'symbol of that victory'.[6] Nationalist party MPs in the Northern Ireland parliament sent Kennedy a congratulatory telegram, claiming that his victory 'finally lays [to rest] a bigoted intolerant, anti-Catholic tradition. We salute with pride this outstanding achievement by the great-grandson of a Famine emigrant.'[7]

Although some newspapers expressed the hope that President Kennedy would visit 'the land of his forebears',[8] the Irish government was slow to issue an invitation. On St Patrick's Day in 1961 T.J. Kiernan presented President Kennedy with an official Kennedy coat of arms and a genealogical tree of the Kennedys in Ireland, but there was a hesitation about inviting him to visit, despite the fact that the President was scheduled to pay an official visit to Paris, for fear that the invitation might be rejected.

Kennedy's visit in June 1963 formed part of a more extensive trip to Europe. By 1963 Ireland had a national television station Telefís Éireann, which meant that many Irish households could share the experience – though as yet only a minority had a television, and the signal did not yet reach many parts of the country. However, television rentals and sales soared; people watched it in the shop windows of electrical suppliers; families without televisions gathered in neighbouring houses. The visit prompted both excitement and some uncertainty. Ireland was trying to establish an image as a modern European nation – this was essential if Ireland was going to secure full membership of the EEC, despite the fact that per capita GNP was roughly half that of existing members. (There was some talk in the early 1960s of Ireland becoming an associate member, a status that the EEC regarded as appropriate for a less developed economy.) The image of modernity was also necessary if Ireland was to attract foreign industrial investment, especially United States investment. At this time American investment in Ireland was limited, and it was almost entirely concentrated in the Shannon Free Airport Development zone, but the announcement in 1963 of a proposed Irish-American Council for Industry and Commerce indicated a determination to expand US–Irish business relations.[9]

The Irish government had limited expertise in dealing with foreign media, though, as Taoiseach, Lemass was very open to doing interviews with foreign journalists. There were acute sensitivities about how Ireland was represented to outsiders, lest their articles/television coverage would challenge the government's efforts to promote an image of modernity and economic growth. In 1961 the Irish Embassy in Bonn asked the German foreign ministry to withdraw the German film *Ireland and her Children*, from the prestigious international television competition the 'Prix du Rome'. Based on the German writer Heinrich Boll's *Irische Tagebuch* (Irish Diary), written in the late 1950s, the film highlighted the poverty and high rate of emigration in the west of Ireland.[10] Irish concerns were not unfounded. In May 1963 under the heading 'The Greatest Event Since Independence' the *New York Times's* story announcing Kennedy's visit to Ireland drew on every American cliché about Ireland.

> If all the leprechauns were tossed off the shamrocks this morning and the mountains trembled from Slieve Naught to McGillicuddy Reeks, it was because of the arrival in Dublin of two advance agents of the White House ... Not only is he coming for sure, but the dates have been arranged. And many's the unearned smile and proffer of a Guinness or a Jameson that has been the reward of the American pilgrim who saw no harm in encouraging as a probability the view expressed that, in all those foreign travels, 'he' was after making, Eire would certainly be included if 'twas God's will'.[11]

Officials in the Department of External Affairs were concerned that American television would show 'pigs in kitchen etc.' when covering Kennedy's visit.[12] As we know the coverage proved overwhelmingly positive and the genuine spontaneity of the Dunganstown tea party exemplified an unpretentious and genuine Irish hospitality. At a more practical level there were concerns that Ireland's primitive tele-communications would be unable to cope with the demands of the United States official party and the foreign media; the number of telephones per head of population was among the lowest in western Europe.

The advance preparations for Kennedy's visit revealed some of the tensions between change and continuity that were continuing to play out within the Irish government. Lemass was determined to promote a closer relationship with the government of Northern Ireland. He believed that the ultimate solution to partition might be found through developing a prosperous Irish economy that would prove attractive to Ulster unionists. But Minister for External Affairs Frank Aiken remained a supporter of the post-war anti-partition campaign, and a key element of that failed strategy was to persuade the United States to use its influence with Britain to urge Britain to support a united Ireland.[13] When T.J. Kiernan, the Irish ambassador to the United States, met Kennedy ahead of his visit to Ireland he broached the possibility that Kennedy might take the opportunity of urging the British that they should indicate publicly that a solution to the partition question 'is desirable from the point of view of both Britain and Ireland'. Kennedy was flying to Britain to meet the Prime Minister Harold Macmillan, following his visit to Ireland, and it was known that the two had a close personal relationship. Kennedy expressed the opinion that 'no British Minister would feel able to make a public statement of the kind suggested'. Kiernan added that:

> He [Kennedy] is by his education, British-inclined. And in the present international conjuncture, he makes no secret of his firm attachment to Britain. So that, to raise a new issue (or renew an old issue) now when Britain has so many pressing problems to solve, is something he would avoid and would seek an alternative. He would, therefore regard our suggestion as embarrassing to the British at this troubled stage in their history.[14]

Kiernan's assessment of Kennedy's attitude was correct, but he failed to convince his minister. Aiken persisted in his efforts to use Kennedy's visit to exert pressure on Britain. Kiernan was sent back to the White House for a further meeting with the President, duly armed with forty-four pages of statements by United States politicians and others, including British Prime Minister W.E. Gladstone, all ostensibly justifying the case for Irish unity. Aiken urged the Ambassador to present these to the President, in the hope of persuading him 'to avail himself of any suitable opportunity with the British to encourage them to play their part in bringing partition to an end'. When Kiernan raised the matter with Kennedy and summarised some of the extracts, he reported that 'The President looked as if another headache had struck him and asked me was he expected to say anything in public. I repeated we were not asking for this but only that we hoped for his continued goodwill towards a solution of the reunification of the country.'[15] Partition did not figure at any point in Kennedy's visit. Although Aiken can be described as 'old guard' Fianna Fáil on this issue, he also had to negotiate the changing relationship between Ireland, the United States and Irish-America. As Minister for External Affairs, and a regular presence at the United Nations General Assembly, Aiken was in favour of the UN debating the question of admitting China to membership of the United Nations, (Ireland did not commit to supporting China's admission, merely to debating the issue), whereas the United States government and Irish-America was strongly opposed to this stance. Aiken and the Irish government faced widespread criticism from the American Catholic hierarchy, many of Irish-American ancestry, for taking this stance. Aiken's persistence in trying to get Kennedy to make a statement about partition might have been designed to rebuild bridges with Irish-America, especially with Irish-American Catholicism.

Most high-profile visits like that of John F. Kennedy to Ireland now conclude with formal announcements of an economic, cultural or diplomatic nature, which are carefully negotiated in advance of the visit. Nothing of that nature happened in 1963, and there is no evidence that the Irish government sought any such outcome – with the possible exception of Aiken's wish for a statement about partition. However, the trip undoubtedly resulted in Seán Lemass featuring in a cover story in *Time* magazine within a month of Kennedy's Irish tour. Lemass was pictured against a garish green curtain, covered with shamrock motifs and the inevitable leprechaun in traditional red and green costume, which opened to reveal chimneys from an electricity generating station and modern high-rise buildings. The inside story, headed 'New Spirit in the Ould Sod' juxtaposed traditional images of Ireland, such as the Lakes of Killarney, horse racing and Gaelic football, with shots of a factory assembling Volkswagen Beetles, a traffic jam in Dublin's O'Connell Street and a vegetable processing plant. The text was replete with clichéd images of a Celtic Ireland with references to the 'swarthy chieftains and pale queens who … still clatter across the country', the 'landscape dreamily unreal' and much more in similar vein, but it did convey the message that Ireland was changing and the economy was expanding.[16]

Lemass's visit to the United States in October 1963 was designed to capitalise on the greater awareness of Ireland resulting from Kennedy's visit, but once again it revealed the need to balance a new economic agenda, with more traditional Irish-American politics. The newly established Irish-American Council for Industry and Commerce aimed to attract a membership among affluent business circles, with some links to Ireland,

Patrick Kennedy, *c.* 1850. Escaping the Great Famine and leaving behind forever his native Ireland, Patrick Kennedy boarded a ship in New Ross in October 1848. Just over one hundred and twelve years later, Patrick's great-grandson was elected the thirty-fifth President of the United States of America.

The grove where Bridget Murphy's house once stood, Cloonagh, Co. Wexford, 22 June 2019. Without Bridget's perseverance, work ethic and ingenuity, the Kennedy family may well have perished.

Joseph P. Kennedy, United States Ambassador to Great Britain, 20 June 1938. His own presidential ambitions ran aground, but were reborn in his sons.

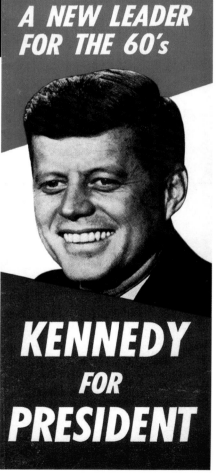

A pamphlet for the 1960 election campaign. Joseph P. Kennedy spent at least $10 million ($86 million in 2020 terms) on his son's 1960 presidential bid.

President-elect John F. Kennedy meeting with President Dwight D. Eisenhower in the Oval Office, 6 December 1960. Eisenhower was unfavourably compared with Kennedy during the period of the JFK presidency.

President John F. Kennedy meeting with the Director of the Federal Bureau of Investigation J. Edgar Hoover (centre) and Attorney General Robert F. Kennedy in the Oval Office, 23 February 1961.

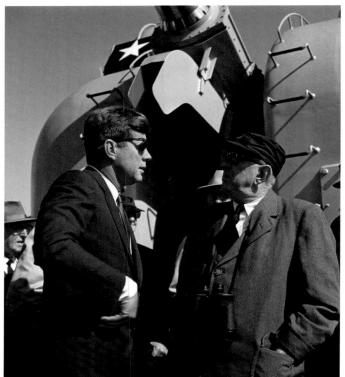

President Kennedy talkin[g] with Senator Richard [B.] Russell aboard the cruis[er] USS *Northampton* at s[ea] off the coast of Virgin[ia] and North Carolina, [14] April 1962.

The Irish Ambassador to the United States of America, Thomas J. Kiernan, presents a gift of shamrocks to President Kennedy for St Patrick's Day at the White House's West Wing Colonnade, 15 March 1963.

Caroline Kennedy (left), daughter of President John F. Kennedy, and Kerry Kennedy (right), daughter of Attorney General Robert F. Kennedy, hiding under President Kennedy's desk in the Oval Office, 22 June 1963.

President John F. Kennedy and other distinguished guests attending a welcome ceremony for the United States President at New Ross Quay, County Wexford, 27 June 1963. The President delivered an address at the quay from where his great-grandfather, Patrick Kennedy, commenced his emigrant journey.

President John F. Kennedy placing a wreath at the Commodore John Barry memorial statue at Crescent Quay, Wexford Town, 27 June 1963.

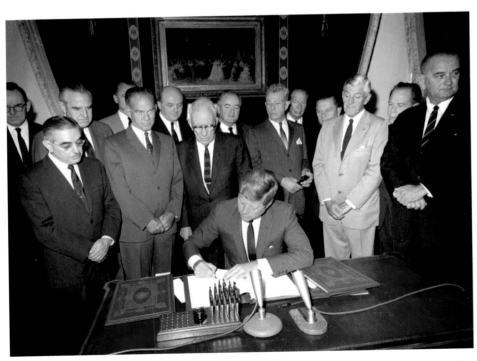

President John F. Kennedy signing the Nuclear Test Ban Treaty in front of a distinguished audience of invited guests, in the Treaty Room of the White House, 7 October 1963.

Senator Ted Kennedy meeting with President Ronald Reagan in the Oval Office to discuss the situation in Northern Ireland, 1 June 1981.

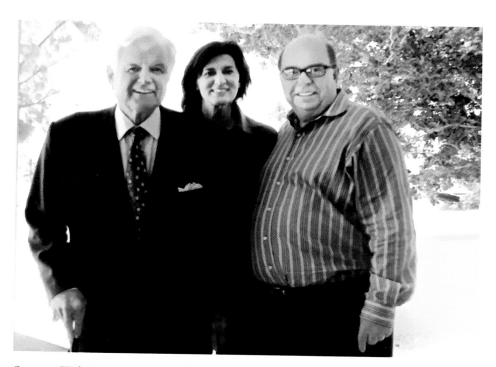

Senator Ted Kennedy, Vicki Kennedy and Bob Shrum at Key Biscayne, Florida, April 2009.

President Barack Obama talks with his Director of Speechwriting Cody Keenan in the Oval Office, 23 July 2013. President Obama said that he relied on Keenan 'to help tell America's story'.

Bernie Sanders speaking at a campaign rally in Traverse City, Michigan, 4 March 2016.

probably economic, as opposed to ethnic. Irish diplomats were also beginning to fashion a new narrative associated with the Irish in America, one that moved the Great Famine back into a new central space. An official in the Irish embassy in Washington reported that Cecil-Woodham Smith's best-selling book, *The Great Hunger* – published in 1962 – had a positive impact on American attitudes towards Ireland because it succeeded 'in putting into focus Irish emigration into the United States and generally of winning a sympathy and respect for the Irish emigrant'. The Famine had always formed part of the Irish-American story. The election of John F. Kennedy, a descendant of Famine-era emigrants whose family rose to the pinnacles of economic and political success in the United States, coupled with the success of Woodham-Smith's book, appears to have prompted Irish officials to identify successful Americans with distant Irish ancestry who might potentially be invited to participate in cultural or business networks. Their success was more in keeping with Ireland's current mission than the modest achievements of more recent Irish emigrants to the United States that Irish consular officials had described in their briefings.

During his visit Lemass met many prominent business figures with some links to Ireland. He travelled to Chicago where he addressed a more traditional Irish-American audience. In advance of this meeting, the Irish consul-general in Chicago warned that in order to placate his audience the Taoiseach would have to say something about partition and 'the need for territorial re-unification ... as Taoiseach Mr Lemass will represent the integral Irish tradition. Moreover, any old IRA men and Old Clan na Gael men present ... will be interested to hear it as the *Time* Magazine article, which so many read, was a bit out of focus on the non-economic side of pre-1959 history.'[17] Lemass addressed the question of partition in a speech at the Washington Press Club. He borrowed the phrase 'Winds of Change' which British Prime Minister Harold Macmillan had used very effectively when referring to British decolonisation in Africa, and called on Britain to issue a statement agreeing that it would abandon partition in Ireland 'when Irishmen want to get rid of it'. (Such a statement was eventually made by British Prime Minister John Major as part of the 1993 Downing Street Declaration.) But in 1963 Britain did not respond. This is not surprising because the speech came shortly after Harold Macmillan's resignation and his succession by Sir Alec Douglas-Home. Regardless of the timing, a response would have been unlikely. However, Lemass's remarks aroused the anger of Northern Ireland Prime Minister Terence O'Neill and his cabinet. It is widely acknowledged that this speech delayed the first O'Neill–Lemass meeting by some time.

Kennedy's visit and his brief presidency undoubtedly impacted on Ireland, on Irish–US relations and on Ireland's relationship with Irish-America. The campaign by Fine Gael candidate Tom O'Higgins to become President of Ireland was modelled on Kennedy's election campaign; the photograph of the extended Lemass family in *Time* magazine is yet another example of Kennedy's influence on the style of Irish politics.

Although Kennedy did not press the British government with regard to partition, arguably he played a more important role in persuading Prime Minister Harold Macmillan to apply for British membership of the EEC.[18] Kennedy's presidency prompted Irish politicians and officials to think again about the Irish in America, and most especially the larger community, whose Irish roots were several generations past. Irish-America was changing; the traditional Irish-American communities were dissolving as people moved to the suburbs and by the late 1960s the impact of the civil rights movement and emphasis on integration would destroy many traditional Irish schools and parishes. The mid-1960s marked the peak in the numbers of Irishmen and women entering religious life; in the early to mid-1960s, Ireland was sending a regular stream of young priests and nuns to the United States, but that ended within a decade.

Changes in Ireland and the United States meant that by the 1960s Ireland had to develop new methods of engaging with the United States and Irish-America at multiple levels – communicating the pragmatic economic arguments about Ireland as a destination for United States investment and a modern society; beginning the process of developing an Irish-American network that was more focused on economy and culture than traditional Irish politics, and learning to make productive use of what Jack Conway described as 'a sentimental regard for their ancestry which does not involve financial expenditure'.[19] These relationships underwent much greater challenges after Kennedy's presidency. The removal of ethnic quotas – which Irish authorities did not oppose – effectively ended legal Irish emigration to the United States after almost 200 years,[20] and the onset of violence in Northern Ireland meant that Irish politicians and officials had to communicate Irish policy towards Northern Ireland in a much more forthright manner than Lemass did in 1963. They had to re-engage with Clan na Gael, the Ancient Order of Hibernians and the County Associations, while simultaneously maintaining relationships with potential United States investors and forging relationships with a new generation of Irish-American politicians.

CHAPTER 9

THE LEGACY OF A THOUSAND DAYS

Robert Schmuhl

By the time John F. Kennedy arrived at the 1960 Democratic National Convention in Los Angeles at the age of 43, he had achieved recognition as a Second World War hero, defeated opponents in elections to the House of Representatives three times and to the Senate twice, and written a best-selling book, *Profiles in Courage*, that brought him a Pulitzer Prize. He had also endured scarlet fever, Addison's disease and life-threatening back surgery, as well as other physical maladies – which led to him receiving the last rites of the Catholic Church on three occasions before he was 35 years old.

At the convention – after assuring several of his staff and potential supporters that he would never select Senate Majority Leader Lyndon B. Johnson as his vice-presidential running mate – he selected Johnson as his choice for the second spot on the national ticket. Kenneth O'Donnell, a close and long-time aide to Kennedy, was apoplectic. In the book *Johnny, We Hardly Knew Ye*, O'Donnell recalls how he reacted and what he said to JFK about the decision:

> 'This is the worst mistake you ever made,' I said to him. 'You came out here to this convention like a knight on a white charger, the clean-cut young Ivy League college guy who's promising to get rid of the old hack machine politicians. And now, in your first move after you get the nomination, you go against all the people who supported you. Are

we going to spend the campaign apologising for Lyndon Johnson and trying to explain why he voted against everything you ever stood for?'[1]

Kennedy, however, strongly and in personal terms defended his pick in words O'Donnell reports he 'never forgot':

'I'm forty-three years old, and I'm the healthiest candidate for President in the United States. You've travelled with me enough to know that. I'm not going to die in office. So the Vice-Presidency doesn't mean anything. I'm thinking of something else, the leadership in the Senate. If we win, it will be by a small margin and I won't be able to live with Lyndon Johnson as the leader of a small majority in the Senate. Did it occur to you that if Lyndon becomes the Vice-President, I'll have Mike Mansfield as the leader in the Senate, somebody I can trust and depend on?'[2]

Of course, and regrettably, all of us know the vice presidency did mean something after the fateful day in Dallas on 22 November 1963, but so, too, did the elevation of Mike Mansfield in the Senate on 3 January 1961. The son of two Irish immigrants, Mansfield ultimately became the longest serving Senate Majority Leader in American history, sixteen years, from 1961 until 1977.

By contrast, Kennedy served the shortest length of time of any Democratic President – 1,036 days. His shadow, though, remains both long and large, and his legacy deserves serious and sustained probing to identify:

- What endures from his life and his career?
- What contributions he made to the work and thought of future generations?
  and,
- What changes he initiated in American political life, especially in relation to the presidency and to the role of the United States in the world?

Back in the late eighteenth century, as the American colonies in the New World were becoming the United States, the French emigrant St Jean de

Crèvecoeur composed a series of *Letters from an American Farmer* about his experiences and reflections on 'this great American asylum' across the Atlantic Ocean. In one epistle, he famously inquired, 'What then is the American, this new man?' That question took on modern and political relevance with the appearance of Kennedy on the national stage in the late 1950s and into 1960. In several specific ways, he personified a 'new man' in the nation's civic and electoral life. He was dramatically different from the presidents who preceded him, and he arrived at the White House after pursuing a course never followed by anyone in previous campaigns.

The first president born in the twentieth century, JFK represented youth, vitality and vigour. It was as though America's politics switched overnight from broadcasting in black and white to Technicolour. In his memoir, *In Search of History: A Personal Adventure*, Theodore H. White observed:

> It is quite obvious now, of course, that he was the man who broke up the old pattern of American politics. All the sophisticated technology of election campaigning and analysis that has come since then has been just that – technology. He was the man who ruptured the silent understanding that had governed American politics for two centuries – that this was a country of white Protestant gentry and yeomen who offered newer Americans a choice for leadership only within their clashing rivalries. He made us look at ourselves afresh. Kennedy ended many other myths and fossil assumptions, and with him, an old world of politics and government came to a close.[3]

This new political man was impatient and willing to seek the nation's highest office in an unconventional way. Until 1960, only one senator (Warren Harding in 1920) had made the jump directly to the presidency. However, it is critical to observe that Kennedy had published *Profiles in Courage* at the beginning of 1956, and it occupied a place on bestseller lists for many weeks before winning the Pulitzer Prize for biography in 1957. The book's popularity helped to make Kennedy a political celebrity, and *Time* put him on that newsweekly's cover for its issue of 2 December 1957. The first sentence of the second paragraph in the nearly five-page article ('Man Out Front') drives home its *raison d'être*, 'In his unannounced but unabashed run for the Democratic Party's nomination for President in 1960, Jack Kennedy has left panting politicians and swooning women across a large spread of the US.' Rather than building an extensive legislative record in Congress, JFK was touring the country to become prominent as a politician-cum-public intellectual and positioning himself for a potential White House candidacy well in advance of the next election.

Kennedy had turned just 40 in May 1957 and ambition animated what he did during this period of his life. In *President Kennedy: Profile of Power*, Richard Reeves astutely observes: 'Looking back, it seemed to me that the most important thing about Kennedy was not a great political decision, though he made some, but his own political ambition. He did not wait his turn. He directly challenged the institution he wanted to control, the political system. After him, no one else wanted to wait either … He believed (and proved) that the only qualification for the most powerful job in the world was wanting it.'[4]

John Kennedy did not wait – and neither did several of his successors. Jimmy Carter in 1976, Bill Clinton in 1992, George W. Bush in 2000, Barack Obama in 2008 and Donald J. Trump in 2016 – all were first-time presidential candidates who refused to stand in line and allow others to go ahead of them. They felt their time had arrived and took on more established and experienced opponents to win the White House. JFK proved that, if you think your moment has arrived, you take the chance and follow your own star wherever that takes you. Lightning might strike and set you off from other aspirants.

Kennedy was also the harbinger of the importance of winning primaries to capture a party's nomination for the White House. Though rule changes by both Democrats and Republicans in the 1970s would make the results of primaries and caucuses decisive in determining the parties' standard-bearers, in 1960 JFK targeted two primary contests – Wisconsin and West Virginia – to show his strength in winning the voters' support. In both states, Senator Hubert Humphrey of Minnesota was the opponent, and Kennedy defeated him each time. Wisconsin was critical because of the state's position in the Midwest right next to Humphrey's. Could a candidate from Massachusetts on the east coast beat an almost favourite son? Kennedy prevailed 56 per cent to 44 per cent. In West Virginia, JFK's Catholicism was the principal factor. Would anti-Catholic bias prevent a candidate from winning a heavily

Protestant state? Kennedy defeated Humphrey again and even more soundly: 61 per cent to 39 per cent.

Besides rewriting some of the unwritten rules for a White House campaign, Kennedy's impact on political culture was hugely consequential, too. He was the first celebrity president of the modern era and he brought the image of a political figure to centre stage in the American consciousness. In that regard, needless to say, there's been no turning back from the early 1960s to today. Indeed, all one has to do to see how Richard Nixon's approach changed from his race against JFK in 1960 (which featured four nationally televised debates) to his campaign in 1968 against Humphrey (with heavily produced programmes for the candidate instead of any debates) is to read Joe McGinniss's book, *The Selling of the President 1968*. It explains in eye-opening detail how the *image* conveyed by television had come to dominate American political communication after the Kennedy years staked out this new territory. In an appendix, McGinniss reprints a memorandum from a top communications adviser, Ray Price, to illustrate the central role television had assumed since JFK took on Nixon eight years earlier. Price wrote: '*We have to be very clear on this point: that the response is to the image, not to the man,* since 99 per cent of the voters have no contact with the man. It's not what's *there* that counts, it's what's projected – and, carrying it one step further, it's not what *he* projects but rather what the voter receives. It's not the man we have to change, but rather the *received impression*.'[5] (Italics in original.)

Another effect on the political culture pertained to how the public viewed the presidency and how that perception changed during JFK's time in office. The 'leader of the free world' was portrayed from several vantage points: as a statesman, as a politician, as a husband, as a father, as a brother, and so forth. The 'mass media' of the time – especially network television, which was developing technologically and becoming the primary source of what was occurring in public affairs – created a new bridge between the president and the citizenry, making a stronger and more direct connection. Five days after he was inaugurated in 1961, he conducted a news conference on live television, and he continued this practice an average of two times a month (for a total of sixty-four) throughout his presidency. In exchange after exchange, Kennedy provided a sense of command in terms of his knowledge of policy and contemporary situations. He also injected wit into his responses that made him more appealing both to the reporters asking the questions and to those watching at home. He was reducing the distance between himself and everyone else.

Through the news conferences and other television coverage, Kennedy appeared more accessible, and how he was perceived and interpreted evoked a certain sense of complexity rather than simplicity among observers. The *Time* cover story in 1957 notes that JFK 'imparts a remarkable quality of shy, sensemaking sincerity'. The suggestion of shyness or self-effacement for a constantly photographed and heavily covered figure became a refrain in the judgements of those watching from afar. Noted communications scholar and media guru of the 1960s, Marshall McLuhan, watched the debates between Kennedy and Richard Nixon in 1960, seeing in JFK 'an image closer to the TV hero … something like the shy young Sheriff' – while Nixon came across to McLuhan 'with his very dark eyes' as 'the railway lawyer who signs leases that are not in the interests of the folks in the little town'. (In *Understanding Media*, where these remarks appear, McLuhan explains his overall reaction to the debates by stating: 'Without TV, Nixon had it made.')[6] Three decades later, Nigel Hamilton in *JFK: Reckless Youth* wrote about Kennedy's 'shy charisma',[7] and *Wall Street Journal* essayist Peggy Noonan in a column ('The Little Clintons') that came out on 12 February 1999 pointed out his 'diffidence', 'ironic shyness' and 'detached amusement'.

Interestingly, in addition to identifying a certain reluctance to bask in public acclaim, observers affixed another, though related, word to appraisals of Kennedy. That word is 'elusive'. In an often-cited and much-discussed essay, 'Superman Comes to the Supermarket', that appeared right before the 1960 election, Norman Mailer wrote of JFK:

> Yet there was an elusive detachment to everything he did. One did not have the feeling of a man present in the room with all his weight and all his mind. Johnson gave you all of himself, he was a political animal, he breathed like an animal, sweated like one, you knew his mind was entirely absorbed with the compendium of political fact and manoeuvre; Kennedy seemed at times like a young professor whose manner was adequate for the classroom, but whose mind was off in some intricacy of the Ph.D. thesis he was writing. Perhaps one can give a sense of the discrepancy by saying that he was like an actor

who had been cast as the candidate, a good actor, but not a great one – you were aware all the time that the role was one thing and the man another – they did not coincide, the actor seemed a touch too aloof (as, let us say, Gregory Peck is usually too aloof) to become the part. (*Esquire*, November 1960)[8]

A half-century later, author and television personality Chris Matthews published *Jack Kennedy: Elusive Hero* in 2011, and early on he admits that he's tackling a perplexing person, '... my fascination with the elusive spirit of John F. Kennedy has remained an abiding one. He is both pathfinder and puzzle, a beacon and a conundrum.'[9]

To dilate on someone's shyness or elusiveness derives, in large part, from the new multi-directional attention to the presidency that the burgeoning media outlets, especially television, provided. That attention, moreover, took the media into areas previously considered professionally off-limits, even taboo, for a public figure. However, in late 1975, a dozen years after the assassination, journalists detailed the findings of the Senate Select Committee to Study Governmental Operations with Respect to Intelligence Activities (colloquially called the 'Church Committee' for its chair Senator Frank Church), and it raised speculation that President Kennedy had been involved in a relationship with a woman, who was simultaneously philandering with major players in organised crime.

The New York Times (on 16 December 1975) published under the headline 'Section of Report Referring to Kennedy Friendship' an extract from the Committee's official record that included this paragraph: 'Evidence before the Committee indicates that a close friend of President Kennedy had frequent contact with the President from the end of 1960 through mid-1962. FBI reports and testimony indicate that the President's friend was also a close friend of John Rosselli and Sam Giancana and saw them often during the same period.' (Both Rosselli and Giancana were well known for their participation in the American mafia, and both were subsequently murdered in gangland style.) The quoted extract even provided the text of the footnote supplied at the end of the paragraph for clarification and amplification: 'White House telephone logs show seventy instances of phone contact between the White House and the President's friend whose testimony confirms frequent phone contact with the President himself.'

The next day's edition of the same newspaper carried a column, 'The President's Friend,' providing opinion writer William Safire's additional reporting and commentary about the committee report, complete with the detail that '"the President's friend" was a beautiful girl who divided her time between the Chicago underworld leadership and the President of the United States'.

In relatively short order, more stories about additional affairs involving JFK appeared – and the image of a martyred leader and devoted family man now competed with the less appealing perception of someone given to reckless behaviour and insatiable appetites. For better or for worse, it is possible to trace several roots of the private becoming public to the presidency of John Kennedy. The media were adjusting themselves to having a genuine celebrity in the White House. In addition, the many lies that circulated during the Vietnam War and Watergate contributed to more probing scrutiny of government by American journalism. The days of shielding a president from information in conflict with someone's projected persona came to an end after the posthumous revelations about JFK and his involvement with women other than his wife.

Reporting that examines what might be behind the mask of someone with power and prestige has become much more common since 1975. (Both Bill Clinton and Donald Trump can attest to that.) Indeed, in this regard, history can even become newsworthy. Six years before Jacqueline Kennedy Onassis's death in 1994, the cover of the celebrity-obsessed magazine *People Weekly* (for 29 February 1988) featured a smiling picture of John Kennedy along with these words: 'Twenty-five years later, his mistress admits she was the link between JFK & THE MOB.' The principal lesson to keep in mind from what was learned about Kennedy's personal life is this: If the image and the reality are ever in conflict, we can now expect the revelation of documented discrepancy. That might be unfortunate for the person involved and his or her family; however, it is a darker, though noteworthy, legacy of the concern for image and celebrity, particularly in relation to modern political figures.

Kennedy's image – smiling yet serious, commanding without being domineering – was just one dimension of his talent for communicating. He also wrote and spoke unforgettable sentences, graced with originality and power, not matched to date by any of his successors. Indeed, seven statements from just his inaugural address in 1961 are carved in granite near his grave at Arlington National Cemetery. One inscription reads:

> Let the word go forth
> From this time and place
> To friend and foe alike
> That the torch has been passed
> To a new generation of Americans

Those words – still vivid and stirring – set the tone for a presidency much different from the one before it: the eight years of Dwight D. Eisenhower in the White House. The youngest elected president (at 43) was succeeding the oldest at that time, who was 70. (Ronald Reagan became the oldest – at 77 – when he concluded his second term in 1989, prior to the election of Joe Biden.) For the first time a Roman Catholic was going to occupy the Oval Office in majority-Protestant America. A Democrat from the legislative branch of government was replacing the five-star US Army General and the Supreme Allied Commander during the Second World War, who was widely known for his executive expertise and was also a Republican. The contrast in figures could not have been more pronounced, and Eisenhower's two terms concluded a twenty-eight-year period with just three presidents: Franklin Roosevelt, Harry Truman and Eisenhower. Kennedy's 'new generation' of seven presidents – all with birthdays between 1908 and 1924 and White House service between 1961 and 1993 – were strikingly dissimilar from the preceding trio.

To consider briefly how each left office:

- Kennedy was assassinated in 1963;
- Lyndon Johnson, with approval ratings sinking below 40 per cent in 1968, decided not to run for re-election that year to avoid defeat;
- Richard Nixon, elected twice, was forced to resign in 1974 because of the misdeeds lumped together under the catch-all scandal heading of 'Watergate';
- Gerald Ford, Nixon's unelected successor, lost his campaign to continue in office in 1976;
- Jimmy Carter endured the Iranian hostage crisis and other trials before being defeated for re-election in 1980;

- Ronald Reagan – became the only two-term president in between the 1950s and the 1990s – but he was seriously injured in an assassination attempt in 1981 and politically wounded by the Iran–Contra affair during his second term;
- George H.W. Bush was elected once but then beaten for re-election in 1992.

For JFK's 'new generation', here is the reckoning: The United States had three Democratic and four Republican presidents with six of the seven having either tragic or forced endings. Why do we see that stretch of difficulty and disruption in America's highest office? Was the assassination and its aftermath so wrenching for the nation that it took decades to recover? Were other serious dislocations, including the Vietnam War and Watergate, more centrally responsible?

What is, curiously, fascinating is that since 1993, up to the election of Donald Trump in 2016, which includes the generation following Kennedy's, the country had three straight two-termers who served the full eight years: Bill Clinton, George W. Bush and Barack Obama. Of course, to be fair, the recent years for White House occupants have not exactly been cakewalks. Not one of those two-term presidents was succeeded in office by the candidate of his party. Clinton in 1998 became, at that time, the only elected president in United States history ever to be impeached. George W. Bush's second-term approval average (36.5 per cent) was the lowest number recorded by Gallup since Nixon's days. Obama departed the White House with his Democratic Party in its weakest position in decades and with both chambers of Congress in the control of Republicans.

From the vantage point of over a century since his birth in 1917, what is the most deliberate and dispassionate way to assess John Kennedy and his legacy? Robert Dallek titled his fine biography *An Unfinished Life*,[10] and that is an honest and straightforward approach for anyone to take. At the time of his death, he was still learning to be president, and his 'New Frontier' still encompassed vast territory yet to be explored. In 1962 Kennedy told the historian David Herbert Donald, 'No one has a right to grade a president – not even poor James Buchanan – who has not sat in his chair, examined the mail and information that came across his desk, and learned why he made his decisions.'[11] To carry Kennedy's own judgement forward: No one really has any right to speculate how a Kennedy presidency of four, or eight years, might have unfolded and turned out. We have no definite way of knowing.

Theodore H. White wrote *The Making of the President, 1960*, which created a new genre of political books in America: the 'insider' chronicle about presidential campaigns. White picked a perfect race to follow – one with vivid characters, seesaw action and high stakes. He also had the opportunity to interview Jacqueline Kennedy shortly after the assassination. As he describes the scene in his memoir, *In Search of History*, Mrs Kennedy wanted to talk with him but then struggled to find the words for her loss and the nation's. White writes:

> Interspersed with the memories, spoken so softly, in the particular whispering intimacy of Jacqueline Kennedy's voice, was constantly this effort to make the statement – the statement she had asked me to come and hear. It would stutter out over and over again with an introductory: 'History! ... History ... it's what those bitter old men write,' or just: 'History ...' But that was what she wanted to talk about; so, thus, I pull together here fragments of disjointed notes; and as I run the notes through my retrieval of memory for meaning, her message was quite simple: She believed, and John F. Kennedy shared the belief, that history belongs to heroes; and heroes must not be forgotten.[12]

White spoke with Mrs Kennedy for almost four hours and then quickly dictated his story for *Life* magazine immediately afterwards. One frequently cited statement that did not appear in the article, or in his memoir, or even in his typed notes (contained in a file as part of the 'Theodore H. White Personal Papers' and available in the John F. Kennedy Library) comes from an interview with White that was conducted by author C. David Heymann for his book, *A Woman Named Jackie* (1989). According to Heymann, White told him: '"Only bitter old men write history," she [Mrs Kennedy] said. "Jack's life had more to do with myth, magic, legend, saga, and story than with political theory or political science." That's when she came out with her Camelot theory.'[13] It's a revealing and significant observation. As a result of the interview and the subsequent article, *Camelot* (a popular musical play first produced in 1960) began to be associated with the assassinated president. In White's words, which appear in his memoir, 'the epitaph on the Kennedy administration became Camelot',[14] which is based on the legend of King Arthur and the knights of the round table.

Of course, the Camelot analogy is, by and large, mythological. But the reality behind this myth-making does not seem to affect public opinion. In November 2013, fifty years after his death, the Gallup polling organisation surveyed Americans for their opinions about all the presidents since Eisenhower and how they 'will go down in history'. Kennedy ranked the highest with 74 per cent placing him as 'Outstanding' or 'Above Average'. Reagan was next at 61 per cent, and Clinton third at 55 per cent. The other eight presidents failed to reach 50 per cent, with Johnson languishing at 20 per cent and Nixon the lowest with 15 per cent.[15]

John Kennedy's 1,036 days in the White House might seem to most people an ice age ago, but the idealistic heroism he evoked and the words he spoke still echo and inspire many who study his life and legacy. For Americans and millions throughout the world, he was the epitome, even the archetype, of a political leader in the prime of life and in command of his nation's destiny. And then, suddenly and tragically, he was gone. However, memory and history still dance together to tell his story and to suggest what might have been.

CHAPTER 10

BUSING IN BOSTON AND SENATOR EDWARD KENNEDY

Larry Donnelly

Introduction: some personal context

In Ireland, one does not have to search very far to find someone with strong connections to and a genuine affinity with Boston, the city I was born in and the place that will remain my favourite on the planet always. Random encounters with men and women, especially in Galway and environs, who hear my accent have unearthed unexpected commonalities and created lasting friendships. They know the pubs I drank (and still drink) in as a young man; they know every inch of the wonderful neighbourhoods that make our city great; and they still follow our incredibly successful sports teams who are simultaneously envied and despised by Americans from everywhere else. Think the Dublin footballers.

In my capacity as a law lecturer at the National University of Ireland, Galway, I have taught first cousins and close friends of people I grew up alongside in East Milton, formerly the 'most Irish' area in the United States. In my idyllic childhood in that community, located on Boston's southern fringe, a mere seven miles from the city centre, approximately half of my friends' parents were Irish emigrants, and the overwhelming majority of them were from Galway. My slightly more distant Galway ancestry never made me feel any less Irish there, especially because of the role played by my uncle, former Congressman Brian Donnelly, in securing tens of thousands of green cards for young Irish in the 1980s. What became known as the 'Donnelly Visa' is a source of tremendous pride to me and my family to this day.

In East Milton back then, a regular refrain from my generation was that our parents were almost all from one of three places: the city neighbourhoods of Dorchester and South Boston or Ireland. Very few originally came from east, central or west Milton, a town that would have been regarded – mistakenly to some extent – as a wealthy enclave favoured by Boston Brahmins, who had moved 'out the country' from the city's fashionable Beacon Hill and Back Bay sections. By way of example, Milton is the birthplace of George Herbert Walker Bush, the forty-first American president.

Why our parents left the city neighbourhoods they were so deeply rooted in and wound up in Milton (and other suburban cities and towns) is the subject of this essay. Busing and the chaos that ensued from it changed Boston forever. There were a number of protagonists in this regrettable affair, who will be discussed herein. Three who will feature prominently are W. Arthur Garrity, the federal judge responsible for busing and a long-time close associate of the Kennedy family, Senator Edward Kennedy, widely recognised as one of the finest legislators in the history of the United States Senate, and Boston School Committee chairwoman, city councillor and US representative during that time, Louise Day Hicks.

As with anyone from Boston of a certain age, and particularly those of us from politically active families, busing was a pivotal happening in my life and is something that still provokes a visceral reaction all these years later. What follows is an examination of the busing crisis and its complex dimensions, including the relationship between the Kennedy family and the Boston Irish.[1]

This is not an instance where the author of a historical essay can purport to be neutral. I simply cannot be when it comes to the merits of busing. It is too personal. I believe that busing may have been well-intentioned (although that is eminently disputable), but that it was ultimately a profound tragedy that destroyed the formative educational experiences of thousands of black and white schoolchildren and wreaked havoc on the lives of countless others. Readers, of course, are free to disagree.

Boston, September 1974

Parents of school-aged children in Boston in September 1974 were gripped by fear and desperation as to what might lie ahead. Their annual late summer routines had been rendered infinitely more complicated and fraught by a ruling from federal judge, W. Arthur Garrity, that the city's public schools were racially imbalanced. That finding was undeniably correct. But the remedy that Judge Garrity chose to desegregate the schools was more controversial. He ordered students to be bused across the city, i.e., white students from mainly white neighbourhoods would have to attend schools in predominantly black neighbourhoods and vice versa.

Put simply, many Boston public school students could no longer walk to the school they lived across the street or down the road from. Instead, they were forced to board at least one bus and embark upon a journey to a different, maybe far-flung part of the city. This was despite the fact that their parents might have attended the same school themselves and bought or rented a home so that their children could have the same educational experience they did. And these children had to get on a bus and face a far longer and more turbulent school day through absolutely no fault whatsoever of theirs or their parents.

These facts are unassailable. Yet as ever, there is more to it than that. First, who was Judge Garrity? W. Arthur Garrity was a native of Worcester, Massachusetts, a city some forty miles away from Boston, and a graduate of the College of the Holy Cross (my own alma mater) and Harvard Law School, who went on to be a dependable aide to John F. Kennedy in his 1960 presidential campaign. That valued service led to his being appointed a federal judge by President Kennedy. As J. Anthony Lukas writes in *Common Ground*, Judge Garrity was part of a cadre of second and third generation Irish Americans who had found 'homes in the suburbs', were 'making their way in law, medicine or business' and were 'too assimilated to enjoy the raucous, boozy and sometimes violent celebration (of St Patrick's Day) in South Boston'.[2]

His critics allege that it was a consequent combination of ignorance, indifference and condescension with respect to the working-class Boston Irish that animated his thought processes in devising a plan for forced busing. Indeed, the plan was implemented by the judge in 1974 and, thereafter, it impacted most heavily upon two largely Irish-American neighbourhoods: South Boston and Charlestown. The Italian-American neighbourhood of East Boston, home to Logan International Airport and connected to the rest of the city by a tunnel under Boston Harbour, was left untouched, while the picturesque streets of the Italian North End, adjacent to the city centre, received only a small influx of Asian-American students from nearby Chinatown.

It was very strongly – and convincingly – signalled to Judge Garrity and to city politicians by organised crime figures and others that the tunnel would be blown up if buses were sent through it en route to schools in East Boston. Given that the airport was located there, this would have had a crippling effect on the local economy. Moreover, the potential for a truly metropolitan solution never seems to have featured on any collective radar screen. Boston, by American standards, is a tiny city geographically. There seems to have been no good reason why surrounding, then virtually all-white, suburban communities with outstanding school systems could not have been incorporated into the plan. That they were not and that Judge Garrity resided in one of the most affluent of these towns provided plenty of fodder for city politicians who vehemently opposed busing and who appealed to the Boston families most affected by it.

These families lived in neighbourhoods like South Boston, Charlestown and Dorchester. In lots of ways, these sections of the city – I was born and baptised in Dorchester, where my father's family lived since emigrating from the west of Ireland – were defined by the core values of hard work, civic mindedness and generosity. Irishness featured prominently as well, and still does, albeit to a lesser extent, today. For many who originally hailed from there and prospered economically, the lure of the suburbs – larger homes, big back gardens, less urban noise and hustle and bustle, better schools – prevailed and they moved out. Others, however, were committed to staying. Busing changed that for a significant portion of that cohort. Once Judge Garrity decreed that their children could not as of right, attend the school nearest to where they lived, many parents who could afford to do so fled. Those who had no choice stayed and did the best they could.

Boston was rapidly diversifying in the years prior to 1974. The African American population in the city's Roxbury and Mattapan sections, as well as parts of Dorchester, expanded enormously in that time. Sadly, city politicians, especially the then elected members of the school committee, did not welcome these newcomers and instead pandered to the fears of city residents about them. One aspect of this was the deliberate neglect of schools in these areas. Typically, black boys and girls went to public schools in buildings that were crumbling and often poorly staffed. Their educational experience and attainment paled by comparison to white students in the city as a result. The school committee would not budge, even when pushed by forces in the city and well beyond its boundaries. That school committee was comprised of several politicians who played to their constituents' worst instincts. According to J. Anthony Lukas in *Common Ground*, one, Elvira 'Pixie' Palladino was heard muttering about 'jungle bunnies' after her election.[3] Another, John Kerrigan, once described a black ABC News correspondent as 'one generation away from swinging in the trees', a remark, Lukas recounts, 'he illustrated by assuming a simian crouch, carving his hands upward, and scratching his armpits'.[4]

In the end, these self-interested politicians actually betrayed the Bostonians they claimed to want to protect. For if they had not been so recalcitrant and had provided the badly needed resources to schools attended by African Americans in a city that was changing and diversifying inevitably, the lawsuit that precipitated Judge Garrity's order might never have come to fruition. Additionally, it is worth pointing out Boston's evolution as a city of ethnic neighbourhoods. The city may have been segregated racially, but it was also segregated ethnically. Dorchester, South Boston and Charlestown celebrated their Irish heritage; East Boston and the North End revelled in their Italian roots. The neighbourhoods acquired their ethnic character as immigrants settled and wanted to retain a piece of the old world in a new country. If the school committee engaged constructively in this vein, things may have played out very differently and more satisfactorily from their own vantage point. Instead, they were horribly bigoted and played lowest common denominator politics in front of a constituency that was afraid and did not know where else to turn.

There is no denying that some of the men and women who elected candidates with disturbing and hateful views shared those sentiments. Yet on the other hand, many likely saw these candidates as the only ones who would look out for them and for their interests at a time when money and power were flowing out of city neighbourhoods. A host of influential observers, locally and nationally, reached the same conclusion about these Boston residents: they were racists and deserved whatever they got. Their assessment is manifest in the media coverage throughout the busing crisis. What it overlooks, though, is that these working-class people – who had been judged so harshly by the Boston cognoscenti – only wanted the same thing that the cognoscenti had already obtained for their own children: the best education possible. When pushed, outsiders could not say that they thought it would be good for their own children to be forced to get on a bus and travel away from a school in their own locality. Anti-busing activists rallied around politicians who recognised that injustice. Some initially thought Senator Edward Kennedy, from a storied political clan with a commendable track record of fighting for the marginalised and vulnerable, would see it and help figure out a better way forward. The senator had actually indicated on more than one previous occasion that he opposed the forced busing of students to achieve school desegregation. But the anti-busers were wrong.

Senator Kennedy's intervention and the 'war zone'

The main citizens' organisation established to fight the implementation of busing in Boston was known as ROAR (Restore Our Alienated Rights). ROAR planned massive demonstrations in the city just prior to the start of the school year in 1974. The group had invited Senator Kennedy to its prior gatherings, but he had declined to turn up. On the eve of this one, however, the popular *Boston Globe* columnist Mike Barnicle wrote a piece called 'An Open Letter to Senator Kennedy.' In it, he employed these rousing and persuasive words.

> Tomorrow, they'll be marching … people who have worked hard to stay even, never mind get ahead. Many of their minds can still race back in time and history to the night that 'one of their own,' John Fitzgerald Kennedy, became the President of the United States of America. That was an earlier, easier time for them, a time when it was easy to smile and laugh. But there will be few smiles tomorrow and little laughter … Senator, you are the one man who can heal the divisions that have arisen over the issue of busing. You have the one voice that can help keep this city calm, leaving the clear ring of

justice and common sense … You could recall your memories of your brother, Bob, being driven through the streets of Gary, Indiana, with hands reaching out to touch him, hands that came out of a grey factory dusk and touched him in a night of brotherhood, hands – black and white – that were alive with hope. You could tell them, Senator, that law knows no neighbourhood, that justice is not confined to any one block, that fear must be put aside and the fact of law adhered to. And to you, Senator Kennedy, they would listen.[5]

Of the three Kennedy brothers who served in elective office, Edward (hereinafter Ted) was the least likely politician. From the beginning, his capacity was questioned and many observers did not think he had anywhere near the 'fire in the belly' for the toughest business of them all. While history ultimately proved his critics were far off the mark, in his first campaign for the United States Senate seat once held by President Kennedy, he became extremely – his foes would say pitifully – upset when his Democratic primary opponent, Massachusetts Attorney General Edward McCormack, unsurprisingly asserted that 'if your name was Edward Moore, not Edward Moore Kennedy, your candidacy would be a joke'. It was that display of emotion and a resulting sympathy from the public that political analysts attributed to Ted Kennedy's eventual victory. He was, naturally, shattered by the assassinations of his two older brothers and damaged in myriad ways by the drowning of Mary Jo Kopechne after the car he was driving, in which she was a passenger, plunged off a bridge on Chappaquiddick Island near Martha's Vineyard in 1969. As he continued to try and put that awful incident behind him, politically and otherwise, busing was a crisis that Ted Kennedy did not need.

Whether he read Mike Barnicle's column or not, he did attend the ROAR rally the following day. Almost immediately after arriving at it, Senator Kennedy had to know that he had made a huge mistake. He was jeered incessantly. 'Impeach him. Get rid of the bum.' 'You're a disgrace to the Irish!' 'Let your daughter get bused, so she can get raped.' 'Why don't you let them shoot you, like they shot your brother?' 'Kill him!' He was shouted down when he took a microphone and attempted to address the thousands gathered there. He reluctantly left the podium and, surrounded by police, strode towards the nearby federal building named after his brother.

Members of the crowd advanced towards him, throwing tomatoes, eggs and other projectiles in his direction. News bulletins uniformly announced that a Kennedy had never been greeted with such hostility on home turf.[6]

If anything, the hot-tempered backlash from the crowd revealed the distance that had grown between the Kennedy family – comprised of national political figures, the closest thing to royalty in American history – and the Boston Irish. For Ted Kennedy, busing was a civil rights issue, one on which he had to be seen as standing up for minority schoolchildren against bigotry and oppression if he were to have any chance of being elected president. That stark political reality, combined with a genuine abhorrence of racism and segregation as well as a reasonably close personal relationship with Judge Garrity, probably meant that he really had no choice but to back busing. Again politically speaking, Ted Kennedy was nonetheless mistaken to allow the perception to take root that he was an enthusiastic supporter of busing and broadly indifferent to the legitimate concerns of the Boston Irish and others about what was an inherently unsettling and disruptive situation for their children. If he had adopted a tenor more akin to 'I understand your anger, but busing is a necessary evil,' he might not have lost the backing of so many who were formerly his most ardent followers. From 1974 onwards, though, these Bostonians harboured an intense personal dislike for Ted Kennedy that bordered on the vicious. He never really faced a serious challenger (Mitt Romney came the closest in 1994, but that initially tight race turned into a 58 to 41 per cent victory for Senator Kennedy) and was repeatedly re-elected until his death in 2009, yet the sense that they had been betrayed by one of their own people, sacrificed at the altar of national political ambition, is palpable among the Boston Irish, even decades later.

Returning to 1974 and the years following, the city often did resemble a 'war zone', as one mother memorably put it in a television interview at the time in a very strong Boston accent. The 9 September surge against Senator Kennedy was only the tip of the iceberg. A quick Google search for Boston and busing will bring up grainy footage of anti-busing demonstrations with angry hordes of men and women of all ages protesting, getting into skirmishes with police in full riot gear, hurling objects at buses, law enforcement officials and black schoolchildren and yelling racial epithets laden with obscenities. When it became clear that peaceful protests would not stop the buses from dropping students at schools, some ridiculed the tactics of the mainstream anti-busing movement and agitated for violence. J. Anthony Lukas recalls one such exchange between Gloria Conway, the secretary of Massachusetts Citizens Against Forced Busing, and a Charlestown activist.

> 'What the hell have you done?' asked Tom Johnson, a burly ex-longshoreman. 'A lot of talking and marching, none of which has made a bit of difference. The time has come for some action.'

> 'What kind of action are you talking about, Mr. Johnson?' asked Gloria Conway, her voice tinged with sarcasm.

> 'I'm talking about action on the streets.'

> 'But our children are going to be on the streets,' Gloria said. 'Would you sacrifice one of our children?'

> For a moment the room was still, as all faces turned towards Tom Johnson. 'Yes,' he said, 'if necessary.'[7]

Louise Day Hicks's Anti-Busing Movement: fighting an unwinnable battle

It was sentiment like this that most worried the woman who was the *de facto* leader of the anti-busing movement, Louise Day Hicks of South Boston. The daughter of a judge, Mrs Hicks became a lawyer herself and was elected to the Boston School Committee throughout the 1960s before an unsuccessful run for mayor in 1967. She served one term in the United States House of Representatives from 1970 to 1972 and was a member of the Boston City Council for much of the 1970s. She started off as a liberal, but her popularity skyrocketed when she opted to become the face of resistance to pressure from within and without to undertake proactive measures to desegregate the school system. Her campaign slogan – 'you know where I stand' – allowed voters to read into it whatever they wished and, more often than not, what they feared. Her critics alleged it was a 'bigot's code'. Some of her rhetoric gave their interpretation credence. She repeatedly said that 'I am alarmed that I, as a woman, can no longer walk the streets in safety ... I am alarmed to see lifelong Bostonians moving out of Boston in disgust.' She also claimed that, if elected mayor, she would ensure 'the parks, streets and subways of Boston will no longer be a jungle of lawlessness' and attacked 'a justice (system) which means special privileges for the black man and the criminal'.[8] Whether she was a racist herself or an astute politician who exploited racist sentiment is a debatable question.

On the flip side, Louise Day Hicks was a proud Democrat who was highly rated by the leftist Americans for Democratic Action organisation for her stances during her single term in Congress. She had also said she did not want to be connected in any way to George Wallace, the segregationist Alabama governor who asked her to be his running mate when he sought the presidency in 1968.[9] She and her supporters were lampooned in the national media, most offensively, J. Anthony Lukas points out, in an arguably anti-Irish 1967 *Newsweek* magazine story on her quest to become mayor.

> They looked like characters out of Moon Mullins, and she was their hometown Mamie made good. Sloshing beer at the long tables in the unadorned room of the South Boston Social and Athletic Club sat a comic-strip gallery of tipplers and brawlers and their tinselled, overdressed dolls ... After Mrs. Hicks had finished off reading off her familiar recitation of civic wrongs the other night ... the men queued up to give Louise their best, unscrewing cigar butts from their chins to buss her noisily on the cheek, or pumping her arm as if it were a jack handle under a trailer truck.[10]

As a Bostonian and an Irish-American, reading these words makes my blood boil. But like any good politician, Mrs Hicks sought to use it to her benefit. In a responsive full-page newspaper advertisement, she said 'I deeply resent your insults to Boston and its residents ... I am proud of my heritage. No article of yours can lessen that pride.'[11]

So much of Mrs Hicks's political appeal flowed from her persona and her refusal to apologise for who she was. 'Boston for the Bostonians' was another of her rallying cries and it was an intentional rebuke to 'do gooders' and outsiders. While she built her political career around busing, one suspects that she knew deep down that the fight was futile and would inevitably be lost. As a lawyer and the daughter of a judge, she had a stronger understanding of the rule of law than most in the anti-busing movement. She also rejected the more violent and anarchic *modus operandi* which radicals in ROAR and the groups that splintered off the organisation favoured. She typically urged conflict avoidance and was attacked by some allies for doing so. Ultimately, as the years and buses continued to roll by, the war against busing subsided and Bostonians got on with their lives as best they could.

The damage was considerable, however. The compelling personal stories of both black and white students in Boston in the mid-1970s paint a terrible picture. Many white students, who were often encouraged to boycott school, either dropped out without obtaining a high school diploma or just about scraped by and never made it to college. Black students, far from getting the superior education busing was intended to deliver, were subjected to racist taunts on a daily basis and had to try to learn in an environment where security invariably trumped pedagogy. There was a litany of racially motivated, violent incidents. A high percentage of Bostonians who could afford to leave the city did so. The crucial middle class was diminished. I have never heard anyone argue credibly that it worked well. In fact, it is a lot easier to make the case that it was a total disaster, a failed experiment in which black and white students and their parents without economic means were unwitting pawns.

That is why I side with the anti-busing movement, notwithstanding my serious misgivings about the racism that undeniably animated elements inside it. But I think fear and desperation were the most prominent emotions felt by the majority. They were not all haters. Fear and desperation united them. They fought busing with everything they had. They fought the system and the outsiders who controlled the system. Those outsiders included Judge Garrity, the *Boston Globe* and, yes, Senator Ted Kennedy. It was a fight they could not win. Yet they still fought to the end. In their conduct of this doomed struggle, I concur with the assessment offered by the former President of the Massachusetts State Senate and of the University of Massachusetts, South Boston's William Bulger: 'They were courageous. They were steadfast. And they were right.'

Conclusion: some final thoughts nearly fifty years on

At the outset, I mentioned that busing had an impact on the trajectory of my life. That is because my family never would have left the city for the suburbs had it not been for Judge Garrity's decision. My father is a proud Bostonian and has a begrudging attitude to Milton. Tales about him and his friends being followed by the town's police after they crossed over the city line from his native Dorchester and snarls that my brother and I were 'helpless Milton kids' when we acted up were a common feature of our childhood. While we were raised only a brisk half-hour walk from his old stomping grounds, it was a world away in some respects and we will eternally wonder at how our lives would be different if we had stayed there. And there are tens of thousands just like us. A further musing, then, is what the city of Boston would be like today if all these families remained in Boston?

The city in 2020 is so radically different at every conceivable level to Boston in 1974. The city is now minority-majority and far more fully integrated. There are no politicians who remotely resemble John Kerrigan, Elvira 'Pixie' Palladino or Louise Day Hicks. The school committee is no longer an elected body. The city council has a majority of women and its president is a woman of colour. Irish surnames are not omnipresent. The mayor, Martin Walsh, whose parents are emigrants from Connemara, may look and sound just like a quintessential 'old Boston' politician, but is an unabashed liberal. The formerly working-class neighbourhoods of South Boston, Charlestown and Dorchester, where most of the dangerous clashes over busing occurred, have been gentrified to the point that they are unaffordable for all except the well to do. Income inequality, not racial strife and division, is the most vexing issue facing the city at present. Boston truly is a forward-thinking, progressive city where lots of people want to live. It has a vibrant and enviable atmosphere. But that does not mean that what was visited upon Boston and its citizens in the 1970s in the wake of forced busing should ever be forgotten. Regardless of one's perspective on the issue and the main protagonists in a tortured series of events, it was, without question, one of the saddest chapters in the otherwise storied history of a city that the eminent American jurist Oliver Wendell Holmes once famously labelled 'the hub of the universe'.

CHAPTER 11

TED KENNEDY: DISTANT PEACEMAKER

Alison Meagher

The contemporary body of literature surrounding the role of diasporas in conflict resolution generally tends to focus on diaspora communities as a 'spoiler', or obstacle to the pursuit of peace. Irish-America during the period of the Northern Ireland conflict is often pointed to as a notable case of diaspora involvement in conflict, due to the economic and ideological support for paramilitary activity that flowed across the Atlantic Ocean. However, from the late 1970s onwards, a more moderate Irish-American group began to emerge in the form of Ted Kennedy and his Democratic Party colleagues Tip O'Neill, Daniel Moynihan and Hugh Carey, who, acting in accordance with the Irish government and under the tutelage of John Hume, successfully lobbied the Carter Administration to break the United States's strict policy of non-involvement in the Northern Ireland conflict.

This essay draws upon the theoretical framework of Camilla Orjuela, that where there exists a diaspora population, in this case Irish-America, with a conflict situation going on in the native homeland, as was the case with the Northern Ireland 'Troubles', members of that diaspora have the opportunity to act as either spoilers, aka distant warriors, or, conversely, as distant peacemakers.[1] Distant warriors are those people who participate in the armed hostilities, without actually being present in the theatre of conflict – their actions could include the importation of arms and money to sustain armed conflict, or the spread of propaganda and moral support. The exile mentality of much of Irish-America, arising as it did from the upheaval and displacement that took place on a massive scale during and after the Famine, gave rise to an immense anti-British sentiment amongst the Irish diaspora. When the conflict in Northern Ireland broke out in the late 1960s, many amongst this exiled diaspora were therefore ready and willing to mobilise in distant warrior mode.

It should be emphasised that Senator Kennedy was never, ever a distant warrior. Given his own family's tragic history at the hands of gunmen, he could not possibly have been. The sole surviving son and heir to Joe Kennedy's 'Camelot' dynasty, and lone bearer of the residual burden of Irish-American interests which this brought with it, Senator Kennedy had first been drawn to the Northern Irish cause after the outbreak of the Troubles. However, his input towards finding a solution had not always been as supposedly productive or as welcome as it became in the latter half of the 1970s. Prior to his change of tack, it has been intimated that he was 'the darling of militant irredentist groups when he proposed British withdrawal in his 1971 congressional resolution and campaigned for the Fort Worth Five'.[2] By advocating such a traditionally nationalist reaction towards British policy in Ireland, and by supporting individuals accused of paramilitary activity, Kennedy embodied an outdated mode of thinking and took on the role of what C.L. Sulzberger termed 'American politicians who see this island's troubles against an outdated Abbey Theatre backdrop.'[3]

The congressional resolution alluded to above took place in 1971 when Kennedy, along with Senator Abe Ribicoff and then Congressman Hugh Carey, introduced a resolution into the Senate and House respectively, calling for, amongst other things:

- dissolution of the Parliament of Northern Ireland;
- withdrawal of all British forces from Northern Ireland; and
- convening of all interested parties for the purpose of accomplishing the reunification of Ireland.[4]

As Orjuela has noted, canvassing international support is one of the principal ways in which a diaspora can influence a homeland conflict and 'international support is crucial ... for influencing the parameters for potential peace settlements'.[5] In seeking to project his own diasporic ideal of a reunified homeland on any agreed settlement for Northern Ireland,

Kennedy displayed a lack of understanding of the complex nuances of the Northern Ireland conflict. His uncompromising stance also gave ideological succour to hardline paramilitary groups. The Senator and his colleagues here certainly did not intend to occupy the role of distant warrior, but by aligning themselves with the main proposed solution of militant republicans, it can be argued that they, by default, lent a tangible degree of moral support to this faction.

It is also highly significant that this 1971 resolution directly resulted in the House of Representatives' Sub-Committee on Europe holding hearings on Northern Ireland in early 1972. This was the first and only time such hearings would take place on Capitol Hill, and both the British and Irish governments looked upon the process with a great deal of unease and scepticism. Despite the unificationist stance of the Fianna Fáil government at the time, it did not support the position of militant nationalists in the same way that Kennedy and his colleagues did through their rhetoric, putting them out of step with the Irish government of the day. The hearings took place at a time when Anglo-Irish relations were at a particularly low ebb in the aftermath of the Bloody Sunday shootings in Derry.[6] Although no discernible repercussions flowed from the hearings, one should take into consideration Andrew Sanders's assertion that 'throughout the 1970s, as the United States struggled to adopt a policy towards the rising Northern Ireland conflict that would satisfy their close diplomatic ties with the British and Irish Republic, as well as the large and increasingly vocal Irish-American population, the persistence of the threat of congressional hearings posed problems for all three governments'.[7]

Yossi Shain contends that, 'in confronting the kin state's conflict, the diaspora attempts to promote its own view of the ethnic community's identity and interests, a view which is not always congruent with the view of the homeland authorities'.[8] Certainly, members of Dáil Éireann disparaged the outlook of Senator Ted Kennedy in the early 1970s. In a supposedly informal interview with the *Washington Post*, the then Taoiseach Jack Lynch condemned the lack of informed knowledge behind Kennedy's call for a withdrawal of British troops. Some controversy surrounds this interview and its subsequent re-hashing in the *Irish Press*, but Lynch would later go on to solidify his opinion on the Dáil record as being the following: 'in so far as Senator Kennedy advocated an immediate and total withdrawal now, that was not my opinion. I said I could understand Senator Kennedy saying such a thing because he was not as well informed of the situation as we were here.'[9]

Essentially, Kennedy was considered a thorn in the side of those who sought freedom and justice through peaceful and parliamentary means. Although he did not endorse the violence of republican paramilitaries, his public pronouncements equipped them with vital ideological succour. However, a meeting between the senator and a leading member of the Northern Irish civil rights movement was to have a profound effect on the events under consideration here. It would turn a hawk into a dove by setting in motion a process whereby Senator Kennedy would transform from a de facto 'distant warrior' into a more effective distant peaceworker.

John Hume of the SDLP understood Senator Kennedy's desire to help the Northern Nationalist cause, however misguided his attempts may have previously been. Towards the end of 1972, Hume was able to impart some advice regarding the true nature of the conflict when the two men met on the fringes of a conference in Bonn, Germany. To declare that the meeting between the pair, held at the Irish Embassy, was the catalyst for the subsequent moderation of Kennedy's views towards nationalists in the region might potentially be deemed as oversimplifying. However, Kennedy himself would later declare that 'it was really in late 1972 that John began the great education of Edward Kennedy about Northern Ireland and established the seeds that grew into a wonderful relationship'.[10]

Hume's engagement with Kennedy did not take place in isolation and, certainly at this point in the early 1970s, both the Irish and British governments recognised the value of beseeching such a high-profile figure as the senator to adopt a more constructive approach towards Northern Ireland. Alan MacLeod has elaborated on how both Lynch and British Prime Minister Ted Heath, in their respective engagements with Kennedy in early 1973, sought to moderate the senator's views. He points, in particular, to advice doled out to Kennedy by two officials at the British Embassy in Washington, Donald Cape and Pauline Neville-Jones, who suggested to the senator's aide, Carey Parker, that 'Senator Kennedy would be well advised to think twice if, on any issue he found that his position was different to that of Mr Lynch and the Irish government.'[11]

An article penned by the senator and published in *Foreign Policy* a few months later demonstrated that such interventions were beginning to have an impact on his public stance on the Northern Ireland conflict. Although still somewhat sceptical of a number of aspects of British policy measures to deal with the conflict, the ideology he articulated drew far more in line with that of Lynch's government at this point. Although re-stating his earlier comparison between the British in 'Ulster' and the United States in Vietnam, he no longer called for the immediate withdrawal of Britain from the region and contended instead that while he would advocate the reunification of Ireland, it should only come about with the consent of the majority of people in Northern Ireland. His vision for the role that America could potentially play in tempering the conflict was of an equally moderate tone. He stated that:

> We should establish a continuing public tone in the foreign policy of the Administration, a tone that reflects the legitimate concern of millions of American citizens for an end to the violence in Northern Ireland and a recognition that the minority in Ulster is entitled to participate fully in the government of their province. To this end, we should convey to Britain our concern for effective and even-handed peace-keeping arrangements and for the fair implementation of the power-sharing arrangements to be established in the legislative committees and the executive departments of government once the new Northern Ireland Assembly is elected.[12]

Essentially, at this point, Kennedy articulated a vision that was based on his fundamental concern for the case of the Catholic minority in Northern Ireland whereby the United States would aid the British government in bringing about an agreed solution amongst all parties to the Northern Ireland conflict and encouraging an end to violence. It was a vision that would be refined and ultimately come to fruition in subsequent years and decades.

Hume had effectively brought Kennedy into the fold of constitutional nationalism, represented as it was at that time by the ideals of the SDLP, as well as involving him in a strategy that was, at this point in the 1970s, being devised by civil servants at the Department of Foreign Affairs in Dublin, key amongst them Seán Donlon and Michael Lillis. As Donlon would later elaborate:

> The DFA policy had a negative side and a positive side. The negative side was stop supporting the Provisionals. The positive side was we cannot deliver a negative message unless it has a positive element and the positive element was to get the American political system interested and involved in, and not with a view to put pressure on the Brits – this is a very important distinction to make. We never ever asked American politicians to put pressure on the Brits to do X, Y and Z. Because those of us who had read history and, as it happens, quite a number of us were historians by background ... knew that by going right back to Charles Stewart Parnell, successive generations of Irish nationalist leaders had sought to put pressure on the Americans to put pressure on the Brits. We knew that it did not work. We could look back eighty or ninety years and see no results, we could not get Ireland raised at the Peace Conference after World War 1 in Paris. When NATO was being established, we could not get Ireland put on the agenda. When Ireland tried to join the UN, and eventually did join the UN, we could not get American support for anything involving Ireland. So we came up with the tactic of, 'let us get the United States interested in the problem but do not ask the USA to intervene on either one side or the other.'[13]

This moderate strategy, articulated here by Donlon, was based on the legal principle *amicus curiae*, a Latin term meaning 'friend of the court'. In legal proceedings, 'frequently, a person or group who is not a party to a lawsuit, but has a strong interest in the matter, will petition the court for permission to submit a brief in the action with the intent of influencing the court's decision'.[14] The Department's strategy envisaged a role for the United States as an honest broker in the search for a peaceful and agreed solution to the Northern Ireland conflict. Indeed, as Donlon understood the term, the United States would be 'a friend who understands the issue and who understands the nature of the conflict between the principals – in this case between London and Dublin – and have the friend sitting at the table metaphorically, as a mediator. And a mediator must understand both sides before both he or she gets involved.'[15]

In the aftermath of the election of Jimmy Carter as President in November 1976, Kennedy brought together three other high profile Irish-American politicians to form 'The Four Horsemen', namely House Speaker Tip O'Neill, fellow senator Daniel Moynihan and newly elected Governor of New York, Hugh Carey. These four Democratic politicians were brought together by a common interest in their ancestral homeland of Ireland in general, and in the Northern Ireland conflict in particular. What marked them apart from other concerned public representatives at that time was the political weight which they each respectively carried within their own parties and throughout the institutions of power in Washington and beyond, as well as the fact that they were willing to adopt a moderate stance, seeing this as a more effective way to help. Andrew J. Wilson's assertion that they were 'the most influential Irish-American Democrats' during the Carter presidency certainly rings true.[16] Ögelman et al. argue that two factors limit the ability of diaspora groups to influence policy-making in the host country. These are, firstly, 'the ... group's cohesion, based on organisational and material capabilities' and, secondly, 'the group's access to the corridors of political power'.[17] Kennedy, Moynihan, Carey and O'Neill were unified by their commitment from this point to moderate their Irish nationalist stance and to operate within the Hume/Dublin doctrine, while working towards a peaceful conclusion to the conflict in Northern Ireland.

As their efforts became more high profile, the four politicians earned themselves the nickname of 'The Four Horsemen', a moniker derived from the successful 1924 University of Notre Dame football team. They were the first four Irish-American disciples of *amicus curiae* and their first joint St Patrick's Day Statement in 1977 bore out their collectively moderate stance. They proclaimed that:

> Each of us has tried in the past to use our good offices to help see that the underlying injustices at the heart of the Northern Ireland tragedy are ended ... continued violence cannot assist the achievement of such a settlement but can only exacerbate the wounds that divide the people of Northern Ireland ... We appeal to all those organisations engaged in violence to renounce their campaign of death and destruction and return to the path of life and peace. And we appeal as well to our fellow Americans to embrace this goal of

peace and to renounce any action that promotes the current violence or provides support or encouragement for organisations involved in violence.[18]

Amidst the usual celebrations of the Irish national holiday, a celebration so very rooted in American soil since the mid-nineteenth century, the four politicians not only denounced the paramilitary groups who perpetrated violence and killing in Northern Ireland, but also the American groups who provided funding and support to further perpetuate these aims. This signalled a radical break from traditional Irish-American political oratory and was, crucially, the first public avowal of their collectively moderate stance. R.J. Briand has described the issuing of this statement as 'a watershed for constitutional nationalism', as 'Kennedy and the three other Horsemen were not just senior figures in the Democratic Party and key figures on Capitol Hill but also exerted influence at a governmental level both within and beyond the United States.'[19] It signified the official starting point of their role as distant peace workers and acted as a platform from which all further lobbying efforts and initiatives could be launched.

It was a brave stance to take – condemning the IRA did not go down well with large swathes of the Irish-American constituencies that these men represented. Two months after the St Patrick's Day Statement, a 2,500 strong crowd demonstrated outside Carey's New York office. The protest was organised by the Irish-American Committee for Human Rights in Ireland, an umbrella body for NORAID, the Ancient Order of Hibernians and the United Counties Association of New York. Those in attendance included New York City Council President, and Mayo native, Paul O'Dwyer; Congressman Mario Biaggi; Jerry O'Callaghan, a Cork-born judge of the Supreme Court of New Jersey; and Mike Flannery, a high-profile NORAID campaigner. The criticism of the Horsemen from the podium was particularly vitriolic. Insisting that the politicians had little to be proud of, the District Attorney of Nassau County, Denis Dillon, asserted that 'there's nothing in the backgrounds of [the Horsemen], in their character or their intellect or in their leadership abilities to make us think that they'll even be remembered 100 years from now'.[20] Portraying Kennedy as a spineless British lackey, motivated entirely by personal monetary gain, O'Callaghan proclaimed that

'Kennedy is tied up and makes millions on Scotch ... Years ago he was pretty good. But now I'm afraid the British way to hold him is to cut off his commissions, and he can't afford that – poor man!'[21]

Such occurrences exemplify the process described by Feargal Cochrane, whereby, 'the Irish-American consensus over the Northern Ireland conflict (and Britain's role in it) ... began to fracture after the mid-1970s'.[22] While O'Dwyer, O'Callaghan et al. embodied the faction still effectively behind militant Irish republicanism and the romantic ideals it espoused, a new group had emerged in the form of Kennedy and his fellow Horsemen. The latter clearly subscribed to the message articulated by Hume, Lillis, Donlon and the Irish government, that 'by supporting achievable reformist objectives and by helping to cut off support from Republicans in Northern Ireland, Irish-America would have a better chance of challenging British policy through their own administration'.[23] This substantiates Steven Vertovec's argument that 'we should resist assumptions that views and experiences are shared within a dispersed population despite their common identification'.[24] His consideration of the vast ideological difference between anti-Castro pre-'62 Cuban-Americans and the so-called 'Children of the Revolution' echoes the divergence between hardline distant warriors and moderate distant peaceworkers then emerging in Irish-America.

Essentially, the Horsemen instigated a process of moderating the pro-nationalist and, in many cases, pro-republican stance adopted by Irish-American politicians since the outbreak of the Troubles. The aim of this moderation was to achieve greater engagement by the United States and the United Kingdom governments regarding Northern Ireland. There was a very specific rationale behind the stance advocated by Hume and the Dublin government. They worked towards bringing the Horsemen around to this point of view with the intention of setting them apart from the pro-republican sympathisers, whose contributions the State Department could more easily reject. The actions of the Horsemen, and the way in which they generated vehement resistance amongst their own grassroots voters, made it difficult to dismiss them as simply engaging in a vote-getting exercise. They also gained the moral high ground in both condemning the IRA and pressing for an agreed accommodation in Northern Ireland – the former message made it significantly harder for US and UK officials to ignore the latter.

On 18 May 1977, the Ireland Fund held a second annual fundraising dinner dance in the Waldorf Astoria ballroom and, in the words of its co-founder Anthony O'Reilly, it constituted 'an evening in which two men recorded their awareness of the complexity of the Irish problem and of the need for peace above all else in present day Ireland'.[25] The two men to whom O'Reilly referred were Ted Kennedy and John Hume.

Unabashed by the protests just weeks before, Kennedy re-stated the essence of the St Patrick's Day statement of the Four Horsemen, specifically beseeching that 'those engaged in violence return to the path of peace'.[26] The senator sought to further underscore his moderate stance, and consequently retract his more hardline outlook of the early 1970s, by appealing directly to the Protestants of Northern Ireland. He stated that 'the overwhelming number of Irish-Americans and others in the US wish them well as they embark on the common search for peace'.[27] He also continued to act as a loyal proponent of both the Irish government and Hume's stance on republican fundraising activity, issuing the following dictum: 'Let no American have it on his conscience that his efforts or his dollars helped to make the violence worse.'[28]

Hume, the de facto leader of Northern Irish nationalism at this point, was able to augment this message in person at the fundraiser, also addressing the assembled crowd. He publicly endorsed the St Patrick's Day statement and insisted that, in propagating a moderate stance, the Four Horsemen spoke 'for the vast mass of the people of Ireland'. 'Their words were widely applauded,' he stated.[29]

The rhetoric espoused by these two politicians would soon be accompanied by diplomatic action. Mary Holland has pointed to this particular occasion as the point at which the potential concept of a Presidential statement on Northern Ireland was first discussed between Hume and Kennedy,[30] a notion corroborated by Michael Lillis.[31]

Kennedy was keen to stress to the US State Department that an initiative towards Northern Ireland conformed to President Carter's much publicised emphasis on a human rights-based approach to foreign policy. In his inauguration speech in January 1977, Carter suggested that this would be a cornerstone of his administration's foreign policy agenda 'because we are free we can never be indifferent to the fate of freedom elsewhere. Our moral sense dictates a clear-cut preference for those societies which share with us an abiding respect for individual human rights.'[32]

Carter's human rights emphasis could be exploited by Kennedy, as he implied no intent to bring about either a boundary or political change, as Irish nationalists had traditionally emphasised, and Irish-America traditionally echoed. The White House agenda of the time stressed universal rights that should apply irrespective of political jurisdiction. Framing the proposal this way allowed the Carter administration to sidestep entirely the issue of Irish nationalists seemingly seeking unification. This was a particularly shrewd line for Kennedy and the Horsemen to take in that they could deflect claims from United Kingdom officials and Ulster Unionists that Irish-America was involved in political interference. Human rights was an issue that could transcend politics and one which Carter's own rhetoric obliged him to respond to.

The abstract possibility of an encouraging speech by President Carter was subsequently given credence and eventually made a reality by a series of intricate negotiations and diplomatic manoeuvres through the summer months of 1977. During this period, the Four Horsemen acted upon the distant peaceworker rhetoric they had recently adopted by engaging constructively with the British government, the Department of State and the White House, as well as their allies in the Irish government in order to bring about a historical initiative for Northern Ireland.

On 30 August, Carter's press secretary, Jody Powell, took to the podium in the White House briefing room to issue the final draft of what became known as 'The Carter Initiative' for Northern Ireland, a statement which promised significant United States investment in the region, in the event of 'an agreed solution' to the ongoing political impasse.

To quote Feargal Cochrane, 'The Carter Statement gave Northern Ireland a diplomatic identity that belied its status as an integral part of the United Kingdom and a political presence that took it beyond a matter of purely British domestic concern.'[33] Cochrane here is stressing the way in which the Carter statement explicitly set Northern Ireland apart from any other region in the United Kingdom, areas whose affairs the United States government would never dream of involving itself in. Despite the relative blandness of the statement, it was a comment on the internal affairs of America's key ally – a wholly unprecedented move. The extremely astute tactics of all those involved on the Irish side, key amongst them Kennedy, ensured that this subtly nuanced, but deeply significant, breakthrough was achieved.

Ronan Fanning has asserted how the 'symbolism' of the statement was 'immense'. He noted the way in which 'The United States government's policy had been governed by the principle of non-intervention for over seventy years, ever since the Anglo-Irish settlements of 1920–2 had partitioned Ireland. President Carter had broken that principle beyond repair.'[34]

To celebrate the issuance of the statement, Kennedy hosted a celebration on the evening of 30 August for his fellow peacemakers in Washington. Michael Lillis recalls the feeling of jubilation he experienced, as one of just a few diplomats at the Irish Embassy in Washington who, thanks to the Irish government's political allies in Washington, had successfully out-manoeuvred the British government. The latter's mission in Washington alone at the time housed more staff than the entirety of the Irish Department of Foreign Affairs. Lillis states: 'I was a lucky kid, in the middle of this power maelstrom and we were beating the British in Washington ... you cannot imagine what it felt like!'[35]

In June 1986, immediately after the United States Senate voted sixty-five to thirty-one to approve a special aid package for Northern Ireland worth $250 million, Senator Daniel Moynihan wrote to a constituent, reflecting that

> Nearly a decade ago – on St Patrick's Day 1977 – Senator Kennedy, Speaker O'Neill, Governor Carey of New York and I asked our fellow Americans to stop contributing to the violence in Northern Ireland, and to look to peaceful means for eliminating injustice and resolving the conflict. Since that day, President Carter, President Reagan and both Houses of Congress have declared their willingness to provide tangible support to this search for peace, which took an important step forward with the signing of the Anglo-Irish Agreement last 15 November.[36]

In tracing the sanctioning of this aid package back to the first St Patrick's Day speech of the Four Horsemen, Moynihan acknowledged that this crucial breakthrough was brought about as a result of the strategy of moderation. The United States delivering an incentivised aid package for an agreed settlement (namely, the Anglo-Irish Agreement), as set out almost a decade previously in the Carter Initiative, was a triumph for the distant peaceworkers in Irish-America.

In the intervening years, Kennedy had been instrumental in swelling the ranks of the distant peacemakers on Capitol Hill. From 1978, many more Irish-American politicians began to add their names to what had become the annual St Patrick's Day statement – still condemning support for paramilitaries, but increasingly also the excesses of the British security forces, and the political inaction of the London government. Moreover, the power of this moderate movement was greatly enhanced with the launch of the Friends of Ireland on St Patrick's Day in 1981.

Throughout the turbulent years of the 1980s and early 1990s, Kennedy remained a rock for the distant peacemaker cause and an ever-steady presence during the peace process. While Bill Clinton, post-Cold War, could afford to be far bolder than either Carter or Ronald Reagan in relation to his administration's engagement with the Northern Ireland issue in the 1990s, it can be argued that he was building on a platform constructed initially by the endeavours of the Horsemen. Indeed, before arguably Clinton's most vital, and undoubtedly his most controversial, contribution to the Northern Ireland peace process – his granting of a United States visa to the Sinn Féin leader, Gerry Adams, in January 1994 – he had first sought approval from Ted Kennedy.[37] Kennedy himself had first sought the assent of Hume, and it is perhaps fitting that the two men had met and discussed the topic at the funeral of Tip O'Neill, who had passed away earlier that month.[38]

When drafting their 1986 St Patrick's Day statement, Senators Kennedy and Moynihan sought to reflect on their peacemaking work of the previous decade. Negotiating the wording of the statement, Kennedy crafted a paragraph, ultimately left out of the final draft, but entirely representative of the task the Horsemen had undertaken since 1977, recalling how they had been

> reviled, hooted, and harassed for daring to stand for peace and for love ... No matter, [we] prevailed; and peace and love will prevail if there are men and women with the courage to stand for them. We remind our fellow Americans that it takes no great courage to send others to their death. Courage is the badge of honour awarded to those who stand for life.[39]

And it was a badge of honour worn so proudly by that most courageous of politicians, and that most spirited of peacemakers, Senator Ted Kennedy.

CHAPTER 12

SHARING THE PASSION AND ACTION OF OUR TIMES

Robert Shrum

Dr Brian Murphy (BM): Given that this is the Kennedy Summer School, and you're probably one of the few people in this room who's had a conversation with John Kennedy, my first question is: could you tell us what meeting him was like?[1]

Robert Shrum (RS): It was entirely accidental. I was 16 years old, living in Los Angeles, and I volunteered at the Democratic National Convention. Campaigns then were a lot more porous in terms of security and access. I worked in the office as an intern for Pierre Salinger, who was the press secretary, and the staff decided I could write. So what I did, aside from getting coffee and collating paper, was to rewrite statements from third or fourth tier politicians. But I had one other assignment, which was to take visitors up to what was supposedly JFK's secret suite. The truth is, pretty soon, people figured out where it was. So I would escort designated visitors up and I would leave them at the door. I was taking up Averell Harriman, the former Governor of New York and Ambassador to Britain and the Soviet Union, who had been an early Kennedy supporter. He asked whether I had ever met Senator Kennedy? I said no. So we knocked on the door and JFK answered it. That would never happen today. Security is far tougher. JFK said something like: 'Who's this?' So I told him I was a volunteer for Pierre Salinger and he asked how did I get to the office each day. I explained that I took the first bus in the morning and the last bus at night.

Then we talked about where I was going to go to college. He told me that Steve Smith, his brother-in-law, had gone to Georgetown. What he did not tell me was that Steve hated Georgetown. (I loved it myself when I went there.) I can tell you that JFK's presence entirely filled the room. When you were talking to him, you were the only person there. I went back downstairs and Pierre Salinger said: 'You're supposed to take people up to see the candidate, not to talk to the candidate. What's your mother's phone number?' So I gave him our home phone number, which I still remember today. He called her and said: 'Look, is it alright if we give Bob a hotel room and a little bit of money for food so that he doesn't have to go back and forth on the bus every day?' My mother was quite surprised, but said sure.

When I went to Dunganstown yesterday, to the Kennedy family homestead, I was powerfully touched by the sense of the place that Patrick Kennedy had left behind and what that walk down to the docks must have been like. I was moved by the mementos and especially, and personally, moved when I pushed the button on the video about Ted Kennedy. So much of what was there covered things in which I was privileged to be involved. It was an unforgettable experience. I hope more Americans and tourists come here and share that experience.

BM: I know how deeply you felt about Ted Kennedy. It struck me yesterday that you also met another legendary political figure. I saw you talking to our former Taoiseach, Bertie Ahern, who said to me, 'Bob was John Bruton in 1997.' Do you want to tell people about that?

RS: When my partner Tad Devine and I became involved in Irish politics, advising Fianna Fáil, one of the common assumptions about Bertie, because he hadn't gone to university, because he wore an anorak, (which I had never heard of before by the way), was that somehow or other he wasn't up to the job of Taoiseach. But my calculation, and Tad's, was that as Bertie came from the people, this could be a huge asset, as long as voters came to the conclusion that he not only passed the threshold test for a prime minister, but, in fact, could be a very good one. The acid test would come when he debated the incumbent Taoiseach, John Bruton. I was asked to play Bruton in the debate preparation, an intense preparation of the kind you would engage in during an American presidential campaign. The legendary P.J. Mara[2] borrowed the

U2 studio in Dublin for two or three days of debate preparation. I studied Bruton and we pretty much anticipated what he would say, and hour after hour practised back and forth. Bertie did extraordinarily well in the debate. He was kind enough to say to me yesterday, 'You were a tougher John Bruton than John Bruton was.'

BM: I'm going to jump to American politics. If you could tell me about the first person you worked for professionally. He was actually a Republican, wasn't he?

RS: Yes, John Lindsay, the Mayor of New York. He was the kind of Republican who doesn't exist today. He was a civil rights pioneer. He was actually pushing President Kennedy early on to move on civil rights. Against all the odds, he was elected Mayor of a very clannish New York and he opened up agencies like the police and fire departments to minorities. He also had this habit of walking a different neighbourhood every night. He would just go almost alone, often with just one aide and a plain clothes police officer. In 1968, when Dr Martin Luther King Jr was killed – I wasn't working for Lindsay yet – most American cities burned. There were two that did not – New York was one, Indianapolis the other.

Robert Kennedy happened to be campaigning in Indianapolis, and there were about 15,000 people waiting for him in the street, most of them African American. It was the era before mobile phones. So the crowd didn't know that Dr King had been assassinated. Robert Kennedy spontaneously gave one of the greatest speeches of his life, the beginning of which is: 'I have bad news for you, for all of our fellow citizens, and people who love peace all over the world, and that is that Martin Luther King was shot and killed tonight.' You could hear the intake of breath from the audience and then the screams, but by the time RFK was finished, he had persuaded people to go home peacefully.

John Lindsay did something similar in New York. Despite the counsel of the police and some other advisers, he and his plain clothes police guard, Pat Vecchio, walked alone into Harlem, where angry people were gathering in the streets. He kept stopping and talking to them and he, too, convinced them not to turn tragedy and anger into violence. Later on, he became a Democrat and ran for president.

BM: Was that under your influence, Bob?

RS: No. In fact, I think Lindsay should have become a Democrat earlier. He should have switched during the midterm election of 1970, when Spiro Agnew and Richard Nixon were spewing vitriol at the Democrats, and there was every reason for him to move. Instead, he did it in the summer of 1971 and, shortly thereafter, he announced that he was running for the Democratic nomination for president. Frank Mankiewicz, who was George McGovern's press secretary – and ultimately, I worked for McGovern in that campaign – made the comment that it was alright to be a convert to the church, but you couldn't ask to lead the choir the next Sunday.

BM: The reason you left John Lindsay was that you wanted to campaign against Richard Nixon. First you went to work for Ed Muskie. His campaign faltered, in part, because he seemed to be more about removing Richard Nixon from office than giving reasons why Ed Muskie should be president. Are there similarities to Hillary's campaign?

RS: Yes, and I had never thought of that until you asked the question. In assessing Hillary Clinton's defeat in 2016, you can point to the probably decisive damage done by James Comey and the FBI, you can focus on Russian interference,[3] but in campaigns you have to concentrate on what you have control over, not the events you don't. Hillary Clinton became the first Democratic nominee in my lifetime who did not communicate an economic message. She did have one on her website. As President Obama's speechwriter Cody Keenan said earlier, she had 70,000 pages of material on that website. Most voters don't go there. Only 9 per cent of the Clinton advertisements were about jobs and the economy, usually in the context of renewable energy; this was hardly going to move the Obama voters in Rust Belt states who ultimately voted for Trump.

Indeed, the campaign became distracted by two developments.

One was the 'Access Hollywood' tape.[4] When that came out, it became a bright shiny object, and almost all of the Clinton advertising focused on what a bum Donald Trump was. That might not be inaccurate, but in a sense it was irrelevant to some of these Rust Belt voters. Donald Trump, and his message was effective but wrong, gave them an explanation for their economic anxiety and alienation – that immigrants and trade deals were at the root of their economic distress. And he promised to fix that and drain the swamp. Clinton had no economic message to offset Trump's that ever reached voters. What I thought Clinton would do was move on from arguing that Trump's a bum – the 'Access Hollywood' tape – to what Senator Ted Kennedy did in 1994 and then what Barack Obama did in 2012 to Mitt Romney – that he was an exploitative businessman who had callously mistreated those who worked for him. And then the last stage of the argument: in fact, Trump's not on your side; his economic programme will benefit the wealthy, not you.

The Clinton campaign never got there. All the way to the election they were running on what a despicable character Donald Trump was. A lot of voters who marked a ballot for him didn't personally approve of Trump, but thought he might do something about their economic situation. The Trump attacks, her alleged opportunism, and the faux email scandal rendered her increasingly unlikeable. Today she has an approval rating lower than Trump's.

Clinton's slogan, 'Stronger Together', was not about her. It was about Trump. Underneath its positive veneer, its message was: this guy will tear us apart and we will be weaker because we will be divided. The Clinton campaign focus-grouped dozens of different slogans. If you're doing that, you're probably searching for a reason for why you're running.

Second, the Clinton campaign bought into the theory that Barack Obama had been elected in 2008 and re-elected in 2012 because of data analytics, the capacity to micro-target and deliver very precise messages to very discrete groups. Political scientists in the United States debate whether that's worth between 1 per cent and 0 per cent of the vote, but it became the Clinton campaign's driving modality. The person who could certainly have been in charge of data analytics was elevated to campaign manager. In the last several weeks, the Clinton campaign took no conventional polls in the major swing states. I had a friend who went out to Michigan – we used to send him there every four years – and he called the Clinton headquarters and said: 'You're in trouble in Michigan.' They replied, no, no, we've run thousands of simulations through the computer and we win there in 98.8 per cent of them. And he replied, well you better start worrying about the other 1.2 per cent. Bill Clinton knew in 1992 – we knew in 2000 and 2004 – that we were likely to carry Pennsylvania, Wisconsin and Michigan, but we advertised heavily there on the economy, on issues like healthcare and drug benefits under Medicare, and we spent a lot of candidate time there. We also had strong organisations on the ground.

Hillary Clinton objects to the view that she didn't have an economic argument and has criticised Joe Biden for saying the same kind of things that I have. She has responded: well, we had Biden all over the midwest, and he talked about the economy and the middle class, but Biden wasn't the candidate. If he had been, I think Donald Trump would not have been elected president. The tragedy for Hillary Clinton, and the Democratic Party, and the country, and perhaps the world, since the President of the United States is the president of the world, although we're the only people who get to cast a vote, is that Clinton lost the unlosable election.

BM: By 1976, you were working on Jimmy Carter's campaign, writing speeches. It was pretty clear he was going to win the nomination. You then walked away from the campaign.

RS: I resigned the night he won the Pennsylvania primary, which sealed the nomination for him. Let me add, by the way, that Jimmy Carter's been a model ex-president. He reminds me of the verdict of Tacitus about a Roman emperor: 'All would have thought him fit to rule if he never had.' In 1976, I concluded Carter was not running for any great animating purpose; it was not clear what he believed in other than himself. I thought he would be unsuccessful as president.

BM: Can I read to you what you wrote? 'Your strategy is largely designed to conceal your true convictions, whatever they may be ...'

RS: I didn't give that letter to anyone in the press. I just sent it to him. I believed it. I actually went to stay with a couple of friends in Washington, one of whom later became an assistant to the president under Carter. Then I returned to Massachusetts with Doris Kearns Goodwin and Richard Goodwin.[5] The episode became public because a reporter from the *New York Times*, Homer Bigart, asked what had happened to me – where was I? And Carter denied I had ever worked for him. All the reporters had been on the plane and had seen me there. Hamilton Jordan, Carter's campaign manager, took him aside and Carter came back and said yes, Shrum had worked for me, but is no longer doing so.

It all became public. I thought that I would, perhaps, never be able to work in Democratic politics again, especially after Carter was elected. I wrote for a magazine called *New Times* and we had extraordinarily talented young writers, like Frank Rich and Janet Maslin, who went on to become singularly successful in American journalism. As Ted Kennedy prepared to run for president in 1979, Dick Goodwin said to him: 'You need to hire Bob Shrum.' Kennedy did know who I was. He had campaigned on the McGovern plane in 1972. Steve Smith, who later became a good friend of mine, was doubtful: 'I don't know; look, Shrum quit Carter and maybe he'll quit and attack us.' Ted Kennedy, I was told, replied: 'You know, I'm running against Carter, and if I have the same critique fundamentally that Bob did, what's wrong with hiring Bob?' Dick Goodwin wrote a cheque for $10,000, which he tore in half and gave to Steve, and said, if anything bad happens, you can have my half and cash the cheque. By the way, Dick did not have $10,000 in his bank account at that time.

BM: Was Ted Kennedy right to challenge a president from his own party? And was he outmanoeuvered as Carter pursued what became known as the Rose Garden strategy?[6]

RS: There were really two major reasons that he decided to run. One was Carter's resistance to a comprehensive national health reform. Carter wanted to move in incremental steps and Kennedy's belief was that after the first one or two steps, even if they succeeded, the rest might simply never get done. The other factor was that he became convinced that the Democratic Party would be decimated in 1980, which ultimately did happen – we lost twelve Senate seats, for example. A lot of his colleagues in the Senate pushed him hard to run. When he started running, and I was new to the enterprise, his support was so high that he ran a very cautious campaign. I have to observe that Ted Kennedy was the worst politician I ever met at saying nothing. If he was up there trying to say nothing – vague political BS – he didn't believe it and the audience didn't believe he believed it. That all changed after he lost the Iowa caucus, discarded the caution, and campaigned for issues that were close to his heart that differentiated him from Carter.

I think Kennedy would have prevailed anyway had it not been for the Iran hostage crisis, when American diplomats were seized in Tehran just before Kennedy announced, and then held for 444 days. The irony for Carter is that the hostages probably saved him in the primaries and doomed him against Reagan in the autumn. In the primaries, Carter refused to debate Kennedy. He didn't campaign, which was not a disadvantage for him, because when he hit the trail late in the nominating contest, he wasn't effective. Basically his campaign's message in Iowa, where Kennedy had initially led 2 to 1, but finally lost 2 to 1, was: you have to vote for Carter to send a message to the Ayatollah, to stand in solidarity with the hostages. This game went on for months and months. We had some very surprising victories nonetheless, in New York and Connecticut, for example, and Pennsylvania. Near the end, voters were no longer buying the Carter argument about the hostages and we were winning. But the one state at the end that we didn't contest in a serious way was Ohio, because our polls seemed to indicate Kennedy couldn't carry it. So we were flying back and forth from California to New Jersey with a stop in New Mexico and a stop in South Dakota. We went just once to Ohio. We should have been there constantly. On what was then Super Tuesday, the last day of the primaries, we lost Ohio by six points. Had Kennedy not only won New Jersey, not only California, not only South Dakota and New Mexico, but had won Ohio, people in the party might have said, party leaders might have said, we just can't go down the Carter road.

Carter had enough delegates to secure the nomination. So we tried to change the rule that said delegates had to vote for the person at the convention that they were for in the primary. We nicknamed it the Robot Rule. Our argument was: what if something materially changed? What if someone was found to be corrupt? What if it was unlikely they could win? We tried to free the delegates. The one absolute resolve of the Carter campaign was that they would not let Kennedy speak until after the vote on the Robot Rule. We had our delegates wearing robot buttons.

We lost that vote and Kennedy spoke the next night, in theory about platform amendments. Even then, there had been resistance to him speaking from the Carter forces. They asked for a series of concessions before Kennedy would be allowed to speak and we weren't conceding much. For example, the first gay rights plank in the history of the Democratic Party was advanced by the Kennedy campaign. The Carter people desperately wanted it out.

Kennedy wouldn't give in. The Carter campaign knew a floor fight on that would be a disaster. During the negotiations, Carl Wagner, a gifted political operative who had worked for Kennedy for several years, finally said to the Carter side: 'have you ever heard the sound of these crickets' – and we held one up – a toy you could buy that made a noise like a cricket? And Hamilton Jordan, Carter's campaign manager, said: 'what's that got to do with this?' Carl replied, 'how do you think it'll sound if there are 5,000 crickets going off on the floor of the convention?' So Kennedy was given fifteen minutes to speak. Of course, he spoke for more than forty-five.

BM: That speech has become known as one of the most famous and eloquent speeches in American history and you were the author. How do you feel about that speech?

RS: First, I should note that I always say that I worked on that speech with Senator Kennedy. It's Senator Kennedy's speech. In fact, the reason that people knew I had something to do with it is that I stayed on the platform after the speech, to help enforce a deal we had with the Carter campaign that we would take two of the three minority planks we were demanding and then let the Carter forces prevail on the third. It was clear from the voice vote that they had lost there too, but House speaker Tip O'Neill, the convention chairman, declared that they had prevailed. I was in a cab on the way back to the hotel, where, because the campaign was running out of money and it was illegal for Kennedy to spend his own, Carey Parker, his legislative assistant, and I were sharing a suite with Senator Kennedy and his wife. There was to be a party in the suite. In the cab, I heard Robert Trout, a famous television broadcaster of the 1950s and 1960s, by now consigned to radio, saying that this wonderful speech was written by Bob Shrum and Carey Parker. I thought: 'Oh my God I'm in trouble.' When I came into the suite, I asked Kennedy: 'Can I see you for a minute?' We went over to the corner, I reported what I had just heard on the radio and added that I hadn't said a word to anybody. He smiled and answered: 'Look, I told.' I said: 'What do you mean you told?' He answered: 'Well, I told because if I didn't, Schlesinger would say he wrote the speech, Sorensen would say he wrote the speech and others would say they wrote the speech; so I said you and Carey wrote the speech.'[7]

That speech was a shining moment in what had been an arduous campaign, because the country got to see Ted Kennedy as I wanted him seen, as he wanted to be seen, standing up for the things he believed in, all of which had been obscured by what was perhaps the oddest presidential nominating contest in American history.

BM: You never learned to type?

RS: I had the good fortune and the misfortune to go to a Jesuit high school, where they thought it was pedestrian to teach typing. I learned classical Greek instead. The only use it's had in my life came before Greece was in the EU. On a trip to Greece, I could decipher the road signs and say, get off here it's Corinth. I always wrote in long hand. I work on a legal pad now and a little on an iPhone and iPad if I have to. In fact, I've edited whole speeches on the pad or on the phone, because even though I tried to move beyond being a speechwriter by the mid-1980s I was always working on speeches for Ted Kennedy and for others who said: 'Can you draft or redraft this?' Yellow Pads, as Cody Keenan said, that's how Barack Obama writes.

BM: Can I ask you about Bill Clinton? Your relationship was often complex. When did you first meet him?

RS: At Georgetown, he was a freshman when I was a senior, but I was well known on campus because that year I was the top college debater in the country. My wife went to Yale with Bill and Hillary and she had this wonderful line, when she introduced a friend to Clinton, that everyone at Yale wanted to be president, but Bill Clinton was the only one building his cabinet. At which point, Robert Reich – Clinton's future labour secretary – walked up and joined the conversation.

After college, I didn't see Clinton for years. I went to Harvard Law School. He was a Rhodes scholar, and then went to Yale Law. By 1972 he was the co-campaign manager in Texas for McGovern. It was a thankless job. We made our one campaign stop in Texarkana, which is right on the border with Arkansas. I was coming down the steps of the plane and Clinton was bounding up to brief McGovern. He grabbed me in a big bear hug and said: 'Bob, how are you?' He's a preternaturally gifted politician. Because I wasn't for him initially in 1992, he was angry at me. Then, in 1994, as he was getting frustrated about the deadlock on healthcare, he enlisted me to work on a big healthcare speech and to write and produce some advertisements, but it was too late. Then a consultant named Dick Morris came in. He detested me.

So it was only after the 1996 election that I became involved with President Clinton again. The night before his second inauguration, he told me he was unhappy with the draft of his inaugural address and he wanted me to edit it with him. I said: 'Sure, we are supposed to go to this party, but I'll cancel.' He said: 'Oh, we're going to the same party. Afterwards, we'll go back to the White House.' Suddenly it was the middle of the night and I realised we weren't heading to the White House anytime soon. So the president said I'll call you at six and send a copy of the speech to the house. When he called, Marylouise,[8] who knew him so well, said: 'Oh! Hi Bill!' Not 'Hi Mr President,' just 'Hi Bill.' He never seemed to mind that from her. He said he had to go to a church service with Jessie Jackson that would only last an hour and he would call me right after. I knew Jesse and I knew the service was going to last three hours. Clinton called me about 11:00 and the inauguration was at noon. I didn't think the speech was – how shall I put it? – particularly good. There was one line that I thought had to come out. I told him that and I explained why. Then I said: 'Look, you have to go up there and give this speech with confidence. It's an excellent speech.'

Believe it or not, at that time I was a paid commentator for Fox News, the Democratic window dressing for a Republican-leaning enterprise. I was on all day, talking about the inauguration and the speech, and commentators on other channels who normally should have been very kind to Clinton, like Doris Kearns Goodwin and the historian William Leuchtenburg were decidedly downbeat. Leuchtenburg said this is the worst inaugural address in modern history. I was on the air trying to defend the speech.

When I finally got home, the phone rang and it was the President. I couldn't believe it, but he had been watching the cable channels. He thanked me and added: 'You gave me the right advice, even though it wasn't a very good speech and then you defended me.' He asked: 'Will you start working on the State of the Union message?' I worked closely with him on the 1997, 1998 and 1999 State of the Unions. I was otherwise occupied in 2000 with the Gore campaign.

The Clinton State of the Union that was pivotal came in 1998. The departments of government had been working on it for months and they generally send in all of this material that's nearly incomprehensible. As Cody Keenan was saying, it's generally the kind of stuff that if you put it out there, people's eyes would just glaze over. I was walking up the driveway of the White House after the Monica Lewinsky story had just broken and Sam Donaldson from ABC was chasing me with a microphone to get me to comment. I just kept going. We had our first meeting in the cabinet room and the President was hangdog. Afterwards – and I didn't know this was against protocol and I didn't care anyway because I didn't work on the White House Staff – I asked: 'Can I see you for a minute?' and he said: 'Sure,' and we went into the Oval Office. I said: 'Look, I don't know anything about this and what went on. But I do know this, in eight days, the country is going to decide whether you should still be the President of the United States. So as hard as it's going to be, you really have to focus on this speech.' He said: 'Thank you, we'll be back at it tomorrow.' I went downstairs. Betty Currie, the president's personal secretary, came down and said he wants to see you again. I went back upstairs. Clinton's a pretty big guy and he put his hands over my shoulder and against the wall. He said: 'Bob, I've known you so long and I want you to know, "I did not do this thing."' I was a little sceptical about that. I thought it was possible that something had happened, but was grateful that he told me that it hadn't, because if he had shared the truth, it might have cost me $500,000 to a million dollars in legal fees.

Then I volunteered a caution that I thought was important: no one around here should be emailing about this. Nobody should be trashing Monica Lewinsky to the press; what she says is actually going to matter.

Suddenly he called out for Erskine Bowles, his Chief of Staff. He said to Erskine: 'No one anywhere in the White House is to email anything about this story.' The special counsel never found a trove of emails.

The President worked very hard all through that next week on the State of the Union. The way Bill Clinton edited a speech was to stand at a teleprompter practising and rewriting it. The big debate was whether or not to talk about the Lewinsky story in the speech. I was totally opposed to that. There were people very close to him over the years who thought he had to address it. His pollster Mark Penn and I walked around the Rose Garden with him; Penn and I agreed that if you even mentioned the scandal, then that would become the whole story of the speech. Everything else would be obliterated.

This speech was a test of whether or not people still wanted Clinton to be president. The first thing he had to do was get the Democrats on their feet. So we also had an argument about whether or not Clinton should call for a minimum wage increase. I wanted him to be for it. It was key to energising Democrats. Clinton quickly settled the argument: 'Look, we have to put the minimum wage at the top of the speech,' he said. Then he had to find a patriotic ending. John Glenn, the senator from Ohio, who was also a client of mine and had been the first American to orbit the Earth, was scheduled to go back up into space on the space shuttle. The end of the speech was about him, as Clinton said to rousing applause: 'God speed, John Glenn.' I was working for someone who according to the smart money had no chance to be elected to the Senate, John Edwards in North Carolina. He was upset that I wasn't there, that I was still up in Washington at the White House. When Hillary Clinton said to me, would you travel with us to the Hill, I replied: 'I can't, I have to get the last plane to Raleigh, North Carolina or I'm probably gone from the Edwards campaign.' She said: 'I'll have a car take you to the plane, and the plane will not take off until you're on it. Will you meet us in the map room, and just talk to Bill for five or ten minutes before he gets in the limousine?' I did. He was clearly nervous, but he knew afterwards that the speech had worked and he went on to defy the attempt to remove him from office.

My next encounter with Clinton was the Gore campaign. He wanted the campaign to be all about a third Clinton term. But in the battleground states, we had a sheaf of polling data that showed that while Clinton's job approval was high, his personal approval was very low. In focus groups and polling, we tested bringing him in full scale – into Iowa for example; the idea set off a negative backlash. Iowa senator Tom Harkin, another client, called me and said: 'If you don't send Bill Clinton here tomorrow I'm going to fire you.' I don't think he meant it, but that's what he said. So I read him the data in confidence. He replied: 'Well, can you send Joe Lieberman,' who was the vice-presidential nominee.

BM: So the polling data said Bill Clinton was a liability to Al Gore?

RS: It was mixed. We had a strong economy, but Bush had a very clever campaign, where he basically didn't disagree on much that was substantive except for a promise to share the prosperity with an across the board tax cut and to conduct a humbler foreign policy with less intervention overseas. He also promised to protect the balanced budget Clinton had achieved, but, most of all, and constantly, he pledged to restore honour and dignity to the White House. What was that about? It was a brilliant code phrase for the scandals.

BM: Can I ask you, Bob, about Florida, the ballots ...[9]

RS: Don't you have a pleasanter question? I think Al Gore is the only person in living memory who was elected president and not inaugurated.

BM: You describe him as the winner who lost. Do you believe that election was stolen from him?

RS: Yes. Think about the riot in Miami Dade that successfully stopped the recount there. There were certainly some ballots found later that had never been counted. But the most fundamental problem was the Butterfly Ballot,[10] as they called it, in Palm Beach county. Pat Buchanan, whom I used to debate on television and is probably the most anti-Israel politician in America, a commentator who isn't remotely mainstream, said to me later: 'There weren't thousands of Jewish voters on the gold coast of Florida who were trying to vote for me. They were trying to vote for Gore.'[11] But the way the ballot was constructed, a voter could think you were choosing Gore and end up marking the ballot for Buchanan. If it weren't for the Butterfly Ballot, the Florida result would have been indisputably clear.

The other moment that was decisive was one Sunday morning on *Meet the Press*. Tim Russert asked Joe Lieberman about the military ballots that had been postmarked after the election. They were supposed to be postmarked by election day; 1,500 of them were postmarked in the days afterwards and many weren't being counted. Under Florida law, they weren't supposed to be, but when Lieberman was asked about it, he said they should be. Gore called me and asked if I knew, if Carter Eskew, my partner and Gore's friend as well as a trusted strategist, knew Lieberman was going to say this. I said, no I had no idea. But if those 1,500 ballots hadn't been counted, then Gore would have claimed Florida's electoral votes.

BM: Let me ask you about the Swift Boat advertisements in 2004,[12] which attacked John Kerry's service in the Vietnam war?

RS: The Bush campaign didn't broadcast the Swift Boat advertisements; an 'independent group' did. George Bush piously claimed that he had nothing to do with them, but they were funded by some of the biggest givers to his campaign. I have a number of reactions. First, the advertisement is an obscenity. When John Kerry graduated from Yale, he easily could have manoeuvered his way out of the draft. Instead, he volunteered, went to Vietnam and won the Bronze Star and the Silver Star. Second, this charge had been made in 1996 when Kerry was running for re-election to the Senate and Admiral Elmo Zumwalt, who was a war hero, a household name in America, and the former Chief of Naval Operations, came to Boston and stood on the steps of the State Capitol, and said: 'That is a lie, I have seen the records, and Kerry is a war hero.' Third, think about the one guy in the Swift Boat advertisement who says that Kerry was lying about his Purple Heart; he wasn't injured; I know because I treated him, then what in the world did he treat him for? Fourth, the impact of the advertisement was not felt on Election Day; by then, people had decided that Kerry could be Commander in Chief.

We lost a very close election. Change 60,000 votes in Ohio and Kerry would have won. He would have been the first person to beat an incumbent president in a time of war who had been re-nominated by his own party. What Swift Boats did was disrupt our campaign for two or three weeks, as an argument raged about whether to respond. Our pollster didn't want to respond; Kerry did. Then the polls showed it was having an impact. We fell behind. The first debate, which was on national security and foreign policy, turned things around. President Bush often justified the Iraq war by pointing to 9/11. We were almost certain he would do it in the debate and, about two thirds of the way through, he did. From the debate preparation, Kerry had a mantra in his head: 'He says Saddam, you say Osama.' And when Bush did exactly what was predicted, Kerry looked at him and said: 'The President just said something extraordinarily revealing and, frankly, very important in this debate. In answer to your question about Iraq and sending people into Iraq, he just said the enemy attacked us. Saddam Hussein didn't attack us. Osama bin Laden attacked us. Al Qaeda attacked us.' And Bush, violating the rule that when you're in the ditch, don't dig deeper, snapped: 'Of course I know Osama bin Laden attacked us – I know that.' The polls showed Kerry winning that debate, and the other two – and then he narrowly lost the election.

One last thing, you don't go into politics as I did without learning that every two or four years, events can break your heart. But I wouldn't have chosen any other path. As Oliver Wendell Holmes Jr[13] once said: 'It is required of a man that he should share the passion and action of his time at peril of being judged not to have lived.'

CHAPTER 13

THE DOWNLOAD: WRITING SPEECHES WITH BARACK OBAMA

Cody Keenan

My family left Ireland for America seven generations ago.[1] To the best of our knowledge, Patrick Keenan left Cork sometime in the 1770s. He was counted in the first American census. His son, Peter Keenan, was born in America. On my mother's side, John McThomas left Dublin around the same time, fought for America in the Revolution, and was buried in a national cemetery in Ohio.

As far as I know, I was the first in my family, on either side, to return. My first visit was with my best friend back in 2005. We were broke, relied on the kindness of strangers and camped wherever we could – a town park in Kinsale, a beach outside Galway, a farm in Dingle whose owner was kind enough to tap our tent with his walking stick in the morning to warn us that he was about to bring down his cows.

My second visit, in May 2011, was a bit different. Surely, it was something my ancestors could not imagine. I flew over in a highly modified 747, crossing the sea they had sailed, with the first black president of a country they helped settle, visiting a town where it was discovered he had an ancestor, and teaching him how to pronounce words in the Irish language, even though I have no idea how to pronounce Irish.

What a day that was. Certainly, it was one of the greatest days I had in the White House. And by 'day', I mean day. An erupting volcano in Iceland meant we could not even spend the night. It was heartbreaking. But we made the most of those ten hours, and the President and I both have very fond memories of that visit. Hundreds of people were lined up along Moneygall village's main street, waving Irish and American flags. While the President shook hands and visited Ollie Hayes's pub, the rest of us darted out back to down some pints. I asked Ollie for help with Irish pronunciation, because I was about to force President Obama to step in front of 25,000 people in Dublin, after a pint of Guinness, and say 'Tá áthas orm bheith in Éirinn.'[2]

Oddly enough, Barack Obama is two generations closer to Ireland than I am. And I know people have a laugh at how Moneygall has made the most of that relationship. But it is not a relationship that should be discounted. I remember President Obama visiting the home where his great-great-great-grandfather lived, walking the same floorboards, marvelling that his ancestor, a young shoemaker, trod the same auld wood.

Much has been made of his Kenyan ancestry. But remember, he only met his father twice. He was raised by his white mother and white grandparents. That side of his family is one he holds just as dear. Moneygall's favourite great-great-great grandson really does have a soft spot for Ireland and its people. He revealed as much in his address to the people of Ireland that day, delivered to a throng that had gathered along Dublin's College Green:

> It was remarkable to see the small town where a young shoemaker named Falmouth Kearney, my great-great-great grandfather, lived his early life. He left during the Great Hunger, as so many Irish did, to seek a new life in the New World. He travelled by ship to New York, where he entered himself into the records as a 'labourer.' He married an American girl from Ohio. They settled in the Midwest. They started a family.
>
> It's a familiar story, one lived and cherished by Americans of all backgrounds. It's integral to our national identity. It's who we are – a nation of immigrants from all over the world.
>
> But standing there, in Moneygall, I could not help but think how heartbreaking it must have been for Falmouth Kearney and so many others to part; to watch Donegal coasts and Dingle cliffs recede; to

leave behind all they knew in hopes that something better lay over the horizon.

When people like Falmouth boarded those ships, they often did so with no family, no friends, no money – nothing to sustain their journey but faith. Faith in the Almighty. Faith in America. Faith that it was a place where you could be prosperous, you could be free, you could think and talk and worship as you please – a place where you can make it if you try.

And as they worked, and struggled, and sacrificed to build that better life for the next generation, they passed down that faith, too – to their children, and their children's children, an inheritance that their great-great-great grandchildren like me carry still.

We call it the American Dream. It is the dream that drew Falmouth Kearney to America from a small village in Ireland. It is the dream that drew my own father to America from a small village in Africa. It is a dream that we have carried forward, sometimes through stormy waters, sometimes at great cost, for more than two centuries.[3]

What a day that was. I still have the front page of the next day's *Irish Times* framed in my office in Washington, with the headline 'OBAMA IN IRELAND: A Message of Friendship and Hope,' a full-page photo of sun-dappled masses stretching down Dame Street and out of sight.[4]

It's not something he would have imagined when he was a young Chicago politician, bringing up the rear of the St Patrick's Day parade, followed only by the sanitation workers picking up the pieces. It is not something that, for my first twenty-six years or so, I could have imagined, either.

Growing up, I had always taken a keen interest in politics, because my parents argued about it on a regular basis – but I began university with plans of becoming a surgeon. Chemistry class altered those plans pretty quickly. I dedicated myself instead to political science, and after graduation, I moved to Washington D.C. I had no pull, no connections, just a friend – a school teacher – who let me crash with him until I was up and running. And that took a while. I had nobody to show me the ropes. But I was a cocky kid from a good university who had seen every episode of *The West Wing*. I figured, how hard could it be?

Well, after a dozen failed interviews, I finally became one of 100 interns under someone for whom I will always be grateful: John F. Kennedy's kid brother, Ted.

It remains my best political learning experience. Not only because Teddy Kennedy was one of the best legislators who ever lived, but because there, relegated to his windowless mailroom, I learned that politics is not like *The West Wing* at all. It is not about sexy walk-and-talks, power lunches, or using witty banter to win people over and solve the world's problems in an hour.

No, with each envelope I opened; with each of the hundreds of letters and phone calls a day from people asking a senator for help; with each perfect stranger's private hopes and pains laid bare across the page – I learned how important politics and public service really are. It was equal parts sobering and inspiring. You can't help but learn how much this stuff matters. I threw myself into it. Worked hard, paid attention, and learned. After a few months, I was hired to answer phones for the princely sum of $18,000 a year. Over a few years, I slowly climbed the ranks.

I even went to the Democratic Convention in 2004 when a young state senator from Illinois introduced himself to the country. Here was somebody who saw politics the way I wanted to – as an imperfect but noble endeavour where, together, we can do great things that we cannot do alone. As a way to collectively move the ball forward and change people's lives for the better.

I must have talked about that speech a lot, because that is when I got my shot. One day, my overworked boss poked his head around the corner and asked, 'hey, can you write a speech?'

I had never considered speechwriting. But I lied and said yes. I stayed up all night panicking my way through it. That one led to a few more. And eventually, a colleague connected me with Senator Obama's chief speechwriter Jon Favreau. We hit it off, and I became an intern all over again, this time in Chicago, on an upstart presidential campaign; this time the only intern. And as our poll numbers rose, and our crowds grew, so did my opportunities to write. We won and went to the White House. I moved into a West Wing office with Jon. And I never stopped working my tail off so that when he left, and Obama had to choose a new chief speechwriter, I was the only choice to take his place.

In less than ten years, I went from mailroom intern in Congress to chief speechwriter in the White House. It was a wild ride, even if I am making it sound a lot easier than it actually was. Those two terms were filled with hardship and friendship, crushing stress and soaring achievement. I met world leaders and I met my wife. One of her many duties was to fact-check my speeches. So she lived a spouse's dream: she literally got paid to tell me I was wrong. Today, she still does that for free!

What goes into a good speech? Well, the first thing I can tell you is that there's no alchemy to it; no magic formula. It's more art than science, and after 3,577 speeches in the White House, I admit a lot of it is not art, either.

I have been fortunate, though, to work for someone who views it as a craft; as a way to organise his thoughts into a coherent argument and present them to the world. He takes it seriously. He was anonymous when he walked into that Boston hall in 2004, and a political rock star when he walked out. That is what a speech can do.

To this day, by the way, he reminds me that he wrote that one by himself. All the time.

He's a frighteningly good writer, which makes my job both harder and easier. Harder because I will stay up all night to get him a draft he will be happy with. Easier because if I do not hit the mark, he is there to back me up. And when it came to any speech of consequence, President Obama was actively involved in the product. We would often begin the process for big speeches by sitting down with him in the Oval Office. We called it 'The Download.' He would walk us through what was on his mind, what he wanted to say, and we would type as fast as possible.

He would always begin with the question, 'what story are we trying to tell?' That is what we have always tried to do with our speeches. Paint a picture of how we got to this moment. Present a set of choices about where we can go from here. Try to point people in a certain direction by tapping into shared values and ideals; hopes and fears; passions and contradictions. Tell a story about who we are, and who we can be.

Once we got his download, we would get to work, and get him a draft. He would often work on it himself until well past midnight. And this may sound counter-intuitive, but it was always a good thing to hear that he had a lot of edits. It did not mean he disliked what we put down. It meant we gave him what he needed to do the job.

When I was drafting the Charleston eulogy, for example – the speech in which he sang *Amazing Grace* – I stayed up for three days straight trying to make it perfect. I handed the draft to him the afternoon before the speech and went home to sleep. Right before I turned in, I got an email from him asking me to come back and meet him at 11 o'clock that night.

He told me he liked the first two pages. But he had rewritten the next two pages in just a few hours. It was annoying. Still, I apologised for what I saw as letting him down. But he stopped me and said, 'Brother, we are collaborators. You gave me what I needed. The muse hit. And when you have been thinking about this stuff for forty years, you will know what you want to say, too.'

I think all that was true, but it was also a nice way of saying 'don't worry about it'.

Most of the speeches we wrote at the White House did not require that level of grind. But when they did, I really worked at it. It turned out we had a mailroom at the White House, too. I read a lot of letters to the President for inspiration, and I tried to channel people's stories and anxieties and aspirations into our speeches. Jon was good at building the big case and laying out the big argument. That was not my strength. I went for people's guts. I wanted to build moral and emotional cases. I wanted to make people feel something. A sense of connection. A sense of belonging. A sense of being heard. That's a pretty important part of storytelling.

And I think the best story we ever told came in a 2015 speech in Selma, Alabama.

In 1965, a group of mostly black Americans set out to march from Selma to the state capitol in Montgomery to demand their right to vote. They barely made it across the town bridge before their non-violent protest was met with violent resistance. The images shocked the conscience of the country and pushed President Johnson to call for a Voting Rights Act.

The idea that just fifty years later, a black president would return to commemorate what they did was extraordinary enough. We could have gone with a safe, simple speech commemorating the anniversary. People would have understood the symbolism. It would have been enough.

But the week before, a Republican politician went on television and said this: 'I know this is a terrible thing to say ...' By the way, if you begin a thought that way, you don't *have* to finish it. Free advice. But he continued,

'I do not believe that the President loves America … He wasn't brought up the way you were brought up and I was brought up, through love of this country.'

I was pissed about it. It was more dog whistle nonsense designed to delegitimise the first African American president – and, I might add, the first president to win more than 51 per cent of the vote twice since Dwight Eisenhower almost sixty years earlier.

'No Drama Obama,' true to form, was not ruffled. He thought it was a comment that merited no response. He did, however, think it was an idea worth taking on. Who gets to decide what it means to love America? Who gets to decide who belongs and who does not? Who gets to decide what patriotism is all about? And we came up with the thesis of that speech:

> What could be more American than what happened in this place? What could more profoundly vindicate the idea of America than plain and humble people, the unsung, the downtrodden, the dreamers not of high station, not born to wealth or privilege, not of one religious tradition but many, coming together to shape their country's course?
>
> What greater expression of faith in the American experiment than this, what greater form of patriotism is there than the belief that America is not yet finished, that we are strong enough to be self-critical, that each successive generation can look upon our imperfections and decide that it is in our power to remake this nation to more closely align with our highest ideals?[5]

The rest of that half hour made up my favourite speech. It was our purest collaboration. At one point, I made a joke that our story is too often told, in political speeches at least, as if the Founding Fathers set everything up, some Irish and Italians came over, we beat the Nazis, and here we are. But there is more to our story than that. This felt more complete, more honest.

He said well, let's include some characters from our story. 'Go come up with some America.'

I grabbed my speechwriters, and we came up with: 'Lewis and Clark and Sacajawea, pioneers who braved the unfamiliar, followed by a stampede of farmers and miners, and entrepreneurs and hucksters. Sojourner Truth and

Fannie Lou Hamer, and Susan B. Anthony, women who could do as much as any man and then some.'[6]

We made it a big open casting call:

> Immigrants and Holocaust survivors, Soviet defectors, the Lost Boys of Sudan. Slaves and ranch hands and cowboys and labourers and organisers.
>
> The GIs who liberated a continent and the Tuskeegee Airmen, and Navajo code-talkers, and the Japanese Americans who fought for this country even as their own liberty had been denied.
>
> The firefighters who rushed into those buildings on 9/11. The volunteers who signed up to fight in Afghanistan and Iraq. The gay Americans whose blood ran in the streets of San Francisco and New York, just as blood ran down that bridge.
>
> The inventors of gospel and jazz and blues, bluegrass and country, and hip-hop and rock and roll, all our very own sound with all the sweet sorrow and reckless joy of freedom.
>
> That's what America is. Not stock photos or airbrushed history, or feeble attempts to define some of us as more American than others. We respect the past, but we don't pine for the past. We don't fear the future; we grab for it. America is not some fragile thing. We are large, in the words of Whitman, containing multitudes.[7]

Lately, as you may have noticed, in America, we are still engaged in this struggle, a struggle to define the very essence of who we are – whether we are a static country, wracked by fear and blame and a nationalist longing for some simpler past; or whether we are a country that is diverse and dynamic; that views constant change as the hallmark that sets us apart.

It is a struggle that is playing out in our larger political debates even today. Who belongs? Who gets a say? It is what informs the MeToo movement, and the Black Lives Matter movement, and the immigrants' rights movement. It underpins policy debates, and efforts to constrain or expand voting rights.

And the feeling of all those struggles swirling together inspired me to add a riff I had been playing with for some time:

Selma shows us that America is not the project of any one person. Because the single-most powerful word in our democracy is the word 'We.' 'We The People.' 'We Shall Overcome.' 'Yes We Can.' That word is owned by no one. It belongs to everyone. Oh, what a glorious task we are given, to continually try to improve this great nation of ours.[8]

If there is one Obama speech I could make people watch, that is it. It was the best, most joyous distillation of the way he sees what this country is and can be. It was the idea that through the hard work of self-government, generations of Americans, often young Americans, often without power or title, often at great risk to themselves, have looked upon our flaws and worked to widen the circle of our founding ideals until they include everybody, and not just some.

That is how I see politics. This collective endeavour; the balance between the realism to see the world as it is, and the idealism to fight for the world as it should be anyway.

Yes, politics is messy, and complicated, and often disappointing. Trust me on this. I have raised a glass on the Truman Balcony when we won health insurance for millions of Americans. And I have cried in the Rose Garden with parents whose kids were murdered in their classroom, only to see a minority in Congress shoot down background checks. But we went into it with a boss who told us our efforts would never be perfect, that all we could do was our best – to take up the work of others before us, advance it as far as we could for as many people as we could, and hand it off to a new generation.

It was the exhausting, fulfilling work of those 2,922 days in the White House that gave my career meaning. Overall, it vindicated the belief I had so many years earlier in what politics could be. And you are not always going to win. Sometimes, that boulder you have been pushing uphill slips, and you have got to take a breath, go back down, and get it.

But when I feel the tugging temptation of cynicism, I reach for my proof point that this whole messy endeavour of democracy can work: the ten most hopeful days I ever saw in politics.

They began in the darkest way imaginable – a mass shooting in the basement of a Charleston church. A black church.[9] It threatened to reopen the kinds of wounds and spark the kinds of recrimination we saw more recently in Charlottesville.[10] But it did not unfold that way. The families of the victims forgave their killer in court. Then, there was a public recognition of the pain that the Confederate flag stirs in so many citizens, and actual introspection and self-examination that we too rarely see in public life, to the point where that flag finally came down from the South Carolina state capitol.

At the same time, it was a week when the Supreme Court could rule on any case, at any time, with no heads up. So while we worked on the President's eulogy for Charleston, we were busy drafting several other statements in case he had to speak quickly.

Thursday morning, boom: Obamacare was upheld as Constitutional for the second time. Obama spoke. Friday morning, boom: marriage equality becomes a reality in America. Obama spoke. An hour later, we boarded Marine One to fly to Air Force One, which would ferry us to Charleston. I was still working in his changes to the eulogy for that afternoon. He had added the lyrics to *Amazing Grace* overnight. And just before he stepped off the helicopter, he turned and said, 'you know, if it feels right, I might sing it'. Exhausted, I simply said 'okay'. And that night, we returned to a White House that was no longer white – but bathed in the colours of the rainbow.

We wrote ten speeches in those ten days – plus a few that never had to see the light of day.

They were ten days in America that I think about all the time. Four of our original sins seemed to be coming due at once – racism, violence, bigotry, inequality – and payment could have torn at the fabric of America at any moment. But it did not. It really felt like we were breaking free of our past into something new. And I believe that the right leadership, indeed the right words and actions – even if they were not all his; especially if they were not all his – made a difference.

That was only a few years ago, if you can believe it. It felt like decades' worth of change in one week. But here is the thing: none of that happened because of one week, or one presidency, or even one generation. It happened because people chose to be decent, and big-hearted, and empathetic. It happened because people chose, over years, to protect not only their own rights, but the rights of others; to care not only about their own children, but about each other's. It happened because countless Americans, more often than not young Americans, demanded something more from their country, and pushed relentlessly to change hearts and minds and laws until that arc of history bent.

Those ten days were on my mind as I added these words to President Obama's Farewell Address:

> Ultimately, that's what our democracy demands. It needs you. Not just when there's an election, not just when your own narrow interest is at stake, but over the full span of a lifetime. If you're tired of arguing with strangers on the internet, try to talk with one in real life. If something needs fixing, lace up your shoes and do some organising. If you're disappointed by your elected officials, grab a clipboard, get some signatures, and run for office yourself. Show up. Dive in. Persevere. Sometimes you'll win. Sometimes you'll lose. Presuming a reservoir of goodness in others can be a risk, and there will be times when the process disappoints you. But for those of us fortunate enough to have been a part of this work, to see it up close, let me tell you, it can energise and inspire. And more often than not, your faith in America – and in Americans – will be confirmed.[11]

I still believe that. Because while the levers of power may have changed, America is still big, generous and optimistic. Americans are still hopeful, compassionate, brave and forward-looking. I believe the future is still on our side. As long as there are people who, despite lack of power or wealth or title, still choose to push for progress, no matter how long it takes. As long as there are people who, despite all of our imperfections, decide to press forward, with determination and honest effort, believing that our efforts matter; that there must be an upward trajectory to the human story.

It's as the man said that day on College Green in Dublin: '... If anyone ever says otherwise – that our problems are too big, our challenges are too great, we can't do something and shouldn't try – think about all we have done together. Remember that whatever hardships the winter may bring, springtime is always just around the corner. And respond with a proud creed: *is féidir linn*. Yes We Can.'[12]

CHAPTER 14

THE BERNIE SANDERS CAMPAIGN STORY

Tad Devine

Introduction

In September 2016, my wife Ellen and I travelled to New Ross in County Wexford, Ireland. I had been invited to speak about Bernie Sanders's campaign for President earlier that year.[1] It was our second trip to the Kennedy Summer School – having been there in the autumn of 2012, to discuss the United States presidential election between Barack Obama and Mitt Romney. When I began my remarks in 2012 at St Michael's Theatre, I told everyone that they could do something in Ireland that we could not do in the United States – bet on the outcome of an election. So, I advised the audience to go to the local Paddy Power and put down some money on Barack Obama because I believed he was going to win in November. My talk that day was about why I believed Obama would prevail.

Fast forward four years – and I found myself on the same stage with some of the same people who had been in the audience in 2012. When I started my talk in 2016, I began by referencing my remarks the last time I was there, when I predicted that Obama would be re-elected. But four years later I did not have the same level of confidence that Hillary Clinton would win against Donald Trump.

You could almost feel a collective gasp from the audience, and my wife said that the woman sitting next to her was shaken by my conclusion that it would be difficult for Hillary to win in November.

The source for my pessimism about Secretary Clinton's chances to succeed in the general election were grounded in what I had witnessed on the campaign trail with Bernie Sanders in 2016. What I saw as we travelled across America was an electorate demanding change.[2] And I knew it would be difficult, if not impossible, for Hillary Clinton to be the candidate of change that year. That intense desire for change fuelled Bernie Sanders's run for the Democratic nomination, and my talk in 2016 at the Kennedy Summer School focused on the media and strategy that aided Bernie's campaign. I wanted to try to answer the question everyone was asking: how could Bernie Sanders come from so far behind to achieve a virtual tie in Iowa,[3] a historic victory in New Hampshire,[4] and a surprising challenge to Hillary Clinton, the seemingly uncontested front runner for the nomination?[5] The focus of my talk was on the areas of the campaign where I worked most – the strategy, media and message – as well as the pivotal events and decisions that shaped the outcome.

The speech

First, to understand the Bernie Sanders campaign it is critical to look at what we called, 'The Speech'.[6] Unlike most campaigns that I have been involved in around the world, Bernie's agenda and message were not developed in the usual way – through extensive research – but instead by Bernie delivering 'The Speech' on the road for about a year before he announced his candidacy. 'The Speech' consisted of a longer than usual stump speech – sometimes lasting more than an hour – where he articulated his broad vision for the problems of America's economy and a prescription for the nation's future.

I tell my students at New York University that 'every winning campaign is about the future'.[7] That belief may be the single most important lesson I have learned in working on campaigns for almost forty years. And it is one of the reasons that, when I developed the slogan for Bernie's campaign, it was focused on the future – *A Future To Believe In*.[8]

Announcement

When Bernie Sanders announced for president in front of the United States Capitol[9] his candidacy was seen as a long shot. He was treated as a fringe candidate with little chance of victory.[10] In part, that was because Bernie did not fit the traditional mould of presidential candidates. His at times dishevelled look and his open embrace of Democratic Socialism were seen by most hardened observers in the press and elsewhere as disqualifying. But Bernie's campaign possessed one component that every winning campaign must have – a powerful message that resonated with voters.

Bernie's announcement was unorthodox to say the least. Having promised he would make a decision on running by the end of April, he arrived on the last day of that month in an area in front of the United States Capitol known as 'the swamp', announced he was running for president, said a few things about his campaign, and then promptly left, saying he had to get back to work in the Senate.

The public polling at that time showed Bernie Sanders had little chance of success.[11] The website *Real Clear Politics* publishes an aggregate of polls both nationally and in some of the early primary states. If you look at the average on 30 April 2015, you will see that in the national polling Hillary Clinton led Bernie Sanders by sixty-two points.[12] In Iowa, Hillary's lead at the end of April was fifty-four points. And even in New Hampshire, a neighbour to Bernie's home state of Vermont, Clinton led by forty points.[13] In addition to her enormous advantage in polling, Hillary Clinton and her husband, former President Bill Clinton, had spent decades establishing a powerful fundraising and political network across America, and she raised almost $50 million dollars by the end of the first fundraising report in June. On the day he announced, Bernie's campaign consisted of little more than a single sheet of paper – his Declaration of Candidacy with The Federal Elections Commission.[14]

Campaign launch

After talking to press contacts and watching the coverage of the 'long shot' candidate that permeated the news, I realised that we had about a month to show the political world and early state voters that this was a serious campaign. So, we decided to plan a formal campaign launch at the end of May.

On the morning of 26 May 2015, I directed a film shoot at Bernie's home in Burlington, Vermont. I interviewed him while he was sitting on a deck in the back garden. Later that day we held a campaign announcement event on the Burlington waterfront. Five thousand people showed up and Bernie delivered 'The Speech' in a formal setting as a presidential candidate for the first time.[15] Combining the morning shoot with footage of the event and film from a trip the next day to New Hampshire, I produced a five-minute video which provided the first formal introduction of Bernie Sanders to Democratic primary voters. The video called *Progress*[16] won all three awards in the political advertising business,[17] generated millions of views online, and provided a vehicle for us to combine the long format speech full of issues with biographical details so that we could begin to introduce Bernie to the American people.

The cornerstones of that introduction were not only Bernie's unique personal narrative, but also his powerful explanation of what was happening to so many people in America who felt they were being left behind by an economic system which generated enormous wealth for those at the top but left so many more struggling to get ahead. That message proved to be a simple but powerful touchstone for the Sanders campaign – that America had 'a rigged economy held in place by a corrupt system of campaign finance'.

The *Progress* video began with a scene from our large crowd event that day, as Bernie said: 'This campaign is going to send a message to the billionaire class – you can't have it all.' It then cut to the back deck interview where he said: 'I'm running for President of the United States because we have four beautiful kids and seven incredible grandchildren, and I want to make sure that the country we leave them is a nation that we are proud of.'

Paid media campaign

The television advertising in Iowa and New Hampshire started in early August, when Hillary Clinton's campaign began running advertisements.[18] I met with Bernie and his campaign manager Jeff Weaver that day at our campaign's small townhouse headquarters on Capitol Hill in Washington, DC. I showed Bernie and Jeff the two introductory Hillary advertisements – both sixty-second television spots that set out her story in both personal and professional terms.[19] He asked me what I thought and I said they were excellent, but that there was no way we could join the paid media campaign now. Clinton's campaign had raised tens of millions of dollars by that point[20] and we were just beginning our fundraising efforts and were not yet confident that we could sustain them over the long haul. I also felt very strongly that we needed to conduct survey research before we began the advertisement-making process, and while Bernie disagreed and felt we could make advertising without doing polling, (he told me, 'Tad, go with your gut, that's what I do,') I told him that I needed polling to do my job – to target the media buys to persuadable voters in order to deliver maximum impact and to best utilise the resources that so many people had contributed in small dollar amounts to his campaign.

The Sanders television-paid media campaign did not begin until November. We created a series of advertisements that told Bernie's story, seized the issue terrain of the election, offered reassurance about his capacity to be president, presented a contrast, and concluded with an affirmative vision for an America that could together create: *A Future To Believe In.*

The paid media campaign was essential to establishing Bernie Sanders as a credible, serious candidate for president against a well-liked and well-known front runner.

Our television advertising campaign consisted of five generations of advertising. In each one of these generations we accomplished a specific goal. Sometimes the generations had one advertisement, but most had multiple advertisements along the same storyline.

The first generation consisted of a classic sixty-second biographical presentation.[21] This introductory slot began visually at the Statue of Liberty. I was constantly looking for iconic symbols of America to present in the advertising, in part because I was concerned about the potential attacks against Bernie's identification as a Democratic Socialist. The advertisement moved through images of Bernie as a young boy growing up in Brooklyn, as a high school runner, as a college student leading protests at the University of Chicago[22] and attending Martin Luther King's *I Have a Dream* speech in Washington, as a mayor who after a surprise election victory walked picket lines with people[23] and was recognised by *US World and News* as 'one of America's best mayors'.[24] The narrator began by saying: 'The son of a Polish immigrant who grew up in a Brooklyn tenement, he went to public schools, then college, where the work of his life began – fighting injustice and inequality, speaking truth to power.'

That introduction to Bernie Sanders in the first twelve seconds of his biographic advertisement laid out his story. His own biography and the work of his life merged as proof points that he would fight for the people, not the powerful.

The advertisement then moved to an element of reassurance – that Bernie was effective. Our research showed that his selection as one of the most effective mayors in America was an important proof point of his capacity to govern as president.

The advertisement then turned to the issue terrain of our choosing. We talked about his work in Congress and how he effectively stood up for working families there. We then moved to one of the key contrasts with Hillary Clinton (without ever mentioning her) – the fact that Bernie Sanders, while in Congress, voted against the war in Iraq.[25] We also pointed to his support of veterans and one of his major accomplishments as the Chairman of the Veterans' Affairs Committee in the Senate, where he negotiated a deal with Senator John McCain in the midst of a crisis at the Veterans' Administration.[26]

We then introduced the central positioning in the race – the fact that Bernie was taking on Wall Street which had rigged the economy against ordinary people through its exploitation of a corrupt system of campaign finance. We depicted this by showing the towers of New York and the faces of hundreds of our campaign contributors who sent us their selfies to represent the army of people who were financing our campaign.

Next, we moved to the issues that would animate the primary election: tackling climate change to create clean energy jobs, fighting for living wages, equal pay for women workers and universal, tuition-free college education. We showed Bernie Sanders speaking to a huge crowd in Seattle, Washington, where he laid out the frame of the message: 'People are sick and tired of establishment politics, and they want real change.' The narrator then returned and said: 'Bernie Sanders, husband, father, grandfather. An honest leader, building a movement with you, to give us a future to believe in.'

After a full flight of advertising on his biography, we then moved to the second generation of advertising. The focus of this was the central message of the campaign: America had a rigged economy held in place by a corrupt system of campaign finance.

In the first advertisement of the second generation – *Rigged Economy*[27] Bernie said directly to camera: 'It's called a rigged economy, and this is how it works.' He explained, succinctly and powerfully, how the rigged economy was sending almost all new wealth to the top 1 per cent, in a system that was held in place by corrupt campaign finance that let billionaires buy elections. He then pointed to the millions of small dollar contributions that were funding his campaign and said to camera: 'The truth is you can't change a corrupt system by taking its money.' He concluded by asking people to 'Join us for real change.' Several other advertisements along the same storyline appeared in this second generation, as we sought to establish what we believed was the most powerful message in the election.

In the third generation of advertising, we moved to a series of testimonial advertisements that attempted to make connections with voters, based on issues and shared values. The testimonials were from people who knew Bernie and his work, like a farmer[28] and a nurse[29] from Vermont, and on issues like Social Security[30] and college education,[31] as well as local issues like the Bakken pipeline[32] – a shale oil pipeline that traversed Iowa – which Bernie opposed. Beginning in Iowa, we also heavily rotated in an advertisement about Bernie's effectiveness, an issue that was a challenge with many voters. We needed to provide significant reassurance that he could get things done as their president.

The fourth generation of advertising consisted of one advertisement. It was the closest thing to a negative advertisement that we ran, although it was not labelled as negative since it contained no image of our opponent nor did it name her. In the advertisement called '*Goldman Sachs*',[33] we returned to the frame of our message that looked closely at the role that Wall Street and powerful special interests play in rigging the economy to their favour by making campaign contributions and paying speaking fees to politicians. It was well known that Hillary Clinton had received millions in speaking fees before the election from Wall Street banks and other powerful interests.[34] We focused on one specific case – that of Goldman Sachs – in part because the firm had just been hit with a $5 billion fine for the role they had played in the collapse of the mortgage market during the great recession in America.[35] We identified Goldman Sachs as being at the heart of the financial meltdown. Beginning with a scene at Goldman Sachs headquarters and a headline about their $5 billion settlement, the narrator stated: 'They're one of the Wall Street banks that triggered the financial meltdown. Goldman Sachs. Just settled with authorities for their part in the crisis that put seven million out of work, and millions out of their homes. How does Wall Street get away with it? Millions in campaign contributions and speaking fees. Our economy works for Wall Street because it's rigged by Wall Street. And that's the problem. As long as Washington is bought and paid for, we can't build an economy that works for people.'

That advertisement, along with the fact that Bernie Sanders began to use the speaking fees issue in debates against Hillary Clinton, had a powerful impact on the dynamic of the race in Iowa and elsewhere.

The final generation of advertising in Iowa and New Hampshire, and most of the later primary states as well, consisted of two longer format (sixty-second) advertisements. The first one became well known and was cited repeatedly by the press as the 'best ad of the 2016 presidential campaign'.[36] The *New York Times* recognised this achievement on the basis of research they conducted through the general election.[37] The singer/songwriter Paul Simon had given us permission to use one of the classic Simon and Garfunkel songs, and we decided to use the song *'America'*, an iconic ballad. The advertisement contained no narration, only lyrics, and very little political feel. Instead it focused on the role that people were playing in Bernie's campaign.

While we were making the advertisement I decided to insert some powerful video of Bernie speaking to a town hall in New Hampshire. In it, he talked about people joining a cause bigger than themselves. The insertion of a sound bite from him would have been very similar in technique to what we did in the first biographic advertisement, where we had a clip of Bernie from a speech near the end. I showed a rough cut of that version to Bernie's wife Jane Sanders and Jeff Weaver during debate preparation in Burlington. They both said they thought it was better without Bernie speaking at the end. That is when I realised that the *America* advertisement was not about Bernie, but about people who were looking to join something bigger than themselves – the people who 'had all come to look for America'. I went back to the studio, and inserted bigger and bigger scenes of crowds until finally the crescendo of the advertisement was all those people. *America* resonated powerfully with voters across the country.[38]

My near obsession with presenting Bernie as a distinctly American candidate is reflected in the visual images of the *America* advertisement.

Eleven scenes contain some kind of American flag imagery. *America* begins with a great scene filmed by my business partner, Mark Longabaugh, and our director of photography, Mark Gunning, in Iowa – a rural barn with an American flag on the side, and wind turbines in a field in the distance. Iowa has made major progress in the production of clean energy and now generates almost 40 per cent of its electricity through wind and solar power, so that image would be very familiar to voters there. To me, that scene of the flag on the side of the barn with the wind turbines in the distance perfectly embodied what we were attempting to present – Bernie Sanders as a distinctly American candidate in the context of his vision and values – while constantly looking towards the future symbolised by those wind turbines in the fields. That opening frame epitomised *A Future To Believe In*, a future that could be achieved through Bernie's leadership and the implementation of his visionary plans for the nation.

There was so much attention given to the *America* advertisement that most observers missed the impact of the other one that ran in the final generation with it. The second sixty-second commercial called *American Horizon*[39] was in my mind just as important to our closing momentum as *America*. While *America* was emotional, authentic and told a memorable story, *American Horizon* allowed Bernie Sanders to present his substantive agenda for the future of the nation directly to voters. The horizon metaphor – which was the visual that began the commercial depicting sunrise over a large cornfield – led to Bernie talking about all of the plans for progress he had for the nation's future.

In *American Horizon*, Bernie asserts to camera: 'There are those who say we cannot defeat a corrupt political system and fix a rigged economy. But I believe we need to lift our vision above the obstacles in place and look to the American horizon. To a nation where every child cannot only dream of going to college but attend one. Where quality healthcare will be a birthright of every citizen. Where a good job is not a wish, but a reality. Where women receive equal pay, and a living wage is paid to all. An America where after a lifetime of labour there's time for rest and grandchildren. A nation that defends our people and our values, but no longer carries so much of that burden alone. I know we can create that America if we listen to our hearts, and that journey begins here in Iowa. I'm Bernie Sanders. I approve this message, and I ask you to join with us at the caucuses on Monday night. Thank you.'

American Horizon set forth the substantive agenda for Bernie Sanders's campaign – from dealing with the forces that were creating income and wealth inequality, to providing specific policies and programmes like Medicare for All, universal college education, equal pay, a living wage and a variety of other real-world solutions. It also allowed us to present Bernie in the strongest format in political advertising – a candidate directly to camera, looking voters in the eye. This advertisement outlined his vision for the future of the nation he aspired to lead.

The Iowa results and the road to victory in New Hampshire

As we waited in the suite at the Holiday Inn by the Des Moines airport where the campaign was holding our caucus night event, a snowstorm was barrelling in on Iowa. We needed to get out of town or risk being stranded there. So even though the final results were not in hand we decided to do our event – where Bernie declared 'a virtual tie' – and then headed quickly to our chartered plane to fly to New Hampshire.

Earlier that evening, Jeff Weaver, Mark Longabaugh and I went to an iconic Des Moines hamburger restaurant – Zombie Burger – for an early dinner as the caucuses were about to begin. Sensing that we were on the verge of something big – perhaps even victory in Iowa – we huddled to try to figure out what we could do in New Hampshire that would capture the attention of voters and the media. We decided to try to stage an event near our hotel on the outskirts of Manchester. When we called Julia Barnes, our New Hampshire State Director, she was not happy to hear this news because she had worked so hard to put in place a detailed schedule and 'Get Out The Vote' effort for the final week of the campaign. We assured her that we would not draw resources away from the state organisation. Mark then began calling experienced advance people in Boston who could put together the event without undercutting the ground campaign. After arriving in New Hampshire, we held an event at 5 a.m. that – in the age of phone-held video – wound up dominating television news coverage on the first day of the final week of the New Hampshire primary. The video, captured on reporters' mobile phones, showed an energetic Bernie Sanders climbing on the back of a pickup truck and delivering his message to voters on the ground in New Hampshire. The footage ran all day in most of the television coverage and was just another fortuitous moment for our campaign after many months of hard work climbing back from forty and fifty-point deficits.

Digital communication and events

While the television advertising campaign was the focus of most of our attention, effort and resources, the digital communications campaign that complemented it was critical to Bernie's success as well. That digital campaign consisted of everything from five-second advertisements targeting young people on their phones in Iowa and New Hampshire to 'Get Out The Vote'[40] to five-minute slots that we ran throughout the course of the campaign telling emotional stories of people who supported Bernie Sanders.[41] We used these digital advertisements and videos to make connections with people and to get individuals to share these videos within their own social networks. This sharing gave us the benefit of voters watching our advertising without us having to pay the premium price of television commercials. The digital campaign was one of the keys to our success and its impact throughout the course of many months cannot be overestimated.

In the end, Bernie Sanders won the New Hampshire primary with more votes than any candidate in the 100-year history of that classic event.[42] I never thought anyone would surpass John McCain's total of 110,000 votes when he ran against George W. Bush in the Republican primary in 2000. I had worked for Democrats like Al Gore, John Kerry and Michael Dukakis who each won the Democratic primary in New Hampshire with much lower vote totals. But Bernie Sanders's 152,193 votes shattered the previous vote record in the New Hampshire primary, where independents can vote either for the Democrat or the Republican. I think it was a testament not only to the campaign that we ran on the ground and the air in New Hampshire, but also to the message and the messenger who delivered it with such passion and import.

Bernie Sanders also delivered important speeches at venues like Liberty University, a conservative evangelical Christian college in Virginia, where he called on liberals and conservatives to find common ground,[43] and at

Georgetown University, where he delivered a speech about Democratic Socialism which offered fundamental reassurance that his political philosophy was deeply grounded in the American experience and inspired in large measure by the unfinished agenda of President Franklin Roosevelt.[44] Moreover, his performance in debates improved immeasurably during the course of the campaign. In his first debate with Hillary Clinton, she had the advantage of walking into her twenty-sixth presidential debate, including twenty-five from 2008,[45] while Bernie was on that presidential stage for the first time. But within weeks of that first debate his performances improved so dramatically that debates became moments where he gained ground consistently in his match-ups with Hillary.

The most important part of the broader digital campaign was fundraising. With a $27 average contribution the campaign raised almost a quarter of a billion dollars. Almost all that money came in via email from donors who contributed small amounts on a regular basis. The success of the fundraising was one of the reasons the press began to cover Bernie seriously as a top-tier candidate and provided the resources for us to run an expensive media campaign, not just in Iowa and New Hampshire, but in many later states as well. In fact, despite Hillary Clinton's early fundraising advantage and extensive political network, Bernie Sanders actually began to raise more than she did each month early in 2016 and continued to do so for most of the spring of that year.[46]

While there were many opportunities to complain about the obvious advantages that the Democratic National Committee was giving to Clinton (like the very limited debate schedule),[47] for the most part we avoided protesting that unfairness, until the DNC took away our access to voter files in Iowa and New Hampshire (some Sanders staff members looked at the Clinton voter files to which they were not entitled access after the firewalls built by the DNC broke down). When the DNC imposed the extraordinary sanction of depriving our campaign of the voter files needed to organise in Iowa and New Hampshire, we immediately decided to take on the political establishment and file a case in federal court seeking injunctive relief, which we were about to be granted hours after the court filing, before the DNC agreed to settle the case on our terms.[48]

Bernie also took frequent advantage of media opportunities available for Sunday show interviews, as well as other broadcast opportunities, even moving into the world of late-night television, where the comedian Larry David proved to be not only a Bernie Sanders lookalike but hysterically captured Bernie as a character for all of America to see on *Saturday Night Live*.[49]

A campaign of consequence

By the time we got to the end of the primary voting, there was no one who could deny that Bernie Sanders's impact on Democratic Party politics was indelible. He had managed to move the debate to the ground of his choosing on issues like health, education and the economy.[50] My business partners – Julian Mulvey, Mark Longabaugh and I are proud of the 275 television, digital and radio advertisements that we produced for that one campaign.

While Bernie Sanders's campaign did not succeed by the metric of winning the nomination, it did nonetheless succeed in the sense that he moved America towards an agenda that he had fought for, for decades. His fights for working people, his commitment to healthcare for all, his push towards expanding educational opportunity, and his defence of programmes like Medicare, Medicaid and Social Security that protect senior citizens and working people, became the heart of the Democratic Party agenda heading into the 2020 presidential election cycle. Victory may be the bottom line in politics, but no one can doubt that the impact that Bernie Sanders's 2016 campaign had on American elections was profound and continues to reverberate. And while no one knows what the future holds, I think it is safe to say that the Sanders for President Campaign 2016 was one of the most consequential causes in decades for both the Democratic Party and American politics. Those consequences continue to be felt today, and hopefully will inspire many to be part of an effort to create *A Future To Believe In*.

CHAPTER 15

PEACE, JUSTICE AND COMPASSION TOWARDS THOSE WHO HAVE SUFFERED

Kerry Kennedy

Dr Brian Murphy (BM): Kerry Kennedy, Céad Mile Fáilte.[1]

Kerry Kennedy (KK): Thank you. It's great to be here.

BM: Welcome to Ireland, welcome to New Ross. Earlier today, you visited Dunganstown, the ancestral home of the Kennedys. One hundred and seventy years ago, your great-great grandfather, Patrick Kennedy, left Dunganstown. He walked on the road to this town of New Ross and he made the journey to Boston, Massachusetts, and started a political legend. How did it feel today to be in Dunganstown, where the Kennedy journey to America began? How did it feel to be back?

KK: The first time I went there was in 1974. I was 14 years old. It was deeply moving for me to stand on that ground and imagine what it must have been like to be living in a country where one out of every eight people died during the Great Famine. In just a seven-year period a quarter of the population of this island either died or took off in the coffin ships and sought a new world. Just imagine where you are living off the land and suddenly the land fails you. Where you see your brothers and sisters either flee or die and where there was such an easy solution. That influence is very strong. I met my fourth cousin who is still farming on the exact same land. If you are connected to the land, it never leaves you all these generations later.

BM: I was struck by what you said earlier this evening in the library here in New Ross and I found it quite emotional when you spoke about your own passion and the passion of your father, Robert F. Kennedy, and the passion of your uncle, John F. Kennedy for justice, for peace and for compassion. Does some of that passion come from the Irishness of the Kennedys, especially given those roots in the Famine where a million of our people starved to death, another million were forced into emigration and has that in some way shaped your political leanings?

KK: Absolutely, Brian. I am the seventh child of a seventh child and there are many, many Irish families that are large like ours. That makes you understand what the pecking order is and fairness at a young age. When Daddy ran for President, he said: 'Peace and justice and compassion towards those who've suffered, that is what the United States should stand for.' It's hard to imagine a political leader today getting up and somebody saying 'Why are you running for President?' and having what might be considered a 'weak answer' of: 'Peace and Justice and Compassion towards those who've suffered,' but that's really what we need in our country and that's what we need in our world. There is a direct line of those values from my father to right here in Ireland.

BM: Do you still feel Irish, 170 years on from Patrick Kennedy leaving Ireland?

KK: First of all, my name is Kerry! To understand the history of Ireland and be fully connected to this place was a big part of our upbringing. The first country I came to with that passport was here. I remember as a child, my grandmother, Rose Kennedy – our next-door neighbour in Hyannis Port, Cape Cod – would bring us up into the attic and pull out the scrapbooks where it said in job advertisements in American newspapers that 'No Irish need apply.' There was a clear connection between the values of what it meant to stand up to oppression and to seek, to strive, to create a better world and the civil rights struggle that was going on in our country at that time and is still so present today.

BM: Can I congratulate you on your book? I managed to spend some time yesterday reading it.

KK: Thank you.

BM: Your book, *Robert Kennedy: Ripples of Hope*,[2] it's not a biography of your father. There are many excellent biographies written of your father, but what this book does is it focuses on the inspiration that Bobby Kennedy gave to so many people around the world. I do want to talk about the inspiration of Bobby Kennedy and his legacy, which has inspired generations of people and political leaders, but what struck me, first of all, in reading the book was about your own life growing up as a Kennedy. For many of us, especially historians, we see Bobby Kennedy as a tough campaign manager, an Attorney General, a Senator, a Presidential Candidate but to you he was Dad. You write about growing up as one of eleven children – with seven brothers and three sisters – what was it like growing up on Hickory Hill?

KK: Well, it was loud! My mother, who's now 90 years old, is a lot of fun. My father thrived on that, so there was a lot of openness, a lot of laughter and also a lot of interest in what was going on around the country and around the world. When I was growing up, five or six newspapers circulated around our breakfast table on any given day. Everybody was meant to read them. At dinner, my father would go around the room and ask everyone about a story they'd read and what they thought about it. You couldn't repeat anyone else's story.

Another rule of my father's: whoever walked into our den first got to choose what to watch on television, unless someone wanted to watch the news. There was that sensibility that you need to know what was going on and be responsible for it. There was also a lot of prayer. My father and mother and all of us children said prayers on our knees in the morning and then before and after breakfast, before and after lunch, before and after dinner, and then my father would read the Old Testament. We would kneel around my parents' bed and say the rosary every night. Being Catholic was a big part of our upbringing.

BM: Sure and I think it's very interesting about news taking precedence in your house and how you happened to read the newspapers. I know from reading biographies of your own father and from reading biographies of your uncle, President Kennedy, that the upbringing they got from your grandfather, Joseph P. Kennedy, was that he asked them to read newspapers every day and quizzed them on public affairs as well. In terms of you growing up as a child, you would have had your ninth birthday in 1968. That was a year that America was in turmoil. It's the year Martin Luther King was assassinated in April 1968, the Vietnam War is raging and on 16 March, just prior to St Patrick's Day, your father, Robert Kennedy, in the Senate Caucus room – in the same room that your uncle President Kennedy declared his candidacy for the United States Presidency – announces that he is going to run for president. What are your memories of that campaign? I know you were a young girl at that stage but do you have specific memories you can share with us?

KK: I have. First of all, my father really sought to engage us all in his work. My parents didn't separate their home life from their work lives so we were always very engaged in it and they tried to make campaigning fun, so it wasn't just going from one speech to the next. My father took us to the Bronx Zoo to feed the elephants, and we went rafting down the Hudson River, that sort of thing. I remember in June of 1968 going to Disneyland. It was all a great, great adventure. Shall I tell you a story about not separating home and work?

BM: Yes, please.

KK: When we were really little kids my father was the Attorney General. My mother used to pile six or seven of us into the back of her convertible with two or three dogs and a football and take us down to the Justice Department to visit my father. He had an enormous office. It was really sort of a hallway to other offices but he chose it because he wanted to be some place long enough that he could throw a football. We would run around there, and we would go through a tunnel from the basement of the Justice Department that led to the FBI building, where we could watch sharpshooters at practice. As children, we loved that.

At that time the head of the FBI was J. Edgar Hoover, who had been quoted as saying the two biggest threats to American democracy were Martin Luther King Jr and Robert F. Kennedy. Hoover was not known for his love of children or his sense of humour. My father and mother, on the other hand, were known for both of those things. One day, when my mother went to round us up from the FBI building, she discovered a suggestion box in the basement, pulled out a pen and filled out one of the forms. Shortly afterwards, an astute FBI agent took her suggestion out of the box, which Hoover immediately had sent over to Daddy's office. It read: 'Get a new director!' Shall I tell you another example of this?

BM: Please do.

KK: There is a film called *Crisis*[3] about of the University of Alabama in the early 1960s, an all-white university run by George Wallace, who was the [State] Governor at the time. It did not allow any African Americans to be in the university. My father was trying to integrate it.

Wallace said he would stand in the schoolhouse door to prevent any blacks from coming into the university. 'Segregation now, segregation tomorrow, segregation forever!' he is remembered for saying. When that crisis was beginning, my father went to a film-maker and said 'I want you to film how Presidential decisions are made and what happens.' So they followed him for ten days and they went into the Oval Office and filmed my uncle, President John F. Kennedy, on the phone with George Wallace. They filmed George Wallace in his office and it was really remarkable. It will never, in a million years, happen again to get that intimacy and that immediacy and to hand over all that to a film-maker.

There is this one scene, that was an out-take from the film, where my father is seen talking to his aides, the heads of the Civil Rights Division and he reads a letter. The letter says: 'Dear Attorney General, I am the head of the Alabama Freedom Militia and we have called up every son of Alabama from the age of 16 to the age of 65 and we have asked them to get their guns and come to the capitol and defend Governor Wallace, so no blacks are allowed into the university ...' And then my father is in the film and he is saying: 'Well, how many Federal troops can we call? Where are they stationed? How long will it take them to get from where they are stationed to the university if we need them? How long does it take from the time they are told that they need to be ready until the time that they are in the helicopters and in the trucks?'

My father wants to know the details. He wants to know exactly what's going to happen.

In the midst of this, you see me. I'm 4. I'm running around his office with my two brothers and then you see my father is saying 'hot and cold'. You know that game? It's hide and seek. So then you see my two brothers hiding underneath the desk and my father is saying 'hot' when I walk closely to them and 'cold' when I walk away. I was not really very adept at this game. So it's taking a long time and as you're watching this film, you find yourself saying forget the kids, deal with the crisis and then, as it goes on and on, you realise that he's making these decisions not in spite of the kids ...

BM: But because of them?

KK: Yes, because of the kids. And this is what is so amazing about that [scene]. His humanity was so strong and he was so connected to other human beings and the most vulnerable of us. So my father successfully integrates the University of Alabama. One of the two students who were the first two people to integrate the school had a little sister. That little sister grew up and fell in love with a very bright young African American man. That African American man then went to law school and he became a prosecutor. Then he rose in the ranks of the prosecutors in the United States and he became the first African American Attorney General in the history of our country.[4]

BM: That is a fantastic story.

KK: Thank you very much.

BM: If your father was alive today [September 2018], he would be 92, which would be younger than President George Bush the first and younger than President Jimmy Carter. If he was around today, what would he think of the direction America is going?

KK: Well, I think he would be dismayed and distraught as all of us are really. We have seen and as we read in *The New York Times* just yesterday the top brass in the White House are also dismayed.[5] You know, in terms of my work as a Human Rights activist we have never had a more disastrous president. He shuttered our doors. He has stopped refugees from being able to come to the United States. He's fermented hate speech, even at a time when women, African Americans, people of the Islamic faith, LGBT people are under attack more than they have been for the last forty years. He has increased military spending so it's now over 50 per cent of our discretionary budget. He said, as candidate, we are going, excuse me, to 'bomb the shit out of them'[6] and he's carried that out as president. We now have more civilians' deaths because of bombings than any time in history. He said I'm going to bring back torture, people who get tortured deserve it anyway.[7] He has put the CIA back into the killing business. He's filled his cabinet with people who are anti-justice, anti-human rights. The Attorney General, who has a long history of racist rants.[8] Mike Pompeo, who's the Secretary of State, who said that the people who committed torture 'are not torturers, they are patriots'.[9] I could just go on as we meet here, I could go on and on and on and on. He's embedded himself with some of the worst dictators on earth, people committing horrendous atrocities from North Korea to Putin in Russia to the Saudi Arabians, to Nigeria, to the Philippines and meanwhile he has alienated our greatest allies in the EU. And this is insanity, to make an enemy of the EU, to make an enemy out of Canada, to make an enemy out of Mexico. The strength of the United States has, in so many ways, been because we are so strongly attached to our neighbours. Anyway, he's really horrendous on so many issues but massively on foreign policy.

BM: For the times we live, what you have stated there about, I suppose, what is Trump's legacy at the moment, it makes it all the more important the work that you do in terms of human rights. I know that you are looking

for opportunities for working with Irish organisations in human rights. The work you do with the Robert Kennedy Human Rights organisation, I've read a bit about it, is remarkable. It builds on your father's legacy, whom I think is a hero to nearly all of us in New Ross and in Ireland, as well. I want to finish by asking you one final question about another remarkable person and that's Ethel Kennedy, your mother. You dedicate your book to her for raising eleven children with a sense of, I think you say, 'rollicking adventure'. In 2013, your sister Rory came here to the Kennedy Summer School and she screened her Emmy Award nominee documentary on your mother's life. She was interviewed by my good friend Richard Aldous and we all got a sense of getting to know your mother from that documentary and that interview.[10] I know she had a significant birthday this year, so how is your mother?

KK: I was just with her last week for about three-and-a-half hours on a sailboat. We had her 90th birthday in April and she left the party at 12.45 in the morning and the police came at 12.50 to quiet it down! She really is so fantastic and full of life. I called her the other day and she said I really want to talk to you sweetheart, but I am in the middle of a backgammon game and I am about to beat my grandchild so I just cannot talk now. She didn't say I am about to lose to him, she said I am about to beat him so she's just got this great, keen sense of fun and has not lost the competitive edge whatsoever.

BM: Was there a story about her that she hijacked a scooter?

KK: She did! She's done a lot of things. Now as a kid, she actually, was accused, in fact, she was rightfully accused of horse thievery, which is a hanging offence in Virginia. There was a neighbour of ours who was starving his horses and she went in the middle of the night, took them out of his barn and brought them over to our barn and tried to bring them back to life. And anywhere she sees wrong she is going to try and right it. She's great.

BM: She's a remarkable woman and you are a remarkable woman as well.

KK: Thank you.

BM: It's been an absolute pleasure to talk to you, Kerry, and to talk about your father's legacy. I encourage everybody to buy the book and Kerry Kennedy, I would love to talk to you all night but we do have to push on. It's been a pleasure, an absolute pleasure.

KK: Thank you, Brian.

ACKNOWLEDGEMENTS

This book owes its existence to the generosity of the authors of each of the individual essays for taking the time out of their busy schedules to contribute to this project. The views of each author are their own and are not necessarily those of the editors.

Each of the essays in this book have their origin in papers delivered at the Kennedy Summer School, New Ross. The book is dedicated to the Summer School's late founder Noel Whelan, who was a force of nature, an intellectual giant and a loyal and generous friend. Noel is dearly missed by many, many people. We would also like to acknowledge Noel's wife Sinéad McSweeney, his son Seamus Whelan, his mother Myra Whelan and the wider Whelan family.

Noel was passionate about the Kennedy Summer School and he worked closely with Willie Keilthy, the Chairman of the Kennedy Summer School, in leading this vibrant community project. Willie's strong work ethic, energy and organisational and diplomatic skills are integral to the continued success of the Kennedy Summer School, which has developed into the number one forum of its type in Ireland.

This book would not have come to fruition without the support of Noel, Willie and all of those whose work underpins the Kennedy Summer School, including Larry Donnelly, Eileen Dunne, Bob Mauro, Carmel Delaney, Tom Redmond, Emma Lane, Richie Kirwan, John O'Donohoe, John Roche, Declan Rowsome, Ann Power, Gail Conway, Karen O'Connor, Myles Courtney, Jamie Long, Eileen Morrissey, Seán Reidy, Delia Hickey, John Michael Porter, Tomás Kavanagh, Eamonn Hore and Sinéad Casey.

The editors would like to thank the CEO of the JFK Trust Seán Connick, Chairman of the Board Colm Caulfield and other directors, Walter O'Leary, Seán Furlong, Myles Courtney, Willie Fitzharris, John Fleming, Frances Ryan, Anne Tubritt, George Walsh and Jim Walsh and Marcella Butler, administrative assistant to the board. We would also like to acknowledge the work of Patrick Grennan at the Kennedy Homestead, Dunganstown, New Ross, which is a fantastic cultural museum that plays a vital role in the continued preservation of the Kennedy legacy in Ireland.

We would each especially like to thank our families and friends for their support and patience while we committed time to this project.

Brian would like to express his deep gratitude to his parents Eddie and Kathryn Murphy for all they have done for him. He also wishes to thank his brother John, sister-in-law Cathy and his Boston-born and raised niece Madeleine and nephews Luke and Owen (who sound like JFK!) and the wider Murphy and Moran families. Brian would like to make special mention of his godson Kaleb Cooper-Fitzpatrick, Evan Cooper-Fitzpatrick, Alexa Cooper-Fitzpatrick and Liam Cooper, who keep him young! Brian would also like to record his appreciation for the always clear and thoughtful advice of Eoin O'Shea and the support of colleagues in Technological University Dublin.

Donnacha's most sustained debt is to Karolina and their daughter, Gaia, who are at the centre of all his endeavours. Without their loving presence, very little would be possible. He would also like to pay tribute to his parents, Deirdre and Brendan, grandmother, Kathleen, aunt Medb and sister, Caoilfhionn. Donnacha has also greatly appreciated the support of his colleagues in the School of Law and Government, and the wider community at Dublin City University (DCU), especially successive heads of school, Professor Robert Elgie, Professor Gary Murphy and Professor Iain McMenamin, faculty dean (and former head of school), Professor John Doyle, and university president, Professor Brian MacCraith. DCU's Institute for International Conflict Resolution and Reconstruction (IICRR) has also been a major resource for facilitating and disseminating research.

We would like to express our gratitude to Conor Graham, managing director of the Irish Academic Press, for his faith in this book from the outset. We are also grateful to Patrick O'Donoghue, Maeve Convery and Dermott Barrett from Irish Academic Press, whose professionalism and attention to detail have made this book a far better final product.

We are obliged to those who assisted us in obtaining the photographs included in this book and for permission to reprint them. Steve Branch, Ronald Reagan Presidential Library, and James B. Hill, John F. Kennedy Presidential Library and Museum, were extremely kind in that regard.

Guy Holland undertook the difficult task of proofreading the final manuscript. He was diligent and dedicated in this work and made many useful suggestions towards improving the final text.

The royalties from this book are being donated to New Ross Community Hospital. We want to express our admiration for Frances Ryan, the board members and all the staff at the Community Hospital for the valuable care and services they provide.

Other friends, family members and colleagues who we wish to acknowledge are Bertie Ahern, Richard Aldous, Stephanie Allibone, Diyar Autal, Nevan Bermingham, Paschal Bolger, Colm Brady, Royston Brady, Michael Carr, Tom Clarkin, Eileen Connolly, Niamh Cooper, Brian Cowen, Mac and Jerry Crean, Kevin Cullen, Kirk Curnutt, George Delaney, Loughlin Deegan, Michael Devereux, Dominic Dillane, Erhan Doğan, John Dolan, John Downing, Allen Dunne, Gerry Farrelly, Tony Feeney, Leonard Fitzpatrick, Diarmaid Fleming, Martin Fraser, Margaret Geoghegan, Deirdre Gillane, Frank Gillespie, the Goldenberg family from Nepolokovcy, Wanda and Andrzej Grześkowiak, Mary Hannon, Philip Hannon, Mark Hennessy, Gerard Howlin, Florian Hummel, Mandy Johnston, Susan Kiernan, Eibhlin Keilthy, John Keilthy, Paul Kelly, Stuart Kenny, Rob Kevlihan, Dáithí Kuijper, Jennifer Langan, Elaine Larkin, Joe Lennon, Zi Liang, Deirdre Lillis, Ralf Lissek, Michael Lonergan, David Looby, Kevin Lu, Shenghe Lu, Fiona Lyons, Liam MacMathúna, David McCullagh, Paul McGuill, Nick McStay, Martina Mastandrea, Angus Mitchell, Derek Mooney, Cormac Moore, Richard Moore, Betty Moran and the staff of the Theatre Tavern, Anna Moran, Eva Moran, Joe Moran, Mary Murphy, John O'Brennan, Mark O'Brien, Ciaran Ó Cuinn, Jerry O'Connor, Mike O'Connor, Kieran O'Grady, Art O'Leary, Eoin O'Leary, Rossa Ó Muireartaigh, Eoghan Ó Neachtain, Mary O'Rourke, Cuan Ó Seireadáin, Des Peelo, Abel Polese, John Pollock, Marie Porter, Allison Ryan, Dermot Ryan, Fionnan Sheahan, Padraig Slyne, Gëzim Visoka, Brendan Walsh, Zhen Yao and Katherine Zappone.

A special thank you to all our friends, colleagues and relatives we have not mentioned explicitly. Many people played a role in shaping the output of this work and we ask for the indulgence of anyone we inadvertently forgot to include here.

In conclusion, the editors wish to recognise all of those who have contributed to an existing wide canon of literature on the Kennedys. We hope this book creates new understanding and we look forward to other authors bringing forward further, fresh insights and new interpretations into the future. In the words of John F. Kennedy, 'history is not something dead and over. It is always alive, always growing, always unfinished.'[1]

Brian Murphy
Donnacha Ó Beacháin

NOTES

Introduction

1 Foy, M. & Conway, N. (1963). 'Freedom's Cry – "Remember the Irish."' *Irish Times*, 28 June 1963.

2 Foy & Conway. 'Freedom's Cry.'

3 Ibid.

4 Tubridy, R. (2010). *JFK in Ireland: Four Days that Changed a President*. London: HarperCollins, p. 138; Foy & Conway. 'Freedom's Cry.'

5 Remarks at Redmond Place, Wexford, 27 June 1963, full text available in Kennedy, J.F. (1963). *Public Papers of the Presidents of the United States: John F. Kennedy, 1963*. Washington: United States Government Printing Office, p. 532.

6 Carroll, J. (2003). *One of Ourselves: John Fitzgerald Kennedy in Ireland*. Vermont: Images from the Past, p. 77.

7 Maier, T. (2003). *The Kennedys: America's Emerald Kings*. New York: Perseus, p. 3.

8 'Remarks on the Quay at New Ross, 27 June 1963,' full text available in Kennedy, J.F. (1963). *Public Papers of the Presidents of the United States: John F. Kennedy, 1963*. Washington: United States Government Printing Office, p. 531.

9 Maier. *The Kennedys*, p. 26.

10 Maier. *The Kennedys*, pp. 26–7; Klein, E. (2003). The *Kennedy Curse: Why America's First Family Has Been Haunted by Tragedy for 150 Years*. New York: St Martin's Press, p. 94.

11 Maier. *The Kennedys*, p. 606. About 6 per cent of the Irish who came to America during this period died on board of cholera, dysentery, yellow fever, small pox or measles. Kessler, R. (1996). *The Sins of the Father: Joseph P. Kennedy and the Dynasty He Founded*. New York: Grand Central Publishing, p. 2.

12 Abrams, R. (2003). *The First World Series and the Baseball Fanatics of 1903*. Boston: Northeastern University Press, p. 87.

13 Klein, E. (2019). 'Patrick Kennedy: The Forgotten Founding Father.' [online] *Catholic League*. Available at: https://www.catholicleague.org/patrick-kennedy-the-forgotten-founding-father [Accessed 9 February 2020].

14 Churchwell, S. (2018). *Behold America: A History of America First and the American Dream*. London: Bloomsbury, p. 1.

15 Maier. *The Kennedys*, p. 33.

16 Abrams. *The First World Series*, p. 87.

17 Maier. *The Kennedys*, p. 33.

18 Maier. *The Kennedys*, p. 34.
19 Ibid. Depending on the account, Patrick Kennedy's death has been attributed most commonly to cholera and occasionally to tuberculosis, but consumption is clearly stated on his death certificate. See Maier. *The Kennedys*, pp. 33–4; Rachlin, H. (1986). *The Kennedys: A chronological history, 1823–present*. New York: World Almanac, p. 7; Klein. 'Patrick Kennedy'; Galvin, E.D. (1985). 'The Kennedys of Massachusetts'. *New England Historical and Genealogical Register*, vol. 139 (July), p. 211.
20 See for example Klein. 'Patrick Kennedy: The Forgotten Founding Father.'
21 Maier. *The Kennedys*, p. 16.
22 Kessler. *The Sins of the Father*, p. 2.
23 Maier. *The Kennedys*, p. 36.
24 Kiely, D. (2018). *Famous Wexford People in History*. Wexford: Parsifal Press, p. 39.
25 Dallek, R. (2003). *An Unfinished Life: John F. Kennedy, 1917–1963*. New York: Hachette, pp. 8–9.
26 Kearns Goodwin, D. (1987). *The Fitzgeralds and the Kennedys*. New York: Simon & Schuster, p. 256.
27 Kaul, V. (2014). *Easy Money: Evolution of the Global Financial system to the Great Bubble Burst*. London: Sage Publications, pp. 1–2.
28 Ling, P. (2013). *John F. Kennedy*. New York: Routledge, p. 28.
29 Beuchamp, C. (2009). *Joseph P. Kennedy's Hollywood Years*. London: Random House, pp. 352–8; Wapshott, N. (2015). *The Sphinx: Franklin Roosevelt, the Isolationists, and the Road to World War II*. London: W.W. Norton, pp. 42–57.
30 MacGregor Burns, J. (2006). *Running Alone: Presidential Leadership from JFK to Bush II*. New York: Perseus Books, p. 11.
31 Lincoln, E. (1965). *My Twelve Years with John F. Kennedy*. Philadelphia, D. McKay Company, pp. 52–3.
32 Bzdek, V. (2009). *The Kennedy Legacy: Jack, Bobby and Ted and a Family Dream Fulfilled*. St Martin's Press: New York, p. 108.
33 Barrett, D. (2005). *The CIA and Congress: the untold story from Truman to Kennedy*. Lawrence: University Press of Kansas, p. 439.
34 John F. Kennedy Library & Museum. 'Seán Lemass: Oral History Interview,' 8 August 1966.
35 Ibid.
36 Speech by President Kennedy, Dáil Éireann, Dublin, Ireland, 28 June 1963.
37 Fianna Fáil. (2019). 'Speech by Fianna Fáil Leader Micheál Martin TD at the Kennedy Summer School, New Ross, 6 September 2019.' [online] Available at: https://www.fiannafail.ie/speech-by-ff-leader-micheal-martin-td-at-the-kennedy-summer-school-new-ross [Accessed 17 February 2020].
38 Mitchell, A. (1993). *JFK and His Irish Heritage*. Dublin: Moytura Press, p. 73.
39 McGreevy R. (2019). 'The Lemass Tapes: Seán Lemass in his own voice,' paper delivered at the Kennedy Summer School, New Ross, 7 September 2019.
The 'Lemass Tapes' were the subject of a supplement in *The Irish Times* in June 2018. The 'Lemass Tapes' were recorded by Dermot Ryan, a successful Dublin businessman and a

member of Fianna Fáil's National Executive. The tapes were recorded between April 1967 and January 1969 and consist of twenty-two hours of audio.

40   Speech by President Kennedy, Conferring of the Freedom of Limerick, Greenpark Racecourse, Limerick, Ireland, 29 June 1963.

41   McGreevy. 'The Lemass Tapes.'

42   Ibid.

43   'His Enduring Images and Words,' *Life Magazine*, 20 December 1963.

44   'Ted Kennedy: Tributes flow from Republicans and Democrats alike,' *The Guardian*, 26 August 2009.

45   Carswell, S. (2015). 'Edward Kennedy's key role in Northern Ireland revealed.' *Irish Times*, 1 October 2015.

46   'US envoy branded "apologist for IRA" to stay on,' *Irish Independent*, 19 January 1998.

47   Smith, B. and Martin, J. (2009). 'Kennedy legacy shapes Obama path.' [online] *POLITICO*. Available at: https://www.politico.com/story/2009/08/kennedy-legacy-shapes-obama-path-026493 [Accessed 15 February 2020].

48   Smith and Martin. 'Kennedy legacy shapes Obama path.'

49   American political scientist Fred Greenstein quoted in Renshon, S.A. (2012). *Barack Obama and the Politics of Redemption*. New York: Routledge, p. 64.

50   Martin, J. (2010). '"Intellectual Blood Bank" of JFK.' *Financial Times*, 6 November 2010; Schmidt, M. (2015). 'State of the Union Speechwriter for Obama Draws on Various Inspirations.' *New York Times*, 20 January 2015.

51   www.jfklibrary.org. (n.d.). 'Tribute to John F. Kennedy at the Democratic National Convention, Atlantic City, New Jersey, August 27, 1964.' *JFK Library*. [online] Available at: https://www.jfklibrary.org/learn/about-jfk/the-kennedy-family/robert-f-kennedy/robert-f-kennedy-speeches/tribute-to-john-f-kennedy-at-the-democratic-national-convention-atlantic-city-new-jersey-august-27 [Accessed 15 February 2020].

52   Ben-Meir, I. (2020). 'Bernie Sanders Despised Democrats In 1980s, Said A JFK Speech Once Made Him Sick.' [online] Available at: https://www.buzzfeednews.com/article/ilanbenmeir/bernie-sanders-despised-democrats-in-1980s-said-a-jfk-speech [Accessed 16 February 2020].

53   Kennedy, C. (2020). 'Caroline Kennedy: Joe Biden for President.' *The Boston Globe*, 4 February 2020.

54   Kennedy, R. (2016). Tweet from @RobertKennedyJr. Available at: https://twitter.com/RobertKennedyJr/status/707669233140953088 [Accessed 17 February 2020].

55   Hardy, K. (2015). 'Sanders likens his politics to those of Bobby Kennedy.' *Des Moines Register*, 23 December 2015; Delamaide, D. (2016). 'Bernie Sanders's quixotic campaign recalls Bobby Kennedy's progressive dream.' [online] *MarketWatch*. Available at: https://www.marketwatch.com/story/bernie-sanderss-quixotic-campaign-recalls-bobby-kennedys-progressive-dream-2016-03-22 [Accessed 16 February 2020]; Sainato, M. (2015). 'Bernie Sanders' Amazing Parallels to John F. Kennedy and Robert F. Kennedy.' [online] *Observer.com*. Available at: https://observer.com/2015/07/bernie-sanders-amazing-parallels-to-john-f-kennedy-and-robert-f-kennedy [Accessed 17 February 2020]; *New York Times*, 23 August 2019.

56 Smith, D. (2018). 'Robert Kennedy's daughter on his death, Donald Trump and America's future.' *The Guardian*, 5 June 2018.

Chapter 1

1   I would like to thank all my former colleagues in Wexford Library Service, especially County Librarian, Eileen Morrissey; Executive Librarian, Hazel Percival; Local Studies librarian, Susan Kelly, and the staffs of Library HQ, Wexford Town library and Wexford County Council GIS, for the tremendous help, support and encouragement they gave me in researching, writing and presenting this paper. I am also hugely indebted to genealogists Richard Andrew Pierce in Boston and John Grenham in Dublin, not just for their helpful comments on the original research but also for directing me to other possible sources and for suggesting other possible siblings of Bridget Murphy Kennedy.

2   Cathedral Records, 1844–1856: 137, Archives of the Archdiocese of Boston. Cited in Galvin, E.D. (1985). 'The Kennedys of Massachusetts'. *New England Historical and Genealogical Register*, vol. 139 (July), pp. 211–24. The old Cathedral of the Holy Cross was on Franklin Street, Boston. Built *c.*1803, it was demolished *c.*1862 and replaced by a new Cathedral of the Holy Cross on Washington Street, Boston.

3   Massachusetts Vital Records (VR) 53:93.

4   Church records, vol. 1, 92. St Nicholas's church, the first Roman Catholic church in East Boston, was established by Irish immigrants in 1844. After 1856 the church, situated on Maverick Street, became known as the Catholic Church of the Most Holy Redeemer.

5   Vital Records 65:89.

6   Church records, vol. 2: 35.

7   Church records, vol. 2: 75.

8   Burials Cambridge cemetery, 1852–1866.

9   Church records, vol. 2: 145.

10 Vital Records 116:14; Church records, vol. 2: 226.

11 Pierce, R. A. (1992). 'Murphys and Barrons of Cloonagh, parish of Owenduff, Co. Wexford: Further ancestors of President John F. Kennedy.' *NEXUS*, the New England Historic Genealogical Society, vol. 9/1, pp. 23–4.

12 Tithes were a tax on agricultural produce which was payable by all occupiers of agricultural land. They were the main source of income for the parish clergy of the Church of Ireland. They were a source of discontent and resentment, especially by Catholics, who did not see why they should have to pay for the upkeep of the established Protestant church. The Tithe Applotment Books are available online at http://titheapplotmentbooks. nationalarchives.ie/search/tab/home.jsp

13 Griffith's Valuation and maps are available online at http://www.askaboutireland.ie/ griffith-valuation

14 Cloonagh is a townland of some 328 statute acres in the old civil parish of Owenduff, Co. Wexford. It has borders with the townlands of Ballygarvan to the east, Dunmain to the west, Nash to the north, and Rathumney to the south. By 1852 the townland was on the Jane C. Boyce estate but had originally been part of the Colclough (Tintern) estate.

15 The Roman Catholic parish registers are available online at https://registers.nli.ie

16 $75 in 1860 is equivalent in purchasing power to about $2,322 in 2020.

17 Bridget's daughter Joanna had married Humphrey Charles Mahoney in 1872. Margaret Kennedy is living elsewhere. Margaret married John Thomas Caulfield in 1882. See Galvin. 'The Kennedys of Massachusetts'.

18 Philip Kane and Margaret Murphy were married on 21 November 1849 in Ballycullane parish. The marriage record indicates that they were related to each other and required a dispensation to marry. Marriage registers of that parish commence 7 October 1827. About 1864, the family moved to the townland of Newbawn in the Catholic parish of Adamstown.

19 A dispensation to marry in the Catholic church would have been required if the couple were related. Laurence Kane and Mary Kennedy's son, Joseph Kane, became a political strategist with the Democrats in Boston and is sometimes credited with persuading his cousin, JFK, to run for Congress.

20 It is unclear if Bridget's sister Margaret Murphy accompanied her to the United States. She cannot be identified in the 1850 census and first appears in Boston records as baptismal sponsor for John Kennedy in 1854.

21 Moses is a form of the Irish name M'aodhóg or Mogue. It is now usually translated as Aidan.

22 https://www.findagrave.com/memorial/27296311/ann-kennedy As the headstone is relatively modern in appearance – perhaps early twentieth century – and there is little detail in the dates of death, I suspect the ages given at death are guesses. For example, Moses Kennedy was born in 1857 and was therefore 15 years old when he died in 1872, not 13; Patrick's death certificate in Ireland is dated 1870 and gives his age as 75 which makes him born in 1795; Ann's age is recorded as 50 in 1872 on the passenger manifest of the *Tripoli*, as 60 in the 1880 census, and as 59 on her death certificate in 1893!

23 Connell, K.H. (1955). 'Marriage in Ireland after the Famine: The diffusion of the match'. *Journal of The Statistical and Social Inquiry Society of Ireland*, vol. xvix, pp. 82–103.

24 I am unable to locate James Roche's baptism in the Ballycullane registers, but he is listed as part of this family in the 1880 census in Salem.

25 It is axiomatic in genealogical research that reported ages in primary sources, especially before 1900 (e.g. censuses, marriage and death records), are rarely accurate. Bridget Murphy Kennedy is a case in point. In the 1855 United States census her age is given as 28 (born 1827); in 1860 it is 30 (born 1830); in 1865 it is 40 (born 1825); in 1870 it is 45 (born 1825); in 1880 it is 50 (born 1830). Her death record in 1888 records her age as 67 (born 1821). The reason for these discrepancies is simple: neither Bridget nor her family members knew exactly how old she was and made a rough guess for the enumerator or registrar. They were not alone in this: as Irish genealogist, John Grenham has observed, hardly anyone born in Ireland before 1900 knew how old they were. For this reason, I have tried to avoid conjecture based on reported – and especially self-reported – ages.

26 $825 in 1888 is equivalent in purchasing power to about $22,300 in 2020; $1,000 in 1888 is equivalent in purchasing power to about $27,000 in 2020.

27 I am indebted to R. Andrew Pierce for this reference, which is from the Petty Sessions Dog Licences Registers, CSPS 2/0787.

28 As Mary Murphy is a fairly common name in County Wexford, I have so far failed to find a death record for Bridget's mother.

29 The house is described in the House Books of the Valuation Office in 1845 as a single-roomed house, measuring thirty-four feet long by sixteen and-a-half feet deep by eleven feet high, and with three 'offices' or outhouses, and a porch. However, it is likely that the house in 1845 was thatched. The Valuation Office books are available online at http://census.nationalarchives.ie/search/vob/home.jsp

30 *New Ross Standard*, 2 May 1896.

31 Death certificate, 1 November 1896. James's age at death is probably a guess. As mentioned above, ages given on official documents in both Ireland and the United States in the nineteenth century are notoriously unreliable because most people had no idea of when they were born. However, I think it might be possible to speculate on the birth order of Bridget and her known siblings, but with the proviso that there are almost certainly unknown siblings, too. James Murphy is probably the eldest, or at least the eldest male because he is the one who 'inherits' the tenancy of the farm at Cloonagh. His reported age at death in 1896 is 85 years, making him born in 1811, but I tend to think his birth year might be around 1814. Nevertheless, the discovery of one of Bridget's siblings born at such an early date raises again Andrew Pierce's question of whether Patrick Barron Snr was the father or brother of Bridget's mother, Mary Barron Murphy. Married to Nicholas Roche in 1835, Catherine Murphy is probably the eldest female, possibly born 1819, on the basis that, if her reported age in census records was correct, she would have had her first child at 13 years. While that is just about possible, it is very unlikely. Ann, Bridget and Margaret are probably next, although their birth order is impossible to determine. Johanna is likely the youngest female but this is based – somewhat precariously – on the fact that she lived until 1904. Edward was, obviously, the youngest and the only sibling to have verifiable records of his birth and death in the same year. In correspondence with me, John Grenham supplied another possible sibling. An Ellen Murphy married Patrick [O'] Keeffe in Salem in 1869, recording her parents as Richard and Mary Murphy. Her death record, also in Salem in 1894, records her parents as Richard Murphy and Mary 'Burne', an obvious phonetic version of Barron. If Ellen was another sibling, she would probably be included in the 'indeterminable birth order' group with Ann, Bridget and Margaret.

32 The land at Cloonagh is still in the ownership of the Shannon family.

33 Lime kilns were essential in rural Ireland in the nineteenth century when burnt lime was used in many ways, from improving the quality of land to whitewashing the walls of houses to disinfect and make them waterproof, and as a medicine for animals.

34 Two houses and several outbuildings are visibly marked on the 1839 six-inch Ordnance Survey maps. The Griffith's Valuation maps indicate the boundary line separating the two holdings runs between the two houses. The Barron house was probably demolished shortly after the last of the family left for the United States. Griffith's Valuation in 1853 does not detail a house on the former Barron holding.

Chapter 2

1 The text of the agreements and minutes of the conference through which they were negotiated can be found in Kennedy, M., Crowe, C., Fanning, R., Keogh, D., and O'Halpin, E., eds (2006). *Documents on Irish Foreign Policy,* vol. V (1937–9). Dublin: Royal Irish Academy, [hereafter DIFP V], pp. 278–86 and online at 'British–Irish tripartite agreement on trade, finance and defence from Text of British–Agreements – 25 April 1938' – *Documents on Irish Foreign Policy.* [online] Difp.ie. Available at: https://www.difp.ie/docs/1938/British-Irish-tripartite-agreement-on-trade-finance-and-defence/2321.htm [Accessed 27 January 2020]. A full account and analysis of the talks can be found in McMahon, D. (1984). *Republicans and Imperialists: Anglo-Irish Relations in the 1930s.* New Haven: Yale University Press.

2 Speaking in Dáil Éireann on 29 May 1935 de Valera explained that 'our territory will never be permitted to be used as a base for attack upon Britain … we are not going … to allow our territory, under any conditions whatever, to be made use of by some foreign power as the basis of attack against Britain'. See Oireachtas.ie. (2019). *Dáil Éireann debate – Wednesday, 29 May 1935.* [online] Available at: https://www.oireachtas.ie/en/debates/debate/dail/1935-05-29/19 [Accessed 6 March 2019].

3 DIFP V, p. 274, de Valera to Roosevelt, 22 April 1938, https://www.difp.ie/docs/1938/British-Irish-negotiations/2316.htm [Accessed 4 March 2019].

4 For example Maier, T. (2003). *The Kennedys: America's Emerald Kings: A Five-Generation History of the Ultimate Irish-Catholic Family.* New York: Basic Books, p. 121. Earlier references include Vieth, J.K. (1975). *Joseph P. Kennedy: Ambassador to the Court of St. James's, 1938–1940* (Doctoral dissertation, The Ohio State University) and Koskoff, D.E. (1974). *Joseph P. Kennedy: A Life and Times.* New Jersey: Prentice-Hall, p. 132.

5 See *Irish Times*, 10 December 1937.

6 See Kennedy, M. (1996). *Ireland and the League of Nations, 1919–1946: International Relations, Diplomacy and Politics.* Dublin: Irish Academic Press, pp. 234–7.

7 For example, during the state banquet in June 1938, following his being awarded an honorary doctorate by the National University of Ireland, Kennedy eulogised 'This town of Dublin, this land of Ireland is sacred soil to me. From this land my ancestors came to the New World.' *Offaly Independent,* 16 June 1938.

8 Kennedy, J.P. (2001). *Hostage to Fortune: The Letters of Joseph P. Kennedy.* New York: Viking Press, p 127 and p. 134. The quoted text is on p. 134.

9 Cudahy to Hull, 14 January 1938, transcript published in Raymond, R.J. (1984). 'John Cudahy, Eamon de Valera, and the Anglo-Irish Negotiations in 1938: The Secret Dispatches to Washington.' *The International History Review, 6*(2), p. 239.

10 Cudahy to Hull, 14 January 1938 in Raymond, 'John Cudahy, Eamon de Valera, and the Anglo-Irish Negotiations in 1938,' p. 239.

11 McMahon, *Republicans and Imperialists: Anglo-Irish Relations in the 1930s*, p. 238.

12 The land annuities were payments made by Ireland to Britain to repay British loans made to Irish farmers to buy out their holdings via a series of late nineteenth-century land Acts passed by Westminster. De Valera had withheld their payment to Britain since 1932.

13 DIFP V, p. 206, Walshe to de Valera, 22 January 1938, https://www.difp.ie/docs/1938/ Northern-Ireland/2279.htm [Accessed 6 March 2019].

14 DIFP V, p. 215, Walshe to de Valera, 25 January 1938, https://www.difp.ie/viewdoc. asp?DocID=2283 [Accessed 6 March 2019].

15 Cudahy to Roosevelt, 22 January 1938, transcribed in Raymond, 'John Cudahy, Eamon de Valera, and the Anglo-Irish Negotiations in 1938,' p. 245.

16 DIFP V, p. 206, Walshe to de Valera, 22 January 1938, https://www.difp.ie/docs/1938/ Northern-Ireland/2279.htm [Accessed 7 March 2019].

17 DIFP V, p. 213, de Valera to Roosevelt, 25 January 1938, https://www.difp.ie/viewdoc. asp?DocID=2282 [Accessed 8 March 2019].

18 Cudahy to Hull, 16 March 1938, transcribed in Raymond, 'John Cudahy, Eamon de Valera, and the Anglo-Irish Negotiations in 1938,' p. 253.

19 University College Dublin Archives, Papers of Eamon de Valera, P150/2836, Roosevelt to de Valera, 22 February 1938.

20 *Irish Times*, 2 March 1938.

21 Ibid.

22 Ibid.

23 *Irish Times*, 4 March 1938.

24 *Irish Times*, 9 March 1938.

25 Cudahy to Hull, 16 March 1938, transcribed in Raymond, 'John Cudahy, Eamon de Valera, and the Anglo-Irish Negotiations in 1938,' p. 251.

26 DIFP V, p. 260, Dulanty to Walshe, 15 March 1938, https://www.difp.ie/viewdoc. asp?DocID=2301. All quotes in this paragraph are from this source [Accessed 8 March 2019].

27 Bowman, J. (1982). *De Valera and the Ulster Question, 1917–1973*. Oxford: University Press, p. 169.

28 Cudahy to Hull, 19 March 1938, transcribed in Raymond, 'John Cudahy, Eamon de Valera, and the Anglo-Irish Negotiations in 1938,' p. 254.

29 The National Archives, Kew London (TNA), CAB 23/93, Cabinet Conclusions 19(38), 13 April 1938. http://filestore.nationalarchives.gov.uk/pdfs/large/cab-23-93.pdf [Accessed 9 March 2019].

30 See the sources quoted in endnote 4 above.

31 Kennedy, M. (2000). *Division and Consensus: The Politics of Cross-border Relations in Ireland, 1925–1969*. Dublin: Institute of Public Administration, p. 68.

32 Self, R., ed. (2004). *The Neville Chamberlain Diary Letters. Volume 4: The Downing Street Years, 1934–40*. Aldershot: Ashgate, p. 316.

33 McMahon and Bowman agree that Kennedy's intervention achieved little or nothing. See McMahon, *Republicans and Imperialists: Anglo-Irish Relations in the 1930s*, pp 281–2 and Bowman, *De Valera and the Ulster Question*, p. 168.

34 De Valera was Chancellor of the NUI from 1921 until his death in 1975.

35 DIFP V, p. 274, de Valera to Roosevelt, 22 April 1938, https://www.difp.ie/docs/1938/ British-Irish-negotiations/2316.htm [Accessed 9 March 2019].

36 DIFP V, p. 301, de Valera to MacDonald, 30 May 1938, https://www.difp.ie/docs/1938/ Conclusion-of-British-Irish-negotiations/2335.htm [Accessed 9 March 2019].

37   See Vieth, *Joseph P. Kennedy: Ambassador to the Court of St. James's*, pp. 109–10.
38   See Bowman, *De Valera and the Ulster Question*, p. 169.
39   *Irish Press*, 5 July 1938.
40   DIFP V, p. 275, https://www.difp.ie/docs/1938/Conclusion-of-British-Irish-negotiations/2317.htm [Accessed 9 March 2019].
41   *Sunday Independent*, 3 June 1984.
42   Ibid.
43   Quoted by Fanning in *Sunday Independent*, 3 June 1984.
44   *Irish Independent*, 23 June 1938.
45   McMahon, *Republicans and Imperialists: Anglo-Irish Relations in the 1930s*, p. 281.
46   Vieth, *Joseph P. Kennedy: Ambassador to the Court of St. James's*, pp. 109–10.
47   Ibid.
48   Nasaw, D. (2012). *The Patriarch: The Remarkable Life and Turbulent Times of Joseph P. Kennedy*. New York: Penguin.
49   Kennedy, J.P. *Hostage to Fortune*, p. 317.

Chapter 3

1   Chafe, W.H. (2003). *The Unfinished Journey: America Since World War II*. Oxford University Press, USA, p. 181.
2   Axelrod, A. (2015). *Lost Destiny: Joe Kennedy Jr. and the Doomed WWII Mission to Save London*. New York: Macmillan, pp. 65–6.
3   Axelrod. *Lost Destiny*, p. 66.
4   Joseph Kennedy bought 30,000 copies of the book and stored them in Hyannis Port. See Garside, A. (2005). *Camelot at Dawn: Jacqueline and John Kennedy in Georgetown, May 1954*. Baltimore: JHU Press, p. 46.
5   Davis, J.H. (1993). *The Kennedys: Dynasty and Disaster*. New York: SP Books, p. 145.
6   Chafe. *Unfinished Journey*, p. 182.
7   Pietrusza, D. (2008). *1960: LBJ Vs. JFK Vs. Nixon: the Epic Campaign that Forged Three Presidencies*. New York: Union Square Press, p. 4.
8   Chafe, W.H. (2009). *Private Lives/Public Consequences: Personality and Politics in Modern America*. Cambridge: Harvard University Press, pp. 113–14.
9   Weinstein, M.C. (2010). 'The political tipping point: how the Kennedy family defeated the Lodges in the 1952 United States senate election in Massachusetts'. *Concord Review* [pp. 245–83], p. 250.
10 Meagher, M. and Gragg, L.D. (2011). *John F. Kennedy: A Biography*. Santa Barbara: ABC-CLIO, p. 27. At this time, O'Neill supported rival candidate Mike Neville.
11 Busby, R. (2009). *Marketing the Populist Politician*. Basingstoke: Palgrave Macmillan, p. 58.
12 White, M. (2013). *Kennedy: A Cultural History of an American Icon*. London: A&C Black, p. 14.
13 Saxe, R. (2007). *Settling Down: World War II Veterans' Challenge to the Postwar Consensus*. New York: Springer, p. 62.

14 Saxe. *Settling Down*, p. 64.

15 Matthews, C. (1997). *Kennedy & Nixon: The Rivalry that Shaped Postwar America*. London: Simon and Schuster, p. 30.

16 Pietrusza. *1960*, p. 9.

17 Nasaw, D. (2013). *The Patriarch: The Remarkable Life and Turbulent Times of Joseph P. Kennedy*. Apple Books, pp. 2195–6.

18 Saxe. *Settling Down*, p. 64.

19 Dallek, R. (2003). *An Unfinished Life: John F. Kennedy, 1917–1963*. New York: Hachette, pp. 95–8.

20 Cimpean, R.L. (2014). *The JFK Image: Profiles in Docudrama*. Lanham: Rowman & Littlefield, p. 77. They were sent by post and Tip O'Neill recalls it was the first time such literature was sent by first class postage as other candidates did not have the resources.

21 Saxe. *Settling Down*, p. 66.

22 In 1946 the salary for a member of Congress was $10,000. The salary for a senator in 1952, the year JFK entered the chamber, was $12,500. Between 1909 and 1948, the United States President's salary was $75,000 while from 1949 to 1969 it was $100,000.

23 Matthews. *Kennedy & Nixon*, p. 11.

24 Whalen, T.J. (2014). *JFK and His Enemies: A Portrait of Power*. Lanham: Rowman & Littlefield, p. 17.

25 Saxe. *Settling Down*, p. 62.

26 Saxe. *Settling Down*, pp. 61–2.

27 Nasaw. *Patriarch*, pp. 2218–19.

28 Nasaw. *Patriarch*, pp. 2221.

29 Whalen. *JFK and His Enemies*, p. 17.

30 Weinstein. 'The political tipping point', p. 250.

31 Shaw, J. (2013). *JFK in the Senate: Pathway to the Presidency*. Basingstoke: Macmillan, p. 17. Tip O'Neill recalled that the amount Joe Kennedy spent was 'six times what I spent in a very tough congressional campaign ... six years later'. Pietrusza. *1960*, p. 8.

32 Nelson, G. (2017). *John William McCormack: A Political Biography*. New York: Bloomsbury, p. 356.

33 Nelson. *John William McCormack*, p. 356.

34 Matthews. *Kennedy & Nixon*, p. 29.

35 Marlin, G.J. (2004). *The American Catholic Voter: 200 Years of Political Impact*. South Bend: St Augustine Press Inc., p. 241.

36 Hess, S. (2015). *America's Political Dynasties: From Adams to Clinton*. Washington D.C.: Brookings Institution Press. p. 470.

37 Pietrusza. *1960*, p. 10.

38 Dallek. *Unfinished Life*, p. 174.

39 Dallek. *Unfinished Life*, p. 171. Weinstein. 'The political tipping point', p. 265.

40 Dallek. *Unfinished Life*, pp. 173–4.

41 Pietrusza. *1960*, p. 11.

42 O'Brien, M. (2010). *Rethinking Kennedy*. Chicago: Ivan R. Dee, p. 73. Weinstein, 'The political tipping point', p. 256.

43   Pietrusza. *1960*, p. 11.
44   Weinstein. 'The political tipping point', p. 251.
45   Weinstein. 'The political tipping point', p. 252.
46   Ibid.
47   Weinstein. 'The political tipping point', p. 253.
48   Weinstein. 'The political tipping point', pgs. 255, 266.
49   Dallek. *Unfinished Life*, p. 171.
50   Hatch, A. (1973). *The Lodges of Massachusetts*. New York: Hawthorn Books, p. 258. Whalen, T.J. (2000). *Kennedy Versus Lodge*. Boston: Northeastern University Press, p. 163.
51   Whalen. *JFK and His Enemies*, p. 69.
52   Dallek. *Unfinished Life*, p. 173.
53   Dallek. *Unfinished Life*, p. 171.
54   Hatch. *Lodges of Massachusetts*, p. 258.
55   Whalen. *JFK and His Enemies*, p. 69.
56   Weinstein. 'The political tipping point', p. 254.
57   Tye, L. (2016). *Bobby Kennedy: The Making of a Liberal Icon*. New York: Random House, p. 92.
58   Dallek. *Unfinished Life*, p. 174.
59   Joseph Kennedy had been eager to retain Jack's seat for one of his other sons; 'look', he said, 'I spent a lot of money for that senate seat. It belongs in the family.' As JFK had already appointed Bobby as United States attorney-general, that ambition was transferred to the only remaining son, Teddy, despite his inexperience. Once elected President, JFK prevailed upon Massachusetts's Democratic Governor Foster Furcolo to appoint Benjamin Smith, a close friend of the Kennedys, to fill the vacated seat 'in the interest of promoting party unity'. The real objective, however, was to keep the senate seat warm for two years until Teddy reached the minimum threshold for a senator of 30 years-of-age. The *New York Times* editorialised that the manner of his elevation was 'demeaning to the dignity of the Senate and the democratic process'. Hilty, J. (2000). *Robert Kennedy: Brother Protector*. Philadelphia: Temple University Press, p. 266. Corrigan, M. (2008). *American Royalty: The Bush and Clinton Families and the Danger to the American Presidency*. Basingstoke: Palgrave, p. 50.
60   Chafe. *Unfinished Journey*, p. 178.
61   Ibid.
62   See Hohenberg, J. (1997). *The Pulitzer diaries: Inside America's greatest prize*. New York: Syracuse University Press, pp. 47–58.
63   Chafe. *Unfinished Journey*, p. 182.
64   Parmet, H.S. (1983). *Jack: The Struggles of John F. Kennedy*. New York: Doubleday Books, p. 323.
65   Savage, S.J. (2015). *The Senator from New England: The Rise of JFK*. Albany: SUNY Press, p. 100.
66   Ibid.
67   Casey, S. (2009). *The Making of a Catholic President: Kennedy vs. Nixon 1960*. Oxford: Oxford University Press, p. 4.

68 Casey. *Making of a Catholic President*, p. 5.

69 Nasaw. *Patriarch*, p. 2618.

70 Thomas, G.S. (2011). *A New World to be Won: John Kennedy, Richard Nixon, and the Tumultuous Year of 1960*. Santa Barbara: ABC-CLIO, pp. 7–8.

71 Nasaw. *Patriarch*, pp. 2624–5.

72 Torrey, E.F. (2014). *American Psychosis: How the Federal Government Destroyed the Mental Illness Treatment System*. Oxford: Oxford University Press, p. 35.

73 Nasaw. *Patriarch*, p. 2626.

74 Nasaw. *Patriarch*, pp. 2646–7.

75 Boller, P.F. (2004). *Presidential Campaigns: From George Washington to George W. Bush*. Oxford: Oxford University Press, p. 301; Sorensen, T.C. (1999). *Kennedy*. Old Saybrook: William S. Konecky Associates, p. 119.

76 Nasaw. *Patriarch*, p. 2614.

77 Nasaw. *Patriarch*, pp. 2623–4.

78 Humphrey, H.H. (1991). *The Education of a Public Man: My Life and Politics*. Minneapolis: University of Minnesota Press, p. 151.

79 Humphrey. *Education of a Public Man*, pp. 151–2.

80 Humphrey. *Education of a Public Man*, pp. 151.

81 Kallina, E.F. (2010). *Kennedy v. Nixon: The presidential election of 1960*. Gainesville: University Press of Florida, p. 59.

82 Dallek. *Unfinished Life*, p. 251.

83 Kallina. *Kennedy v. Nixon*, p. 63.

84 Friedenberg, R.V. (2002). *Notable Speeches in Contemporary Presidential Campaigns*. Westport: Greenwood Publishing Group, p. 49.

85 Alsop, J. (1960). 'The Question of Bigotry', *The New Republic*, 25 April 1960, p. 5.

86 Kallina. *Kennedy v. Nixon*, p. 65. See Corbin, D. (2015). 'John F. Kennedy Plays the "Religious Card": Another Look at the 1960 West Virginia Primary.' *West Virginia History* 9, no. 2 (Fall 2015): 1–35. Available at https://textbooks.lib.wvu.edu/wvhistory/files/html/19_wv_history_reader_corbin_kennedy/

87 Pietrusza. *1960*, p. 124.

88 Rorabaugh, W. (2009). *The Real Making of the President: Kennedy, Nixon and the 1960 Election*. Lawrence: University Press of Kansas, p. 55.

89 Rorabaugh. *Real Making of the President*, p. 55.

90 Ibid.

91 Pietrusza. *1960*, p. 125.

92 A 'favourite son' is a politician whose electoral appeal derives from their native state or region rather than their political views.

93 Hodgson, G. (2015). *JFK and LBJ: The Last Two Great Presidents*. New Haven: Yale University Press, p. 88.

94 Kallina. *Kennedy v. Nixon*, p. 72. The claims regarding JFK's medical condition, while accurate, were vigorously refuted by the Kennedys and medical specialists in their employment.

95 Shesol, J. (1998). *Mutual Contempt: Lyndon Johnson, Robert Kennedy, and the Feud that Defined a Decade*. New York: WW Norton & Company, p. 57.

96   Donaldson, G.A. (2007). *The First Modern Campaign: Kennedy, Nixon, and the Election of 1960*. Lanham: Rowman & Littlefield Publishers, p. 81.

97   Hess, S. (1995). *Presidents & the Presidency: Essays by Stephen Hess*. Washington D.C.: Brookings Institution Press, p. 81. Hess. *America's Political Dynasties*, p. 484.

98   Black, C. (2008). *Richard Milhous Nixon : The Invincible Quest*. London: Quercus, p. 396, p. 408.

99   So much was made of Kennedy's youth that it was sometimes overlooked that Nixon was only three years his senior and if victorious would be the second youngest candidate ever elected to the presidency, just a few weeks older than Ulysses Grant in 1869.

100   Matthews. *Kennedy & Nixon*, p. 125.

101   See, for example, 'Nixon's Experience?', 1960 Kennedy one-minute commercial. Available at http://www.livingroomcandidate.org/commercials/1960/nixons-experience.

102   Casey. *Catholic President*, p. 177.

103   See Fuchs, Lawrence H. 'Election of 1928' in Hansen, W.P., Israel, F.L. and Schlesinger, A. (1986). *History of American Presidential Elections, 1789–1968*. New York: Chelsea House Publishers, pp. 2585–609 and Moore, E.A. (1956). *A Catholic Runs for President: The Campaign of 1928*. New York: Ronald Press Company.

104   'We can win, says Senator Kennedy,' *Irish Independent*, 16 September 1960, p. 8.

105   *New York Times*, 7 September 1960, p. 1.

106   Black, *Richard Milhous Nixon*, p. 404.

107   Jfklibrary.org. (2020). 'Address to the Greater Houston Ministerial Association.' *JFK Library*. [online] Available at: https://www.jfklibrary.org/learn/about-jfk/historic-speeches/address-to-the-greater-houston-ministerial-association [Accessed 7 February 2020]. Also available in Wilson, J.F. (2018). *Church and State in American History: Key Documents, Decisions, and Commentary from the Past Three Centuries*. Philadelphia: Routledge, pp. 190–1.

108   White, T.H. (1961). *The Making of the President, 1960*. New York: Atheneum Publishers, p. 393.

109   Casey. *Catholic President*, p. 185.

110   This was done in a manner similar to the way that, five decades later, Barack Obama inspired white people to demonstrate their opposition to racism by voting for his candidacy.

111   Thomas. *A New World to be Won*, p. 173.

112   Quoted in Donaldson. *The First Modern Campaign*, pp. 113–14.

113   Lehrer, J. (2012). *Tension City : Inside the Presidential Debates*. New York: Random House, pp. 21–2.

114   In general, those who watched the debate in studio or, who, like Lyndon Johnson, listened to the debate on radio, thought that Nixon had won. Thomas. *A New World to be Won*, p. 212; Lehrer, J. *Tension City*, p. 22.

115   Lehrer, J. *Tension City*, pp. 21–2.

116   Nixon, R. (2013). *Six Crises*. New York: Simon and Schuster, p. 422.

117   Nixon, R. (2013). *RN: The Memoirs of Richard Nixon*. New York: Gossett and Dunlap, p. 221. No doubt influenced by the experience in 1960, LBJ avoided a television debate

with Barry Goldwater in 1964 and Nixon refused to participate in television debates with Hubert Humphrey in 1968 and George McGovern 1972. It was only in 1976, when Jimmy Carter challenged incumbent Gerald Ford that presidential television debates returned and have remained a feature since then.

118 White. *The Making of the President*, p. 323.
119 Donaldson. *The First Modern Campaign*, p. 125.
120 As the first federal civil rights legislation passed by Congress since the Civil Rights Act of 1875, much was initially expected from the 1957 Act. However, the amendment inserted a provision by which defendants charged with denying blacks their right to vote would be entitled to a trial by jury. Because juries in the south were invariably white in composition (jury service was linked to voting rights), and therefore unlikely to convict, this provision would prevent the Act from meeting its stated objectives of ending the disenfranchisement of African Americans. Consequently, civil rights activists and organisations strongly opposed the jury trial amendment, as did the Eisenhower administration, including Vice President Nixon.
121 Donaldson. *The First Modern Campaign*, p. 151.
122 Pietrusza. *1960*, p. 294.
123 Thomas, E. (2002). *Robert Kennedy: His life*. New York: Simon and Schuster, p. 100; Carty, T. (2004). *A Catholic in the White House?: Religion, Politics, and John F. Kennedy's Presidential Campaign*. New York: Palgrave, p. 91.
124 Ibid.
125 Casey. *Catholic President*, p. 194.
126 Smith, R.C. (2013). *John F. Kennedy, Barack Obama, and the Politics of Ethnic Incorporation and Avoidance*. Albany: SUNY Press, p. 132.
127 Savage, S.J. (2012). *JFK, LBJ, and the Democratic Party*. Albany: SUNY Press, p. 84.
128 As Jamieson notes, 'this tightly targeted message distribution ensured that those unsympathetic to the gesture would be un-reminded of it'. Jamieson, K.H. (1996). *Packaging the Presidency: A History and Criticism of Presidential Campaign Advertising*. Oxford: Oxford University Press, p. 144.
129 Rorabaugh. *Real Making of the President*, p. 170.
130 Pietrusza. *1960*, p. 298.
131 Matthews. *Kennedy & Nixon*, p. 173.
132 As of 2020, it has happened only once more, in 1976.
133 Nixon. *Six Crises*, p. 413.
134 Whalen. *JFK and His Enemies*, p. 132.
135 Kallina. *Kennedy v. Nixon*, p. 95.
136 Black, *Richard Milhous Nixon*, p. 397.
137 Letter dated 31 August 1957, King to Nixon. Luther, M., Carson, C., Carson, S., Clay, A., Shadron, V., Taylor, K.W. and Luther, M. (2000). *The Papers of Martin Luther King, Jr.* Volume 4, Symbol of the movement, January 1957–December 1958. Berkeley: University of California Press, p. 263.
138 Aitken, J. (2015). *Nixon: A life*. New York: Simon and Schuster, p. 331.
139 'Mrs. Kennedy Notes Father–Son Difference', *New York Times*, 1 October 1960.

140   Ted Sorensen quoted in Nasaw. *Patriarch*, p. 2671.

141   Donaldson, G.A. (2017). *The Making of Modern America: the Nation from 1945 to the Present*. Lanham: Rowman & Littlefield, p. 130.

142   Adler, B., ed. (1967). *The Washington Wits*. New York: Macmillan, p. 109. Boller. *Presidential Campaigns*, p. 301.

Chapter 4

1   Shesol, J. (1997). *Mutual Contempt: Lyndon Johnson, Robert Kennedy, and the Feud that Defined a Decade*. New York: WW Norton & Company, p. 68.

2   Its first draft written by Senator Strom Thurmond, Sr, of South Carolina and its final by Russell, the Southern Manifesto – or 'Declaration of Constitutional Principles' – was a protest document, signed by nineteen Senators and eighty-two Representatives from former Confederate states and entered into the Congressional Record. With a possible 1960 presidential run in mind, Senator Lyndon B. Johnson did not sign the document, which characterised the Supreme Court's 1954 *Brown* decision against separate school facilities for black and white children as a 'clear abuse of judicial power' because of an 'encroachment on the rights reserved to the States and to the people'. The then-senior senator from Georgia, Walter F. George, introduced the Southern Manifesto in the Senate. (Russell became his state's senior senator upon George's death, in office, in 1957.)

3   Russell's encyclopaedic parliamentary knowledge caused Lyndon Johnson, when Leader of the Senate, to have the Georgian occupy the seat next to him, so as to be able to consult him on rules and precedents.

4   During debate in the Senate on 16 March 1964, Russell opined that the bill would precipitate the 'amalgamation and mongrelisation' of 'both' the races, white and black, currently living under the South's 'separate but equal system'. On the day of – but before – the bill's passage, Russell, speaking from the Senate floor, characterised cloture as 'gag rule' and urged his fellow senators to 'reject this legislation that will result in vast changes … in our social order'. *New York Times*, 17 March 1964; Purdum, T.S. (2014). *An Idea Whose Time Has Come: Two Presidents, Two Parties, and the Battle for the Civil Rights Act of 1964*. New York: Henry Holt and Company, p. 103.

5   Purdum. *An Idea Whose Time Has Come* p. 7. While Johnson's remarks elicited a 'storm of applause' from most of those present, 'Southern members [of Congress] like Russell sat silently' at that time. Walker, T. (1968). *JFK and LBJ: The Influence of Personality upon Politics*. New York: William Morrow, p. 169.

6   Caro, R.A. (2012). *The Years of Lyndon Johnson: The Passage of Power* (vol. 4). New York: Random House, p. 465.

7   Written remark, authored by Johnson in 1959; quoted in Fite, G.C. (1991). *Richard B. Russell, Jr., Senator from Georgia*. Chapel Hill: University of North Carolina Press, p. 375. In response to Russell's reluctance to join the Warren Commission, Johnson insisted, '[Y]ou're going to serve'; however, he sweetened the command by continuing, 'No one has ever been more to me than you have, Dick – except my mother.' Caro. *The Years of Lyndon Johnson: The Passage of Power*, p. 449.

8 *New York Times*, 24 May 1961; John F. Kennedy Presidential Library and Museum. Letter to John F. Kennedy from Richard B. Russell, Jr, 23 May 1961. Presidential Papers, President's Office Files, Special Correspondence, Russell, Richard B., April 1961–August 1962. In his written invitation to Russell, Kennedy acknowledged the Georgian's confederate patrimony; and Russell's response recalled his 'conversations … as a boy' with family members who had seen combat service in the Civil War.

9 Russell chaired the committees on Immigration (75th–79th Congresses), Manufactures (79th) and Appropriations (91st). Two of the his most consequential subcommittee chairmanships were Defence Appropriations and Agricultural Appropriations. Russell was President pro tempore of the Senate throughout the 91st Congress, which began on 3 January 1969. He continued in the role until his death, eighteen days into the subsequent Congress.

10 After the August 2018 death of Republican Senator John S. McCain (Arizona), the Minority Leader, Democrat Charles E. Schumer (New York), called for renaming the Russell Building in McCain's honour. One effect of the proposal was renewed attention on Russell's civil rights stance.

11 Klinkner, P.A. and Smith, R.M. (2002). *The Unsteady March: The Rise and Decline of Racial Equality in America*. Chicago: University of Chicago Press, p. 133. Notwithstanding his avoidance of inciteful speech, Russell could be unequivocal in expression. Responding to Eugene Talmadge's challenge for his Senate seat, Russell wrote to Talmadge on 9 December 1936, 'I am willing to go as far and make as great a sacrifice to preserve and insure white supremacy in the social, economic, and political life of our state as any man who lives within her borders'. Richard B. Russell Memorial Library, University of Georgia, Letter from Russell to Talmadge, 9 December 1936, Russell Papers, Series IV, Box B24.

12 Russell, S. (2011). *Richard Brevard Russell, Jr: A Life of Consequence*. Macon: Mercer University Press, pp. 229–30.

13 Russell, *Richard Brevard Russell, Jr.*, p. 230.

14 Mailer, N. (2014). 'Superman Comes to the Supermarket,' in *Mind of an Outlaw: Selected Essays*. New York, Random House, pp. 110–12.

15 Mailer. 'Superman Comes to the Supermarket,' in *Mind of an Outlaw*, p. 115, p. 119.

16 Jim Crow was the name of the formal, codified system of racial apartheid that operated primarily, but not exclusively in southern and border states, between 1877 and 1965. It mandated segregation in almost every aspect of daily life.

17 In Philadelphia in 1948, Russell lost to Harry S. Truman by 263 votes to 947.5. In Chicago in 1952, he competed through the third round in what became, in essence, a three-person race. Adlai Stevenson, the eventual winner, gained 617.5 third-round votes to Estes Kefauver's 275.5 and Russell's 261.

18 Fite. *Richard B. Russell, Jr., Senator from Georgia*, pp. 377–8. One wonders if Russell's desire not to highlight Kennedy's faith related to his having witnessed the politicisation of anti-Catholicism in Georgia during the 1910s and 1920s. His debut as a 23-year-old representative in his state's General Assembly in 1921 coincided with a revival of the Ku Klux Klan, which abetted Georgia politician Tom Watson's robust advocacy for a

boycott of Catholic businesses across the state. A more personal reason may have been regret that, in 1938, he had terminated his engagement to Patricia ('Pat') Collins, a Catholic Georgian he first met at a Washington function the prior year. In her biography of the senator, his niece, Sally Russell, notes that his mother invited him to contemplate whether he loved Pat 'enough to accept' that her Catholicism might mean his 'never be[ing] elected again to a state wide office in Georgia'. Russell, *Richard Brevard Russell, Jr.*, p. 152.

19   Caro, R.A. (2002). *Master of the Senate* (vol. 3). New York: Borzoi, p. 210.
20   Donaldson, G.A. (2007). *The First Modern Campaign: Kennedy, Nixon, and the Election of 1960*. Lanham: Rowman & Littlefield, p. 137.
21   Donaldson. *The First Modern Campaign*, p. 137.
22   Fite. *Richard B. Russell, Jr., Senator from Georgia*, p. 374. The speaker, Senator Joseph Clark (Pennsylvania), was a leading Democratic liberal.
23   Kennedy was aware of challenges in Russell's home state of Georgia. In response to the 2 January 1960 announcement of his candidacy, he had received a 'Dear Jack' letter from James H. Gray, the state's Democratic Party chair and the editor and publisher of the *Albany Herald* newspaper in Albany, southwest Georgia. Gray's message was stark: '[T]he only issue here, really, is the racial one.' John F. Kennedy Presidential Library and Museum. Papers of John F. Kennedy, Pre-Presidential Papers, Presidential Campaign Files, 1960, Speeches and the Press, Press Secretary's State Files, 1958–60, Georgia. On 10 October 1960, breaking with a quarter-century and better of precedent, Kennedy as the Democratic presidential nominee pressed the flesh in Georgia via two airport rallies, in Columbus and LaGrange, as well as a visit to Franklin D. Roosevelt's Little White House in Warm Springs. The next day, at short notice, Johnson made a whistle-stop speech at Atlanta's Terminal Station.
24   Novotny, P. (2004). 'John F. Kennedy, the 1960 Election, and Georgia's Unpledged Electors in the Electoral College.' *The Georgia Historical Quarterly*, 88(3), pp. 386–7.
25   Novotny, 'John F. Kennedy, the 1960 Election, and Georgia's Unpledged Electors in the Electoral College,' p. 396.
26   Mailer. 'Superman Comes to the Supermarket,' in *Mind of an Outlaw*, p. 124. On 25 September 1957, on orders from President Eisenhower, United States Army soldiers escorted six female and three male African American students, the 'Little Rock Nine', into Central High School in Little Rock, capital city of Arkansas, an event described on the 7 October 1957 cover of *Time* magazine as 'Paratroopers at Little Rock'.
27   Fite. *Richard B. Russell, Jr., Senator from Georgia*, p. 381.
28   A product of Boys' High, Atlanta's most prestigious public school, Rusk had amassed distinctions, including a Rhodes scholarship and the Legion of Merit for infantry service in the Second World War. At the time of Kennedy's coming to power, he was president of the philanthropic Rockefeller Foundation, but, during the early 1950s, he had served as Assistant Secretary of State for Far Eastern Affairs, helping advance, under President Truman, United States intervention in the Korean conflict. Conscious that the Cold War could become hot again, Russell voiced concern to Kennedy over Rusk's decision-making capabilities, respecting combat or potential combat. When chairing a

senate joint-committee into Truman's controversial 1951 relief of Douglas McArthur, commander of forces in Korea, Russell gained awareness that Rusk had advised Truman to fire the popular general.

29 Dean Rusk, Interview with Karen Kelly, Richard B. Russell, Jr, Oral History Project (Athens: University of Georgia), 15 August 1971.

30 Rusk, D, (1990). *As I Saw It*, New York: Norton, p. 227.

31 ExComm was short for 'the Executive Committee of the National Security Council'.

32 Rusk, *As I Saw It*, p. 234.

33 By contrast with their public reticence over Kennedy's decision on the Cuban missiles, Russell and Fulbright 'blasted' the Johnson administration 'from the Senate floor for sending [three C-130 transport] planes to the Congo' in late 1967 'to help that government quell a rebellion of white mercenaries'. Rusk, *As I Saw It*, p. 543.

34 Under pressure because of the Soviet Union's 30 October 1961 detonation of the Tsar Bomba, a hydrogen bomb that remains the most powerful nuclear weapon ever exploded, Kennedy had reluctantly resumed atmospheric testing on 25 April 1962.

35 Fite. *Richard B. Russell, Jr., Senator from Georgia*, p. 400.

36 Once the July 1954 Geneva conference divided Vietnam along the seventeenth parallel, Russell remained opposed to United States military support, which would now be directed to the South Vietnamese, the French having left. Despite his uncompromising stance on US military superiority, Russell was no interventionist. When Kennedy and Khrushchev discussed Vietnam's landlocked western neighbour Laos, during their 4 June 1961 summit in Vienna, the American president was mindful of Russell's opposition to an extension into the military sphere of extant United States support for the Royal Lao government. Kennedy and Johnson had addressed Laos with key congressional leaders on 27 April 1961 and, in contrast to Johnson's view, Russell had opined, 'We should get our people out and write the country off.' Gibbons, W.C. (1988). *The US Government and the Vietnam War: Executive and Legislative Roles and Relationships, Part II*. New Jersey: Princeton University Press, p. 29.

37 McKnight, G.D. (2005). *Breach of Trust: How the Warren Commission Failed the Nation and Why*. Lawrence: University Press of Kansas, p. 45. As a Commission member, Russell was sceptical of the FBI's single-assassin and no-conspiracy theories; furthermore, according to McKnight, he was the sole member 'who actively dug in his heels' against the proposition that 'Kennedy and [Texas Governor] Connally had been hit by the same non-fatal bullet' (p. 283). Russell's investment in opposing the 1964 Civil Rights Bill caused him to miss many Commission hearings. McKnight argues that had Russell been more present, 'he could have had a significant – perhaps decisive – impact on the outcome' of the assassination inquiry (p. 201).

38 Recognising Georgia's potential to become a world leader in egg and (especially) broiler-production, Russell secured funds for the establishment, in 1962, of a major US Department of Agriculture poultry-research laboratory in Athens, Georgia, now the leading such facility in the United States of America.

39 For a broadly contemporary accounting of Kennedy's production-management efforts, especially anent the grain sector, see Hadwiger, D.F. and Talbot, R.B. (1965). *Pressures*

and Protests – The Kennedy Farm Program and the Wheat Referendum of 1963. San Francisco: Chandler.

40 While the phrase, 'Lion of the Senate', is an established formulation, Lyndon Johnson identified Russell with another creature. His political mentor was among the individuals in Johnson's mind when, shortly after the inauguration, he opined that '[o]ne of Kennedy's troubles' was that as regards Congress the new President 'had the minnows but not the whales'. Conley. R. *The Presidency, Congress, and Divided Government: A Postwar Assessment.* College Station: Texas A & M University Press, p. 169.

41 Charles Campbell, Interview with Bob Short, 'Reflections on Georgia Politics' (Athens, GA) 14 May 2009.

Chapter 5

1 An earlier version of this essay was presented at the Kennedy Summer School, New Ross, Co. Wexford on 7 September 2012.

2 Lubin, D.M. (2003). *Shooting Kennedy: JFK and the Culture of Images.* Berkeley: University of California Press, p. 287.

3 Dallek, R. (2003). *An Unfinished Life: John F. Kennedy, 1917–1963.* Boston: Little, Brown, & Co., p. 625.

4 Interview in the documentary film *John F. Kennedy in the Island of Dreams* (Byrne, 1993, Irl.).

5 Schlesinger, A.M. (2002). *A Thousand Days: John F. Kennedy in the White House.* Boston: Mariner Books, p. 885.

6 John F. Kennedy Presidential Library and Museum (JFKPLM), Central Subject Files TR5.

7 Lee, J.J., 1989. *Ireland 1912–1985: Politics and Society.* Cambridge: Cambridge University Press, p. 340.

8 JFKPLM, 'Why are we Going to Europe?', memo by McGeorge Bundy, dated 22 May 1963, Central Subject Files TR56, *Europe Proposed Trip* 1963.

9 The parliamentarians present were not just members of the Dáil, but also members of the Seanad, in a specially convened joint sitting of the Houses of the Oireachtas to mark Kennedy's visit.

10 Speech by President Kennedy, Dáil Éireann, Dublin, Ireland, 28 June 1963.

11 Speech by President Kennedy, Dáil Éireann.

12 JFKPLM, 'Note to Congressman John E. Fogarty,' Pre-presidential papers, *Irish Campaign Files,* 1952.

13 Carroll, J. R. (2003). *One of Ourselves: John Fitzgerald Kennedy in Ireland.* Images from the Past, pp. 58–9.

14 Despite the commentary written by Barry Baker that suggests otherwise, both John F. Kennedy and Eamon de Valera were born in the United States.

15 See O'Brien, H. (2004). *The Real Ireland.* Manchester: Manchester University Press, pp. 86–9.

16 The sense of irony may stem from Robert Vaughn's reading of the script. The actor's usual, slightly askance style lends an air of a raised eyebrow where perhaps the scriptwriter might not have intended this.

17 This is an extensively debated and heavily researched area that includes contributions from several very active advocacy groups continually highlighting issues and struggles in contemporary and historical Ireland.

18 The evidence for this is an anecdotal source at the John F. Kennedy Presidential Library and Museum, Boston, MA. James Robert Carroll records that the President insisted on viewing the European footage at home in Hyannisport shortly after his return. See Carroll, *One of Ourselves*, pp. 178–9.

19 See O'Brien, *The Real Ireland*, p. 51.

Chapter 6

1 Carroll, J.R. (2003). *One of Ourselves: John Fitzgerald Kennedy in Ireland*. Vermont: Images from the Past, p. 172.

2 On his return to the United States, President Kennedy repeatedly showed films of his Irish trip to family and friends. Bobby Kennedy's assessment was that this trip was 'the happiest time of his administration'. In October 1963, President Kennedy told Taoiseach Seán Lemass that his visit to Ireland earlier that summer was 'among the warmest memories' of his life. Kennedy's visit to Ireland was portrayed by his political opponents as a taxpayer-funded holiday. Senator Barry Goldwater stated: 'The leader of the Frontier is in Ireland. I don't know what troubles they have there, but we have a lot of 'em here, and he ought to be home taking care of them.' Maier, T. (2003). *The Kennedys: America's Emerald Kings*. New York: Perseus Books, p. 442; Washington Bureau of The Sun. (1963). 'Sun Shines on The Irish As Kennedy Greets Lemass.' *The Baltimore Sun*, 16 October 1963; United Press International. (1963). 'Goldwater Raps Moral Bankruptcy of Liberal Politicians.' *The (Roseburg) News-Review*, 28 June 1963.

3 O'Donnell, K. & Powers, D. (1970). *Johnny We Hardly Knew Ye: Memories of John Fitzgerald Kennedy*. Boston: Little, Brown and Company, p. 370.

4 O'Donnell & Powers. *Johnny We Hardly Knew Ye*, p. 358.

5 O'Donnell & Powers. *Johnny We Hardly Knew Ye*, p. 370; United Press International. (1963). 'President Leaves Ireland; Flies To London for Macmillan Meet.' *Lead Daily Call*, 29 June 1963.

6 Molumby, G. (2013). 'JFK's historic Derbyshire detour to sister's grave.' *Irish Post*, 22 July 2013.

7 United Press International. (1963). 'JFK, Macmillan to Push for Test Ban.' *Scranton Tribune*, 1 July 1963.

8 New York Times Service (1963). 'U.S. Urges Guiana Rule by Britain.' *The Minneapolis Star*, 10 July 1963.

9 Ironically, Kennedy had come to this meeting with Macmillan from Ireland, where the British had, in 1920, imposed proportional representation with 'the simple logic, from

a British perspective … that it would damage Sinn Féin', the Irish nationalist party, which had won a resounding electoral victory in the 1918 General Election. This tactic did not work in Ireland. Sinn Féin consolidated their gains in the 1920 local elections. The British plan for Guiana was that proportional representation would reduce the strength of single parties and bring a coalition of Jagan's opponents to office. Jagan was ultimately ousted from power by a coalition of his rivals in the 1964 election. Guyana achieved independence in May 1966. Cheddi Jagan was elected as the fourth president of Guyana in 1992. Ferriter, D. (2015). 'How Britain left us with PR voting,' *The Irish Times*, 16 May 2015; Rohter, L. (1997). 'Cheddi Jagan Dies at 78,' *New York Times*, 7 March 1997; New York Times Service. 'U.S. Urges Guiana Rule by Britain.'

10   United Press International, '5,000 Greet JFK in Italy,' *Scranton Tribune*, 1 July 1963.

11   O'Donnell & Powers. *Johnny We Hardly Knew Ye*, p. 370.

12   McGinniss, J. (1993). *The Last Brother*. London: Little, Brown and Company, p. 146.

13   Levin, E. (1963). 'Pontiff and President Talk Peace,' *Corsicana Daily Sun*, 2 July 1963.

14   In 1960, Peale set up an organisation called the National Conference of Citizens for Religious Freedom, which actively campaigned against Kennedy and the prospect of a Catholic president. In 2016, an article in *IrishCentral.com* described South Carolina as 'perhaps the most anti-Catholic state in America'. This was also a common perception in 1960s America. O'Donnell & Powers. *Johnny We Hardly Knew Ye*, p. 373; O'Dowd, N. (2016). 'Trump's anti-Catholic rhetoric rises before South Carolina Primary.' [online] *IrishCentral.com*. Available at: https://www.irishcentral.com/opinion/niallodowd/trumps-anti-catholic-rhetoric-rises-before-south-carolina-primary [Accessed 12 January 2020].

15   Casey, S. (2009). *The Making of a Catholic President : Kennedy vs. Nixon 1960*. Oxford: Oxford University Press; Roos, D. (2019). 'How John F. Kennedy Overcame Anti-Catholic Bias to Win the Presidency.' [online] *History.com*. Available at: https://www.history.com/news/jfk-catholic-president [Accessed 10 January 2020].

16   Kennedy was bruised by the anti-Catholic bigotry thrown at him during the presidential election. In an emotive broadside against his critics in West Virginia, in April 1960, he stated: 'Nobody asked me if I was a Catholic when I joined the US Navy and nobody asked my brother if he was Catholic or Protestant before he climbed into an American bomber plane to fly his last mission.' In another speech, he directly questioned the open-mindedness of non-Catholics in America: 'Are we to say that a Jew can be elected mayor of Dublin, a Protestant can be named foreign minister of France, a Muslim can sit in the Israeli Parliament, but a Catholic cannot be President of the United States?' The anti-Catholic prejudice displayed in the campaign was something that Kennedy's father, Joseph. P. Kennedy, deeply resented. For the rest of his life, he 'kept among his papers a vicious cartoon that had been published in a Baptist periodical during the 1960 campaign. Under the caption "Big John and Little John," it showed Pope John XXIII sitting on his throne with his hand on John F. Kennedy's head, bidding him to "be sure to do what Poppa tells you."' Anderson Yanoso, N. (2017). *The Irish and the American Presidency*. London: Routledge, pp. 189–93; McAuley, J. (2015). 'The solemn

handshake between JFK and Pope Paul VI.' [online] *America Magazine*. Available at: https://www.americamagazine.org/content/all-things/pope-and-president-paul-vi-and-john-f-kennedy-solemn-handshake-and-bittersweet [Accessed 11 January 2020].

17   In Houston, Kennedy said 'I believe in an America where the separation of church and state is absolute, where no Catholic prelate would tell the president (should he be Catholic) how to act, and no Protestant minister would tell his parishioners for whom to vote; where no church or church school is granted any public funds or political preference; and where no man is denied public office merely because his religion differs from the president who might appoint him or the people who might elect him ... contrary to common newspaper usage, I am not the Catholic candidate for president. I am the Democratic Party's candidate for president, who happens also to be a Catholic. I do not speak for my church on public matters, and the church does not speak for me.' For an example of 'the neat narrative' referred to in this essay, see the entry for 'Anti-Catholicism' in Roberts, R.N., Hammond, S.J. and Sulfaro, V.A. (2012). *Presidential Campaigns, Slogans, Issues, and Platforms. Vol. 1: The Complete Encyclopedia*. Santa Barbara: Greenwood.

18   Anderson Yanoso. *The Irish and the American Presidency*, pp. 193–4.

19   In 1951, President Harry Truman decided he would appoint a full Unites States Ambassador to the Vatican and nominated General Mark W. Clark for this role. Following vocal criticism from American Protestants, Clark withdrew from the nomination and Truman dropped the idea. In 1984, President Reagan appointed William A. Wilson as the first United States Ambassador to the Vatican, following the establishment of full diplomatic relations. Rothman, L. (2015). 'The First Time a Pope Visited the US Was Much More Complicated.' [online] *Time*. Available at: https://time.com/4042433/paul-vi-lbj-1965 [Accessed 12 January 2020]; Levin. 'Pontiff and President Talk Peace'; Noland, C. (2009). 'William A. Wilson dies at 95; first US ambassador to the Vatican.' *Los Angeles Times*, 6 December 2009.

20   McAuley, J. 'The solemn handshake between JFK and Pope Paul VI.'; Levin. 'Pontiff and President Talk Peace.'

21   Levin. 'Pontiff and President Talk Peace.'

22   Associated Press. (1963). 'Pope Receives Kennedy, Invokes Blessing Upon All Americans,' *The Bridgeport Post*, 2 July 1963; Levin. 'Pontiff and President Talk Peace.'

23   Levin. 'Pontiff and President Talk Peace.'

24   John F. Kennedy Library & Museum, Speech Files (03): 'Remarks at NATO Headquarters, Naples, July 2 1963.'

25   Oser, A. (1986). 'Ex Gov. Averell Harriman, Adviser to 4 Presidents, Dies.' *New York Times*, 27 July 1986.

26   American Presidency Project Website. (2016). 'Joint Statement by the Heads of Delegations to the Moscow Nuclear Test Ban Meeting, July 25, 1963, "Treaty Banning Nuclear Weapon Tests in Atmosphere, in Outer Space and Underwater."' [online]. Available at http://www.presidency.ucsb.edu/ws/?pid=9358 [Accessed 1 May 2016].

27   Sachs, J. (2013). *To Move the World: JFK's Quest for Peace*. London: The Bodley Head, p. 111.

28   Sachs. *To Move the World*, p, 111; Clarke, T. (2013). *JFK's Last Hundred Days: An Intimate Portrait of a Great President*. London: Allen Lane, p. 22; Dallek, R. (2003). *John F. Kennedy: An Unfinished Life 1917–1963*. London: Allen Lane, p. 628.

29   Sherman Adams was White House chief of staff from 1953 until his resignation in 1958. Adams was reputed to have wielded so much influence in Eisenhower's White House that he was known as 'assistant president'. Eisenhower reportedly did not approve any policy papers that were not initialled 'S.A., O.K.' During Eisenhower's hospitalisation for a heart attack in 1955, a committee of senior officials, with Adams in charge, signed off on key political decisions. Adams's resignation was provoked by revelations that he had accepted expensive gifts from a wealthy industrialist, Bernard Goldfine, who was convicted of tax evasion in 1961. He served six months in prison and was declared bankrupt. He died in 1967. Associated Press. (1986). 'Eisenhower Aide Sherman Adams Dies,' *Victoria Advocate*, 28 October 1986; Anonymous. (1967). 'Bernard Goldfine: Always A Benefactor,' *Boston Globe*, 25 September 1967.

30   Clarke. *JFK's Last Hundred Days*, p. 25.

31   Adams was not indicted and died in New Hampshire, aged 87, in 1986. Upon Adams's death Vice President George Bush described him as 'a longtime friend who brought distinction to his public and private life'. Clarke. *JFK's Last Hundred Days*, p. 25; Associated Press. (1986). 'Eisenhower Aide Sherman Adams Dies'.

32   Clarke. *JFK's Last Hundred Days*, p. 31.

33   Bracker, M. (1963). 'Eisenhower Hints He Backs Treaty.' *New York Times*, 16 August 1963; United Press International. (1963). 'Dirksen Says He'll Vote For Test-Ban Treaty: Indicates Kennedy Will Dispel Doubt On Nuclear Issue.' *The Toledo Blade*, 9 September 1963.

34   United Press International, 'Kennedy Sends Senate Assurances on Treaty.' *The Chronicle (Pascagoula, Mississippi)*, 11 September 1963.

35   McGrory, M. (1964). 'Goldwater Urged To Go After Big Prize,' *The Virgin Islands Daily News*, 13 January 1964; Edson, P. (1963). 'July 4 Rally is Set to Skyrocket Goldwater', *Ocala Star-Banner*, 3 July 1963. Barry Goldwater and Kennedy were personal friends. Both had been elected to the Senate for the first time in 1952 and, despite ideological differences, the two men 'developed a great professional respect and personal fondness for one another', having served together on the Senate Labour Committee (McClellan Committee). Goldwater would occasionally visit the Kennedy White House, 'sitting in the President's rocking chair, talking politics and sipping whiskey'. President Kennedy and Goldwater relished the prospect of running against each other in the 1960 election and had even reached an agreement that they 'would campaign together, at least on occasion, travelling from city to city, perhaps on the same airplane or train, and at each stop would debate the issues'. Ultimately Goldwater would face-off against Lyndon Johnson. In an interview in the 1970s, Goldwater said: 'When Jack Kennedy died, I lost all interest in running … The country wasn't ready for three presidents in three-and-a-half years. And I knew Johnson would not run an honest campaign like Kennedy. Kennedy and I used to talk about running against each other. We came to a tentative agreement that would have revived the practice of the two candidates travelling together around the country and

appearing on the same platform.' A decade later, Goldwater wrote about the agreement in his autobiography, published in 1988: 'Kennedy and I informally agreed – it seems a pipe dream in looking at some of today's negative campaigning – that we would ride the same plane or train to several stops and debate face to face on the same platform.' In an oral history interview for the Kennedy Library in 1965, Goldwater said that he believed he could have beaten Kennedy in 1964: 'Certainly, he couldn't have carried the south. The business fraternity was against him. I felt that I had a fair to middling chance of defeating him.' Kennedy was confident that he would win against Goldwater and told aides that if the Republicans did nominate the Arizona senator 'all of us would get to bed much earlier on election night than we did in 1960'. Kennedy believed that the Republicans would select a more moderate candidate, like Michigan Governor George Romney, 'who could give us more trouble'. Schram, M. (1998). 'A Different Debate.' *The Washington Post*, 20 June 1998; Owen, D. *November 22, 1963: Reflections on the Life, Assassination and Legacy of John F. Kennedy*. New York: Skyhorse, pp. 247–9; O'Donnell & Powers. *Johnny We Hardly Knew Ye*, p. 13.

36 Talbot, D. (2007). *Brothers: The Hidden History of the Kennedy Years*. London: Pocket Books, p. 213.
37 O'Donnell & Powers. *Johnny We Hardly Knew Ye*, pp. 380–1.
38 United States Department of State. (2017). 'Address by President John F. Kennedy to the UN General Assembly, 20 September 1963.' [online] Available at: https://2009-2017. state.gov/p/io/potusunga/207201.htm [Accessed 11 January 2020].
39 United States Department of State. 'Address by President John F. Kennedy to the UN.'
40 Clarke. *JFK's Last Hundred Days*, pp. 101–2.
41 Clarke. *JFK's Last Hundred Days*, p. 221; O'Donnell & Powers. *Johnny We Hardly Knew Ye*, p. 381.
42 Clarke. *JFK's Last Hundred Days*, pp. 183–4; Dallek, R. (2013). *Camelot's Court: Inside the Kennedy White House*. New York: HarperCollins, p. 385.
43 Dallek, *Camelot's Court*, pp. 386–7; McCormally, J. (1975). 'Castro testily denied role in touchy assassination issue.' *The Salina Journey*, 28 May 1975; Attwood, W. (1967). *The Reds and the Blacks: A Personal Adventure*. New York: Harper and Row, p. 288.
44 Guthman, E. & Shulman, J., eds (1988). *Robert Kennedy In His Own Words: The Unpublished Recollections of the Kennedy Years*. New York: Bantam Books, p. 376.
45 Dallek. *Camelot's Court*, p. 387.
46 Dallek. *John F. Kennedy: An Unfinished Life*, p. 662.
47 Guthman & Shulman. *Robert Kennedy In His Own Words*, p. 376.
48 Dallek. *Camelot's Court*, p. 387.
49 Clarke. *JFK's Last Hundred Days*, pp. 250–2.
50 Castro, F. (2006). *My Life*. New York: Scribner, p. 591.
51 Daniel, J. (1963). 'Unofficial Envoy: An Historic Report from Two Capitals.' *The New Republic*, 14 December 1963.
52 Daniel. 'Unofficial Envoy.'
53 Szule, T. (1984). 'Castro on John Kennedy and the Missile Crisis.' *Los Angeles Times*, 15 April 1984.

54 Daniel. 'Unoffical Envoy.'
55 Daniel, J. (1963). 'When Castro Heard the News.' *The New Republic*, 14 December 1963.
56 Daniel. 'Unofficial Envoy.'
57 In this 1984 interview with Ted Szule, Castro portrayed Kennedy's assassination as a major setback for peace. He suggested that both he and Kennedy had politically matured, having learned hard lessons from the events leading to the Cuban Missile Crisis. Interestingly, in this same interview, Castro attributed an unsatisfactory 1959 meeting that he had with the then Vice-President, Richard Nixon, as being at the root of plans that led to the Bay of Pigs invasion, a failed attempt by US-sponsored Cuban exiles to overthrow Castro in April 1961. Szule. 'Castro on John Kennedy and the Missile Crisis.'
58 Clarke. *JFK's Last Hundred Days*, p. 285.
59 Clarke. *JFK's Last Hundred Days*, p. 319.
60 John Foster Dulles was President Eisenhower's Secretary of State from 1953 to 1959. In a speech in 1957 on United States policy towards China, Dulles maintained that the best way to bring about an end to Chinese communism was by refusing to engage with the regime in Beijing: 'The Chinese people are, above all, individualists. We can confidently base our policies on the assumption that international communism's rule of strict conformity is, in China as elsewhere, a passing and not a perpetual phase. We owe it to ourselves, our allies and the Chinese people to do all that we can to contribute to that passing. If we believed that this passing would be promoted by trade and cultural relations, then we would have such relations. If we believed that this passing would be promoted by our having diplomatic relations with the present regime, then we would have such relations.' Hilsman, who resigned from President Johnson's administration after only three months, believed it was Kennedy's intention to change course and reach out to China in his second term. Dean Rusk said that Kennedy had often discussed this with him and Rusk speculated that this would have happened in 1965. Ransom, C. (1967). 'A Kennedy Aide's Book About Policy,' *The Des Moines Register*, 12 August 1967; Liu, D. (1978). *A History of Sino-American Diplomatic Relations, 1840–1974*. Beijing: Academy, p. 355; Hilsman, R. (1967). *To Move a Nation: The Politics of Foreign Policy in the Administration of John F. Kennedy*. New York, Doubleday, pp. 351–3; Clarke. *JFK's Last Hundred Days*, pp. 319–20.
61 Associated Press. (1961). 'Kennedy Plan for China Bid in Second Term told by Aid[e].' *The Toledo Blade*, 26 August 1971.
62 President Nixon stunned the world's diplomatic community when, on 15 July 1971, he announced on live television that he would visit China the following year. Nixon opened this special broadcast by stating that 'I have requested this television time tonight to announce a major development in our efforts to build a lasting peace in the world. As I have pointed out on a number of occasions over the past three years, there can be no stable and enduring peace without the participation of the People's Republic of China and its 750 million people. That is why I have undertaken initiatives in several areas to open the door for more normal relations between our two countries.' Salinger's claims

that Kennedy intended in a second term to open diplomatic relations with China were
first broadcast at the end of August 1971, about six weeks after Nixon's announcement.
Any suggestion that Salinger's prime motivation was to upstage Nixon's achievement
(by saying Kennedy had planned this change in China policy first) are undermined by
the fact that Salinger actually recorded his interview with the BBC on 5 July, ten days
before Nixon's breakthrough with China was announced. Salinger would not have been
privy to the secret talks that led to Nixon's announcement, however, as an astute political
observer, Salinger had clearly picked up on public overtures Nixon's administration were
making about warmer relations with China. Associated Press. (1971). 'Kennedy Planned
China "Bridge," Salinger Says: Interview on 2nd Term Hopes Recorded Before Nixon
Peking Trip Was Announced.' *Los Angeles Times*, 27 August 1971.

63 Kennedy and Tito had actually previously met, in 1951, in Belgrade. As a young
Congressman, Kennedy undertook a tour of Europe to inspect Western defence efforts.
Kennedy said his reason for including Yugoslavia as part of this tour was 'because it is
useless to talk about the defence of Europe without also talking about Yugoslavia in
its position against Russia'. Tito had refused to accept Stalin's authority and Yugoslavia
had been expelled from Cominform in June 1948. In January 1951 Kennedy attended
a news conference hosted by Tito. Kennedy reported back to the United States that
Tito was preparing Yugoslavia against the threat of invasion by the Soviet Union and
its Eastern European allies. Associate Press. (1951). 'This will be Dangerous Year For
Peace, Tito Tells Kennedy,' *Baltimore Sun*, 26 January 1951; Brogan, P. (1990). *Eastern
Europe 1939–1989: The Fifty Years War*. London: Bloomsbury, pp. 156–62; American
Presidency Project Website. (2016). 'Toasts of the President and President Tito, 17
October 1963' [online]. Available at: http://www.presidency.ucsb.edu/ws/?pid=9477
[Accessed 1 May 2016]; Kaufman, B.I. & Kaufman, D. (2009). *Historical Dictionary of
the Eisenhower Era*. Maryland: Scarecrow Press, p. 235.

64 Associated Press. (1963). 'Red Carpet is Out For Tito At White House,' *Council Grove
Republican*, 17 October 1963.

65 O'Neill, M. (1963). 'Tito Gets Our Not-So-Glad Hand,' *New York Daily News*, 18
October 1963.

66 Chicago Tribune Press Service. (1963). 'Peace Bid Urged by Kennedy, Tito,' *The
Spokesman-Review*, 18 October 1963.

67 The Skopje earthquake occurred on 26 July 1963. It destroyed over 80 per cent of the
city. It killed over 1,000 people and left 200,000 people homeless. O'Neill. 'Tito Gets
Our Not-So-Glad Hand.'

68 O'Neill. 'Tito Gets Our Not-So-Glad Hand.'

69 As an example of the level of hostility generated by Tito's visit, *The New York Daily News*
also reported that the United States Federal Aviation Agency had found it necessary to
issue a special regulation prohibiting airplane flights over places on Tito's route. O'Neill.
'Tito Gets Our Not-So-Glad Hand.'

70 Associated Press. 'Red Carpet is Out For Tito At White House.'

71 Maier. *The Kennedys: America's Emerald Kings*, p. 443; John F. Kennedy Library &
Museum. 'Seán Lemass: Oral History Interview,' 8 August 1966.

72 Associated Press. (1963). 'Membrane Ailment Is Death Cause.' *The (Indiana) Times*, 9 August 1963.

73 United Press International. (1963). 'President, Wife Mourn The Death of Their Son,' *The Hartford Courant*, 10 August 1963.

74 Esther Cleveland, born 1893, and Marion Cleveland, born 1895, were respectively the first and second children born to an incumbent President. Patrick Kennedy was the third child born to an incumbent President. Gould, L. (2001). *American First Ladies: Their Lives and Their Legacies*. New York: Routledge, p. 167.

75 United Press International. 'President, Wife Mourn The Death of Their Son.'

76 Dallek. *John F. Kennedy: An Unfinished Life*, pp. 673–84; Reeves, T.C. (1991). *A Question of Character*. London: Arrow Books, pp. 403–12.

77 Jacobs, S. (2006). *Cold War Mandarin: Ngo Dinh Diem and the Origins of America's War in Vietnam, 1950–1963*. Maryland: Rowman & Littlefield, p. 149.

78 Reeves. *A Question of Character*, p. 403.

79 US Congress, Senate, Committee on Foreign Relations, 90th Congress, 1st Session. (1967). *Background Information Relating to Southeast Asia and Vietnam* (3rd Revised Edition). Washington DC: US Government Print Office, p. 115; O'Donnell & Powers. *Johnny We Hardly Knew Ye*, pp. 16–18, p. 382.

80 Hilsman, *To Move a Nation*, p. 221.

81 The 1962 Geneva accords on Laos aimed to end the Laotian civil war. Arising from a conference at Geneva, which went on for fifteen months and in which fourteen countries participated – Burma, Cambodia, Canada, China, the Democratic Republic of Vietnam ('North Vietnam'), France, India, Laos, Poland, the Republic of Vietnam ('South Vietnam'), Thailand, the Soviet Union, the United Kingdom, the United States. Agreement was signed on 23 July 1962. The signatories pledged to respect the neutrality, territorial integrity and independence of Laos. 'Geneva Accords on Laos,' *The New York Times*, 7 March 1970.

82 Jones, H. (2003). *Death of a Generation: How the Assassinations of Diem and JFK Prolonged the Vietnam War*. New York: Oxford University Press, p. 348.

83 Hilsman, *To Move a Nation*, p. 231.

84 Gallagher, P. (1968). 'Viet War Escalation a Real Danger – Hilsman.' *The (Elmira) Star-Gazette*, 28 March 1968.

85 Associated Press. 'Kennedy Planned China "Bridge."'

86 Clarke. *JFK's Last Hundred Days*, p. 108.

87 Beschloss, M. (2008). *Presidential Courage: Brave Leaders and How They Changed America 1789–1989*. New York: Simon & Schuster, pp. 275–6.

88 Beschloss, *Presidential Courage*, pp. 114–16.

89 Beschloss, *Presidential Courage*, pp. 233–4.

90 Goldstein, R. (2008). 'Floyd M. Boring, Agent who Guarded 5 Presidents, is Dead.' *New York Times*, 7 February 2008.

91 Clarke. *JFK's Last Hundred Days*, p. 312; President's Commission on the Assassination of President Kennedy (Warren Commission) Volume VII. (1964). Testimony of Kenneth P. O'Donnell. Washington DC: McGraw-Hill Book Company, p. 440.

Chapter 7

1 Dallek, R. (2003). *John F. Kennedy : an unfinished life 1917–1963*. Camberwell, Vic.: Allen Lane; Reeves, R. (1994). *President Kennedy : profile of power*. New York: Touchstone; Sachs, J. (2013). *To move the world*. London: Bodley Head.

2 Donald, D.H. (2011). *Lincoln*. New York: Simon and Schuster, p. 13.

3 Reeves. *President Kennedy*, pp. 13–14.

4 Mailer, N. (1960). 'Superman comes to the supermarket.' *Esquire* (November 1960), pp. 119–27.

5 Reeves. *President Kennedy*, p. 14.

6 Avlon, J. (2017). 'David McCullough on Reading History as Resistance.' [online] *The Daily Beast*. Available at: https://www.thedailybeast.com/historian-david-mccullough-writes-that-reading-history-may-be-the-smartest-form-of-resistance [Accessed 5 March 2019].

7 Sachs. *To move the world*, p. 51.

8 Parmet, H.S. (1983). *JFK, the presidency of John F. Kennedy*. New York: Doubleday, p. 82.

9 *Irish Independent*, 21 June 2013.

10 Brinkley, A. (2013). 'The legacy of John F. Kennedy', *The Atlantic: JFK in his time and ours* (special commemorative issue), Fall 2013.

11 Wills, G. (1983). *The Kennedys : a shattered illusion*. London: Orbis, p. 16.

12 Fitzgerald, F.S. (1925). *The Great Gatsby*. London: Penguin [1973], pp. 187–8.

13 Dallek. *John F. Kennedy*, p. 631.

14 Clark, C.M. (2014). *The sleepwalkers : how Europe went to war in 1914*. London: Penguin, p. 376.

15 Clark. *The sleepwalkers*, pp. 378–9.

16 For Parnell's speech in which these lines occur, see Travers, P. (2013). 'The march of the nation: Parnell's ne plus ultra speech,' in Travers, P. and McCartney, D., eds (2013). *Parnell reconsidered*. Dublin: UCD Press, pp. 179–96.

17 Collins, S. (2013). 'Romantic Ireland lives on in our fascination with the leaders who left us too young.' *Irish Times*, 3 August 2013.

18 Dallek, R. (2013). *Camelot's court: inside the Kennedy White House*. New York: HarperCollins, p. 35. Parnell's words here are as recorded in O'Brien, W. (1910). *An olive branch in Ireland and its history*. London: Macmillan, p. 47. They were quoted by O'Brien, C.C., (1957). *Parnell and his party*. Oxford: Oxford University Press, p. 145, n. 1.

19 Speech to the joint session of Dáil Éireann and Seanad Éireann, 28 June 1963.

20 Desy, M.M. (2017). 'John F. Kennedy and "Old Ironsides" – USS Constitution Museum.' [online] Available at: https://ussconstitutionmuseum.org/2017/05/29/jfk [Accessed 6 March 2019].

21 *The Guardian*, 18 November 2013.

22 Sachs. *To move the world*, p. 168.

23 Kennedy, J.F. (1956). *Profiles in courage*. New York: HarperCollins [2003], p. 1.

24 Gaddis, J.L. (2011). *George F. Kennan: an American life*. New York: Norton, p. 572.

25   Schlesinger, R. (2008). *White House ghosts: presidents and their speechwriters from FDR to George W. Bush*. New York: Simon & Schuster, p. 113.

26   Reeves. *President Kennedy*, p. 19.

27   Goodwin, D.K. (2018). *Leadership: In turbulent times*. London: Viking, p. 310.

28   The words 'at home and around the world' were, in fact, an eleventh-hour addition to the inaugural address. See 'Poetry and power: the inaugural address of President John F. Kennedy,' a booklet published by the Foundation for the National Archives (Washington, D.C.) for an exhibition which opened at the JFK Library and Museum in Boston in January 2009 to mark the inauguration of President Barack Obama.

29   Lippmann, W. (1945). 'Roosevelt Has Gone,' *New York Herald Tribune*, 14 April 1945.

30   See Caro, R. (2012). *The years of Lyndon B. Johnson*, vol. 4: *The passage of power*. New York: Knopf, especially chap. 23: 'In the books of law,' pp. 558–70.

31   *New York Times*, 10 June 2013.

32   For an interesting overview of and commentary on these polls, see Merry, R.W. (2012). *Where they stand: the American presidents in the eyes of voters and historians*. New York: Simon & Schuster. As regards Kennedy, Merry argues that he 'never had a chance to leave a substantial stamp upon the nation', p. 77.

33   Dallek. *Camelot's court*, p. 1.

34   C-span.org. (2017). 'Total Scores/Overall Rankings | C-SPAN Survey on Presidents 2017.' [online] Available at: https://www.c-span.org/presidentsurvey2017/?page=overall. [Accessed 6 March 2019].

35   Brinkley. 'The legacy of John F. Kennedy'.

36   Shaw, J.T. (2018). *Rising star, setting sun: Dwight D. Eisenhower, John F. Kennedy and the presidential transition that changed America*. New York: Pegasus Books, p. 49.

37   The poll was commissioned by Larry J. Sabato for his book. Sabato, L.J. (2013). *The Kennedy half-century: the presidency, assassination and lasting legacy of John F. Kennedy*. New York: Bloomsbury. For summary data, see Politico.com. (2013). 'Poll: JFK tops presidential rating' [online] *Politico*. Available at: https://www.politico.com/story/2013/10/john-f-kennedy-presidential-rating-poll-098330 [Accessed 6 March 2019].

38   From 'For the fallen', a poem by Laurence Binyon (1869–1943); first published in the (London) *Times*, 21 September 1914.

39   Speech at Amherst College, 26 October 1963.

40   Brinkley. 'The legacy of John F. Kennedy'.

41   Dallek. *Camelot's court*, p. ix.

42   Leaming, B. (2007). *Jack Kennedy: the making of a president*. London: Orion, p. 190.

43   Campbell, J. (2014). *Roy Jenkins: a well-rounded life*. London: Jonathan Cape, p. 699.

44   Lyttelton, G. & Hart-Davis, R. (2001). *The Lyttelton Hart-Davis letters, 1955–1962: a selection*, ed. Roger Hudson, London: John Murray, p. 303.

45   See Kennedy's speech to the General Court of the Commonwealth of Massachusetts at the State House, Boston, 9 January 1961.

46   Dallek. *John F. Kennedy*, p. 711. The words of Lincoln which Dallek borrows here are taken from his first inaugural address and his message to Congress of 1 December 1862.

Chapter 8

1 For further details see Daly, M. 'Nationalism, sentiment, and economics: relations between Ireland and Irish America in the postwar years', in Kenny K., ed. (2003). *New directions in Irish-American history.* Madison: University of Wisconsin Press, p. 264.

2 Brennan, E. 'Television in Ireland before Irish television: 1950s audiences and British programming,' Shared Histories Conference, National Library of Ireland, 6 July 2016; McLoone, M. and MacMahon, J., eds (1984). *Television and Irish society: 21 years of Irish television.* Dublin: RTÉ, p. 7.

3 Kennedy, M. et al. eds (2018). *Documents in Irish Foreign Policy Vol. XI.* Dublin: Royal Irish Academy. Document no 326, 2 November 1960.

4 National Archives of Ireland (NAI), Department of Foreign Affairs (DFA), P115/1.

5 *Irish Independent*, 10 November 1960.

6 *Irish Independent*, 11 November 1960; *Evening Herald*, 12 November 1960; *Cork Examiner*, 12 November 1960.

7 *The Irish Times*, 15 November 1960.

8 *Evening Herald*, 12 November 1960.

9 NAI, S 15245A 'Irish Chamber of Commerce in USA.'

10 Daly, M. (2016). *Sixties Ireland, Reshaping the economy, state and society, 1957–73*: Cambridge: Cambridge University Press, p. 366.

11 As reported by the *Irish Independent*, 15 May 1963, press cutting available on NAI, S17401A 'Kennedy visit.'

12 NAI, S17401A, 17 May 1963.

13 This strategy ignored the fact that the 1949 Ireland Act which Westminster passed in response to Ireland becoming a Republic, stipulated that any decision about the future of Northern Ireland was a matter for the people of Northern Ireland.

14 NAI, S17401B, 'Kennedy visit to Ireland,' Cable, 19 March 1963, Kiernan to McCann

15 NAI, S17401B, 17 June 1963.

16 *Time*, 12 July 1963. At this time there appears to have been a belief that pictures of traffic jams in towns or cities sent a positive message. Officials made a very maladroit attempt to persuade the documentary maker Peter Carey to include pictures of traffic gridlock in Sligo in his lyrical documentary *Yeats Country* released in 1965.

17 NAI, DFA 22/1 Washington.

18 Kennedy et al. *Documents in Irish Foreign Policy Vol. XI.* Document no 385, Hugh McCann (London) confidential report to Con Cremin, 19 April 1961 and Document No. 386, Kiernan to Cremin, 19 April 1961.

19 NAI, DFA Washington Files P 115/1 27 June 1958.

20 In the 1960s, 'when the USA was revising its immigration regulations and removing ethnic quotas, hubris about the growing Irish economy and a belief that emigration had been consigned to history, meant that Ireland failed to lobby for measures to secure a continuing quota for Irish emigrants. Whether political representation would have been effective is not certain, but no effort was made to prevent the abolition of the Irish quota.' See Daly, M. (2018), 'Migration since 1914' in Bartlett, T., ed. (2003).

The Cambridge History of Ireland: Volume 4, 1880 to the Present. Cambridge: Cambridge University Press, p. 341.

Chapter 9

1 O'Donnell, K. & Powers, D. (1972). *Johnny We Hardly Knew Ye: Memories of John Fitzgerald Kennedy.* Boston: Little, Brown and Company, p. 192.
2 O'Donnell & Powers. *Johnny We Hardly Knew Ye,* p. 193.
3 White, T.H. (1978). *In Search of History: A Personal Adventure.* New York: Harper & Row, p. 474.
4 Reeves, R. (1993). *President Kennedy: Profile of Power.* New York: Simon & Schuster, p. 14.
5 McGinniss, J. (1969). *The Selling of the President 1968.* New York: Trident Press, pp. 193–4.
6 McLuhan, M. (1964). *Understanding Media: The Extensions of Man.* London: McGraw-Hill, p. 330.
7 Hamilton, N. (1992). *JFK: Reckless Youth.* London: Random House, p. 780.
8 Mailer, N. (1963). *The Presidential Papers.* New York: Putnam, pp. 45–6.
9 Matthews, C. (2011). *Jack Kennedy: Elusive Hero.* New York: Simon & Schuster, p. 7.
10 Dallek, R. (2003). *An Unfinished Life: John F. Kennedy 1917–1963.* New York: Little, Brown.
11 Donald, D.H. (1995). *Lincoln.* New York: Simon and Schuster, p. 13.
12 White, *In Search of History,* p. 543.
13 Heymann, C.D. (1989). *A Woman Named Jackie.* Lyle Stuart, p. 418.
14 White, *In Search of History,* p. 545.
15 Dugan, A. & Newport, F. (2013) 'Americans Rate JFK as Top Modern President.' [online] *Gallup.com.* Available at: https://news.gallup.com/poll/165902/americans-rate-jfk-top-modern-president.aspx [Accessed 17 January 2020].

Chapter 10

1 Larry Donnelly was born in the city of Boston in 1974, when Judge W. Arthur Garrity's busing plan was implemented. There are two sources for much of the information contained in this essay, which only scratches the surface of a sad chapter in American history. One is the definitive, Pulitzer Prize-winning book about busing in Boston and one of the seminal works about life in the US in the twentieth century, *Common Ground: A Turbulent Decade in the Lives of Three American Families* by J. Anthony Lukas. The other are countless, lengthy conversations with my father, who was a strong advocate against forced busing and still cannot accept what transpired in the 1970s in his city.
2 Lukas, J.A. (1986). *Common ground: a turbulent decade in the lives of three American families.* New York: Vintage Books, p. 227.
3 Lukas. *Common ground,* p. 137.

4 Lukas. *Common ground,* p. 138.
5 Barnicle, M. (1974). 'An Open Letter to Senator Kennedy,' *Boston Globe,* 8 September 1974.
6 Lukas. *Common ground,* pp. 261–2.
7 Lukas. *Common ground,* p. 264.
8 Lukas. *Common ground,* p. 134.
9 Lukas. *Common ground,* p. 128, p. 135.
10 Lukas. *Common ground,* p. 136.
11 Ibid.

Chapter 11

1 Orjuela, C. (2008). 'Distant warriors, distant peace workers? Multiple diaspora roles in Sri Lanka's violent conflict.' *Global Networks,* 8(4), pp. 436–452.
2 Wilson, A.J. (1995). *Irish America and the Ulster Conflict 1968–1995.* London: Blackstaff, p. 114. The Fort Worth Five were five New Yorkers accused of gun running for the IRA. Kennedy declared that the police probe into the men's illegal activities was 'a thinly veiled attempt to harass and intimidate peaceful and legitimate activities by Irish-American individuals … in support of equal justice for the Catholic minority in Northern Ireland.' *Sarasota Herald-Tribune,* 5 August 1972.
3 *New York Times,* 11 July 1972.
4 Hugh L. Carey Papers (HLCP), Accession No. 5, Box No. 4, 'Northern Ireland 1971–72' folder, Press Release on Kennedy, Ribicoff and Carey's Northern Ireland Resolution, 20 October 1971.
5 Orjuela, 'Distant warriors, distant peace workers?', p. 438.
6 On 30 January 1972, the British Army opened fire on a Civil Rights demonstration in Derry, fatally wounding thirteen civilians.
7 Sanders, A. (2016). 'Congressional Hearings on Northern Ireland and the "Special Relationship," 1971–1981.' *Diplomacy & Statecraft,* 27(1), p. 135.
8 Shain, Y. (2002). 'The Role of Diasporas in Conflict Perpetuation or Resolution.' *SAIS Review,* 22(2), p. 116.
9 *Dáil Debates,* vol. 259 no. 9, cols. 1353–5, An Taoiseach Jack Lynch, 9 March 1972.
10 Kennedy, E.M. (2009). *True Compass.* London: Little Brown, p. 355.
11 MacLeod, A. (2016). *International Politics and the Northern Ireland Conflict: The USA, Diplomacy and the Troubles.* London: I.B. Tauris, p. 126.
12 Kennedy, E.M. (1973). 'Ulster Is an International Issue.' *Foreign Policy,* (11), p. 71.
13 Interview with Seán Donlon, 5 July 2016.
14 Legal Information Institute. (2017). 'Amicus Curiae' [online] Available at: https://www.law.cornell.edu/wex/amicus_curiae [Accessed 21 Oct. 2016].
15 Interview with Seán Donlon, 5 July 2016.
16 Wilson, *Irish America,* p. 130.
17 Ogelman, N., Money, J. and Martin, P.L. (2002). 'Immigrant Cohesion and Political Access in Influencing Host Country Foreign Policy.' *SAIS Review,* 22(2), p. 146.

18　National Archives of Ireland (NAI), Dept. Foreign Affairs Files (DFA) 2007/111/1973, 'St. Patrick's Day Appeal for Peace in Northern Ireland by Edward M. Kennedy, Thomas P. O'Neill Jr., Daniel Patrick Moynihan and Hugh L. Carey.'

19　Briand, R.J. (2002). 'Bush, Clinton, Irish America and the Irish Peace Process'. *The Political Quarterly*, 73(2), p. 174.

20　HLCP, Accession No. 5, Box No. 101, 'Irish Topics, 1977' folder, Memo from Erica Teutsch to Governor Carey, 19 May 1977.

21　HLCP, Memo from Erica Teutsch to Governor Carey.

22　Cochrane, F. *The End of Irish-America? Globalisation and the Irish Diaspora*. Dublin: Irish Academic Press, p. 58.

23　Cochrane. *The End of Irish-America?*, p. 58.

24　Vertovec, S. (2005). 'The Political Importance of Diasporas.' Working Paper No. 13. Centre on Migration, Policy and Society, University of Oxford, p. 4.

25　NAI, DFA 2007/59/174, Letter of thanks from A.J.F. O'Reilly in the aftermath of the Ireland Fund Dinner. Undated, circa late May 1977.

26　*International Herald Tribune*, 20 May 1977.

27　*Irish Independent*, 19 May 1977.

28　*Belfast Telegraph*, 19 May 1977.

29　*International Herald Tribune*, 20 May 1977.

30　Holland, M. (1977). 'Jimmy Carter, Edward Kennedy and Ireland: The Inside Story', *Magill*, 2 October.

31　Interview with Michael Lillis, 24 January 2015.

32　Speech by President Jimmy Carter, Washington D.C., 20 January 1977.

33　Cochrane, *The End of Irish-America*, p. 58.

34　Fanning, R. (2003). 'The Anglo-American alliance and the Irish question in the twentieth century', in Devlin, J., Lovett, A.W. and Clarke, H.B. eds (2003). *European encounters: essays in memory of Albert Lovett*. Dublin: UCD Press, p. 209.

35　Interview with Michael Lillis, 24 January 2015.

36　Papers of Daniel P. Moynihan (PDPM), Part 2, Box No. 326, Folder No. 6, Subject File 'Irish Aid General Feb–July 1986', Letter from Daniel Moynihan to unidentified constituent, 27 June 1986.

37　Mallie, E. and McKittrick, D. (2001). *Endgame in Ireland*. London: Hodder & Stoughton, p. 179.

38　O'Clery, C. (1996). *The Greening of the White House*. Dublin: Gill & Macmillan, p. 81.

39　PDPM, Part 2, Box No. 329, Folder No. 1, Subject File 'Northern Ireland, Friends of Ireland/St Patrick's Day Statements 1977–1987,' Letter and attachments from Senator Edward Kennedy to Senator Daniel Moynihan, 11 March 1986.

Chapter 12

1　The following is an edited transcript of a public interview by Dr Brian Murphy, Technological University Dublin, with Robert 'Bob' Shrum, Director of the Jesse M.

Unruh Institute of Politics at the University of Southern California. Shrum worked on numerous Democratic Party campaigns as a political consultant, strategist and speechwriter. Shrum wrote Senator Ted Kennedy's acclaimed speech at the 1980 Democratic National Convention, New York. In May 2004, *The Atlantic* magazine described Shrum as 'the most sought-after consultant in the Democratic Party'. The interview took place at the Kennedy Summer School, New Ross, on 9 September 2017.

2   P.J. Mara was a former Irish Government Press Secretary, and adviser to Charles Haughey. He was the National Director of Elections for Fianna Fáil at the general elections in 1997, 2002 and 2007.

3   In May 2017, Hillary Clinton said: 'I was on the way to winning until the combination of Jim Comey's letter on October 28 and Russian WikiLeaks raised doubts in the minds of people who were inclined to vote for me, but got scared off … If the election had been held on October 27, I'd be your president, and it wasn't.' On 28 October 2016, Comey wrote to Congress saying that the FBI had discovered a new batch of emails that 'appear to be pertinent' to the investigation into Clinton's use of a private email server while she was secretary of state. Shabad, R. (2017). 'Hillary Clinton says she would've won election if it were held Oct. 27.' [online] *Cbsnews.com*. Available at: https://www.cbsnews.com/news/hillary-clinton-says-she-would-have-won-the-election-if-it-were-held-oct-27 [Accessed 13 January 2020].

4   The 'Access Hollywood Tape' was a video recording of Donald Trump and NBC television host Billy Bush having an inappropriate conversation about women in 2005. The tape was released by the *Washington Post* in October 2016, during the US presidential election campaign. A segment of the tape records Mr Trump as saying 'I did try and f–k her. She was married … I moved on her like a bitch, but I couldn't get there.' Mr Trump also talked about his attraction to beautiful women. 'I just start kissing them. It's like a magnet. Just kiss. I don't even wait.' 'And when you're a star they let you do it,' he said. 'Grab them by the pussy. You can do anything.' Halper, D. (2016). 'Trump says he tried to "f–k" a married woman in 2005 video,' *New York Post*, 7 October 2016.

5   Richard Goodwin was a political assistant and speechwriter to President Kennedy, President Johnson and Senator Robert Kennedy. Doris Kearns Goodwin is a Pulitzer Prize-winning American historian.

6   Carter declined to actively campaign or debate Kennedy, citing the need to devote his time to the Iranian hostage crisis. According to one definition, 'the term Rose Garden Strategy refers to the re-election strategy of incumbent American presidents who focus on events in the White House, taking advantage of the grandeur and aura of their office to look presidential. By following this strategy, presidents hope to underscore their competence in office. While challengers must work hard to look presidential, incumbent presidents appear presidential by staying focused on the business of governing, often remaining above the political fray.' Warren, K.F., ed. (2008). *The Encyclopedia of U.S. Campaigns, Elections, and Electoral Behavior*. Los Angeles: Sage, p. 726.

7   Arthur Schlesinger, a distinguished historian, had worked as an adviser and speechwriter for Adlai Stevenson's campaigns for president. He worked as a special assistant in the

Kennedy White House and campaigned for Robert Kennedy in 1968 and Ted Kennedy in 1980. Ted Sorensen was President Kennedy's primary speechwriter.

8   Bob Shrum's wife, Marylouise Oates, a journalist and former society columnist for the *Los Angeles Times.*

9   Although Al Gore had won the popular vote by roughly a half-million ballots, the Electoral College count was so close that whoever won Florida would be the overall winner of the 2000 Presidential Election. After protracted recounting, George W. Bush won Florida by 537 votes out of six million cast and became President-Elect.

10   According to Segers, 'this ballot [in Palm Beach County] differed in its layout from ballots elsewhere in the state [of Florida]. Instead of placing candidates' names on the left and a punch hole to the right of each, as specified by Florida statutes, the butterfly ballot placed some names on the left and some on the right, and all punch holes in the middle. It was difficult to line up a name with the correct punch hole. Moreover, contrary to Florida statutes, the butterfly ballot did not list candidates' names in proper order – the two major-party candidates followed by eight minor-party candidates. Instead, Bush's name was first, with Pat Buchanan below him and Gore listed third. This confusing ballot resulted in the disqualification of 19,000 ballots because citizens voted for two or more candidates.' Segers, M.C. (2002). *Piety, Politics, and Pluralism: Religion, the Courts, and the 2000 Election.* Lanham: Rowman & Littlefield, p. 22.

11   Pat Buchanan ran on the Reform Party ticket in the 2000 election. Segers notes that Palm Beach County in 2000 was 'a largely Democratic county ... populated by Jewish voters living in retirement villages and by African American and Hispanic communities'. Buchanan got 5 per cent of the vote here in 1996, but 20 per cent in 2000. Buchanan himself admitted on television that he had not expected to win so many votes in Palm Beach and 'suggested that something was amiss'. Segers. *Piety, Politics, and Pluralism,* p. 22.

12   Swift Boat Veterans for Truth was a group of United States Swift boat veterans and former prisoners of war formed during the 2004 presidential election campaign. The group campaigned against John Kerry's candidacy.

13   Oliver Wendell Holmes Jr was a member of the Supreme Court of the United States from 1902 to 1932.

Chapter 13

1   This essay is adapted from a speech at the Kennedy Summer School on 8 September 2017, which was accompanied by an audio-visual presentation.

2   I am happy to be in Ireland.

3   Speech by President Barack Obama, College Green, Dublin, 23 May 2011.

4   *Irish Times,* 24 May 2011.

5   Speech by President Barack Obama, Selma, Alabama, 7 March 2015.

6   Speech by President Barack Obama, Selma, Alabama.

7   Ibid.

8   Ibid.

9 On 17 June 2015, nine people were killed at the Emanuel African Methodist Episcopal Church in Charleston, South Carolina.

10 Violence, resulting in serious injuries and deaths, occurred arising from a Neo-Nazi, white supremacist rally, which was held in Charlottesville, Virginia, from 11 to 12 August 2017. Counter-protests included religious groups, local residents and businesses, civil rights organisations and students and staff from the University of Virginia.

11 Speech by President Barack Obama, McCormick Place, Chicago, 10 January 2017.

12 Speech by President Barack Obama, College Green, Dublin, 23 May 2011. The Irish words '*Is féidir linn*' translates as 'Yes we can.'

Chapter 14

1 Carswell, S. (2016). 'The Spin Doctor Who Guided Sanders and Ahern.' *The Irish Times*, 29 August 2016.

2 Murray, M. (2015). 'Poll: Americans Want Change, Not Another Clinton or Bush.' [online] *MSNBC*. Available at: http://www.msnbc.com/msnbc/poll-americans-want-change-not-another-clinton-or-bush [Accessed 19 January 2020].

3 Hardy, K. (2016). 'Bernie Sanders finds victory in "virtual tie" with Clinton.' [online] *Des Moines Register*. Available at: https://www.desmoinesregister.com/story/news/elections/presidential/caucus/2016/02/02/bernie-sanders-finds-victory-virtual-tie-clinton/79620372 [Accessed 19 January 2020].

4 Benen, S. (2016). 'Sanders Makes History with New Hampshire Landslide.' [online] *MSNBC*. Available at: http://www.msnbc.com/rachel-maddow-show/sanders-makes-history-new-hampshire-landslide [Accessed 19 January 2020].

5 Beinart, P. (2014). 'Clintonphobia: Why No Democrat Wants to Run Against Hillary.' [online] *The Atlantic*. Available at: https://www.theatlantic.com/politics/archive/2014/08/why-no-democrat-wants-to-run-against-hillary-fear-of-retaliation/378914 [Accessed 19 January 2020].

6 C-SPAN.org. (2010). 'Senator Sanders Filibuster.' [online] Available at: https://www.c-span.org/video/?297021-5/senator-sanders-filibuster [Accessed 19 January 2020].

7 McManus, D. (2019). 'For a Guy Who's Not Running, Joe Biden Is Having a Tough Campaign.' *Los Angeles Times*, 3 April 2019.

8 Surrey, M. (2016). 'Bernie Sanders Campaign: Logo, Slogan and Campaign Platform.' [online] *Mic*. Available at: https://www.mic.com/articles/133585/bernie-sanders-campaign-logo-slogan-and-campaign-platform [Accessed 19 January 2020].

9 C-SPAN.org. (2015). 'Senator Bernie Sanders News Conference.' [online] Available at: https://www.c-span.org/video/?325700-1/senator-bernie-sanders-i-vt-news-conference [Accessed 19 January 2020].

10 Healy, P. (2015). 'Bernie Sanders's Campaign, Hitting Fund-Raising Milestone, Broadens Focus.' *New York Times*, 1 October 2015.

11 Scribd. (2015). 'National Poll 30 April 2015.' [online] Available at: https://www.scribd.com/document/410998973/National-Poll-4-30-15 [Accessed 19 January 2020].

12 Scribd. (2015). 'Iowa Poll 30 April 2015.' [online] Available at: https://www.scribd.com/document/410998972/Iowa-Poll-4-30-15 [Accessed 19 January 2020].

13 Scribd. (2015). 'NH Poll 30 April 2015.' [online] Available at: https://www.scribd.com/document/410998969/NH-Poll-4-30-15 [Accessed 19 January 2020].

14 Federal Elections Commission. (2015). 'Bernie Sanders Statement of Candidacy, 30 April 2015.' [online] Available at: http://docquery.fec.gov/pdf/533/15031422533/15031422533.pdf [Accessed 19 January 2020].

15 7D Staff (2015). 'Video: Bernie Sanders' Full Campaign Announcement.' [online] *Seven Days*. Available at: https://www.sevendaysvt.com/OffMessage/archives/2015/05/27/video-bernie-sanders-campaign-kickoff [Accessed 19 January 2020].

16 Facebook Watch. (2018). 'Progress: Bernie Sanders Campaign Video.' [online] Available at: https://www.facebook.com/berniesanders/videos/873391986049140 [Accessed 19 January 2020].

17 'Progress' won the 2016 Gold Polly award from the American Association of Political Consultants, The Telly Award and the Reed Award from *Campaigns and Elections Magazine* for the Best Campaign Web Video.

18 Frizell, S. (2015). 'Hillary Clinton: First 2016 Television Ad Focuses on Empathy, Mother.' *Time*, 3 August 2015.

19 Clinton, H. (2015). 'Dorothy: Hillary Clinton Campaign Video.' *YouTube*. Available at: https://www.youtube.com/watch?v=kNLwH8AEa7Q [Accessed 19 January 2020]; Clinton, H. (2015). 'Family Strong: Hillary Clinton Campaign Video.' *YouTube*. Available at: https://www.youtube.com/watch?v=NdKsA4q-FFA [Accessed 19 January 2020].

20 Debenedetti, G. (2015). 'Clinton Raises $28 Million but Sanders' Haul Is Too Close for Comfort.' [online] *POLITICO*. Available at: https://www.politico.com/story/2015/09/hillary-clinton-campaign-raises-28-million-in-third-quarter-214312 [Accessed 19 January 2020].

21 Devine Mulvey Longabaugh (2020). 'Bernie 2016 – Real Change.' [online] *Vimeo*. Available at: https://vimeo.com/144177519. [Accessed 20 January 2020].

22 Skiba, K. (2019) 'Arrest Photo of Young Activist Bernie Sanders Emerges from Tribune Archives.' [online] *Chicagotribune.com*, 6 April 2019. Available at: www.chicagotribune.com/news/ct-bernie-sanders-1963-chicago-arrest-2012219-story.html. [Accessed 9 May 2019].

23 Freyne, P. (2007). 'It's Nine or Never?' [online] *Seven Days*. Available at: https://www.sevendaysvt.com/vermont/its-nine-or-never/Content?oid=2131890 [Accessed 20 January 2020].

24 Seelye, K. (2015). 'As Mayor, Bernie Sanders Was More Pragmatist Than Socialist.' *New York Times*, 25 November 2015.

25 Congress.gov. (2020). 'Text – H.J.Res.114 – 107th Congress (2001–2002): Authorization for Use of Military Force Against Iraq Resolution of 2002.' [online] Available at: https://www.congress.gov/bill/107th-congress/house-joint-resolution/114/text?q=%7B%22search%22%3A%5B%22Authorization+for+Use+of+Military+Force+iraq%22%5D%7D&r=2 [Accessed 20 January 2020].

26 Herb, J. (2014). 'Sanders, McCain Strike VA Deal.' [online] *POLITICO*. Available at: https://www.politico.com/story/2014/06/bernie-sanders-john-mccain-va-deal-107491 [Accessed 20 January 2020].

27 Devine Mulvey Longabaugh (2019). 'Bernie 2016 – This Is How It Works.' [online] *Vimeo*. Available at: https://vimeo.com/146444775 [Accessed 20 January 2020].

28 Devine Mulvey Longabaugh (2019). 'Bernie 2016 – Rock.' [online] *Vimeo*. Available at: https://vimeo.com/148511759 [Accessed 20 January 2020].

29 Devine Mulvey Longabaugh (2019). 'Bernie 2016 – Mari.' [online] *Vimeo*. Available at: https://vimeo.com/150356231 [Accessed 20 January 2020].

30 Devine Mulvey Longabaugh (2019). 'Bernie 2016 - Social Security.' [online] *Vimeo*. Available at: https://vimeo.com/150356230 [Accessed 20 January 2020].

31 Devine Mulvey Longabaugh (2019). 'Bernie 2016 – Universal College.' [online] *Vimeo*. Available at: https://vimeo.com/150691660 [Accessed 20 January 2020].

32 Devine Mulvey Longabaugh (2019). 'Bernie 2016 – Patti And George.' [online] *Vimeo*. Available at: https://vimeo.com/151198000 [Accessed 20 January 2020].

33 Devine Mulvey Longabaugh (2019). 'Bernie 2016 – Goldman Sachs.' [online] *Vimeo*. Available at: https://vimeo.com/165323459 [Accessed 20 January 2020].

34 Chozick, A. & Confessore, N. (2016). 'Hacked Transcripts Reveal a Genial Hillary Clinton at Goldman Sachs Events.' *New York Times*, 16 October 2016.

35 Barlyn, S. (2016). 'Goldman Sachs to pay $5 billion in U.S. Justice Dept mortgage bond pact.' [online] Available at: https://www.reuters.com/article/us-goldman-sachs-mbs-settlement-idUSKCN0X81TI [Accessed 20 January 2020].

36 Pierce, C.P. (2016). 'This Bernie Ad May Be the Best Political Commercial I've Ever Seen.' [online] *Esquire*. Available at: https://www.esquire.com/news-politics/politics/news/a41418/bernie-sanders-america-ad [Accessed 20 January 2020].

37 Vavreck, L. 'The Ad That Moved People the Most: Bernie Sanders's America.' *New York Times*, 30 December 2016.

38 Ace Metrix. (2016). 'Bernie Sanders Continues to Deliver the Most Effective Ads.' [online] *Ace Metrix*. Available at: http://www.acemetrix.com/insights/blog/bernie-sanders-continues-to-deliver-the-most-effective-ads [Accessed 20 January 2020].

39 Devine Mulvey Longabaugh (2019). 'Bernie 2016 – American Horizon IA.' [online] *Vimeo*. Available at: https://vimeo.com/154625810 [Accessed 20 January 2020].

40 Devine Mulvey Longabaugh (2019). '5 Sec Ads.' [online] *Vimeo*. Available at: https://vimeo.com/242789869 [Accessed 20 January 2020].

41 Devine Mulvey Longabaugh (2019). 'Bernie 2016 – Tenemos Familias.' [online] *Vimeo*. Available at: https://vimeo.com/158077547 [Accessed 20 January 2020].

42 Orlin, J. (2016). 'Bernie Sanders Won the Most Votes Ever in a New Hampshire Presidential Primary.' [online] *HuffPost*. Available at: https://www.huffpost.com/entry/bernie-sanders-won-the-mo_b_9228324 [Accessed 20 January 2020].

43 Prokop, A. (2015). 'Bernie Sanders's speech at Liberty University wasn't a stunt. It's core to his campaign.' [online] *Vox*. Available at: https://www.vox.com/2015/9/14/9323041/bernie-sanders-liberty-university [Accessed 25 October 2019].

44 Foran, C. (2015). 'How Bernie Sanders Explains Democratic Socialism.' [online] *The Atlantic*. Available at: https://www.theatlantic.com/politics/archive/2015/11/bernie-sanders-makes-his-pitch-for-socialism/416913 [Accessed 20 January 2020].

45 Enten, H. (2015). 'Is Six Democratic Debates Too Few?' [online] *FiveThirtyEight*. Available at: https://fivethirtyeight.com/features/is-six-democratic-debates-too-few [Accessed 20 January 2020].

46 Yoon, R. (2016). '$182 Million: Bernie Sanders Equals Clinton.' [online] *CNN*. Available at: https://edition.cnn.com/2016/04/21/politics/2016-bernie-sanders-fundraising-hillary-clinton/index.html [Accessed 20 January 2020].

47 Jacobs, B. 'Democratic Primary Debate Schedule Criticized as Clinton "Coronation."' *The Guardian*, 6 August 2015.

48 Taylor, J. (2015). 'DNC Restores Sanders Campaign's Access To Voter Files After Data Breach.' [online] Available at: https://knpr.org/npr/2015-12/dnc-restores-sanders-campaigns-access-voter-files-after-data-breach [Accessed 20 Jan. 2020].

49 Cocca, C. (2015). 'Larry David's "SNL" Impression Of Bernie Sanders Was Obviously Awesome.' [online] *BuzzFeed News*. Available at: https://www.buzzfeednews.com/article/christinacocca/larry-david-appears-as-doppelganger-bernie-sanders-on-snl [Accessed 20 January 2020].

50 Stein, J. (2016). 'Bernie Sanders moved Democrats to the left. The platform is proof.' [online] *Vox*. Available at: https://www.vox.com/2016/7/25/12281022/the-democratic-party-platform [Accessed 20 January 2020].

Chapter 15

1 The following is an edited transcript of a public interview by Dr Brian Murphy, Technological University Dublin, with Kerry Kennedy, President of the Robert F. Kennedy Human Rights organisation. The interview took place at the Kennedy Summer School, New Ross, on 6 September 2018.

2 Kennedy, K. (2018). *Robert F. Kennedy: Ripples of Hope*. New York: Hachette.

3 *Crisis: Behind a Presidential Commitment*, directed by Robert Drew (1924–2014), is a documentary film, which centres on the University of Alabama integration crisis of June 1963. The film was released on 28 October 1963. It was added to the National Film Registry of the Library of Congress on 28 December 2011.

4 The two African American students who Wallace tried to block from entering the university were James Hood (1942–2013) and Vivian Malone (1942–2005). After President Kennedy issued an Executive Order federalising the Alabama National Guard, Wallace was compelled to step aside and Hood and Malone were registered as students at the University of Alabama. James Hood left the university after eight weeks, but returned years later to earn a doctorate there. Vivian Malone went on to become the first African American graduate of the university in 1965. Malone later worked for the US Department of Justice in Washington and for the Environmental Protection Agency in Atlanta. Vivian Malone's sister, Sharon, married, Eric Holder in 1990. Holder served from February 2009 to April 2015 as the United States Attorney General in the

administration of President Barack Obama. Holder was the first black person to hold this post. *Los Angeles Times*, 19 January 2013; *USA Today*, 13 October 2005; *Washington Post*, 10 February 2012; *Washington Post*, 3 February 2009.

5 On 5 September 2018, *The New York Times* published an anonymous op-ed, which was entitled 'I am Part of the Resistance inside the Trump Administration.' The author was identified only as a 'senior official', and stated: 'I work for the president but like-minded colleagues and I have vowed to thwart parts of his agenda and his worst inclinations.' The author described President Trump's leadership style as 'impetuous, adversarial, petty and ineffective'. *New York Times*, 5 September 2018. In October 2020, in the closing days of the presidential election campaign, Miles Taylor, the former chief of staff at the Department of Homeland Security, revealed himself to be the author of the anonymous op-ed. Kayleigh McEnany, President Trump's press secretary, responded by calling Mr Taylor a 'low-level, disgruntled former staffer'. Mr Taylor had earlier that summer endorsed Joe Biden's candidacy. *New York Times*, 28 October 2020.

6 At a campaign rally in Fort Dodge, Iowa, Trump was asked about ISIS. 'I'd bomb the shit out of them,' he said. Wead, D. (2017). *Inside Trump's White House: The Authorised Story*. London: Biteback Publishing, p. 221.

7 Serwer, A. (2017). 'Trump Wants to Bring Back Torture. Can He Do It?' [online] *The Atlantic*. Available at: https://www.theatlantic.com/politics/archive/2017/01/trump-torture/ 514463 [Accessed 6 January 2020]; Jacobs, B. (2015). 'Donald Trump on waterboarding: "Even if it doesn't work they deserve it."' *The Guardian*, 24 November 2015.

8 Jeff Sessions was the Attorney General at the time of Kerry Kennedy's interview in New Ross. In 2017, *The Guardian* reported that at his Senate confirmation hearing, as Attorney General nominee, Sessions would 'face testimony by the ACLU's legal director as the Alabama Senator is accused of [a] "30-year record of insensitivity"'. The same report said that Sessions would be forced to 'defend a career dogged by claims of racism and bigotry'. In 1986, the US Senate had blocked Sessions's nomination by President Ronald Reagan to a federal judgeship after hearing testimony about alleged racist remarks he made to colleagues, as well as a failed voter-fraud prosecution that he brought against black civil rights activists. In 2016, Bakari Sellers, a young African American politician from South Carolina, wrote of Sessions: 'An attorney general with a track record of hostility towards women, communities of colour and the LGTB community is simply unfit to serve.' Swain, J. and Laughland, O. (2017). 'Jeff Sessions confirmation hearing to shine light on history of racism claims,' *The Guardian*, 10 January 2017; Swaine, J. (2017). 'The Key points from Jeff Sessions' confirmation hearing,' *The Guardian*, 10 January 2017; Sellers, B. (2016). 'Jeff Sessions as attorney general: a terrifying prospect for black Americans,' *The Guardian*, 19 November 2016.

9 In 2014, the then Congressman Mike Pompeo defended the CIA after the release of a Senate report on torture, which detailed such practices as waterboarding. He stated: 'These men and women are not torturers, they are patriots'. The CIA tactics, he said, 'were within the law, within the constitution'. BBC News. (2018). 'Mike Pompeo: Trump's loyalist diplomat and ex-spymaster,' [online] *BBC.com*. Available at: https://www.bbc.com/news/world-us-canada-38029336 [Accessed 6 January 2020].

10 *Ethel*, a 2012 documentary directed by Rory Kennedy, was nominated for a Primetime Emmy Award for Outstanding Documentary or Nonfiction Special. In September 2013, at the Kennedy Summer School, *Ethel* was screened before a capacity audience at St Michael's Theatre, New Ross. Rory Kennedy was subsequently interviewed by Professor Richard Aldous, Bard College, New York.

Acknowledgements

1 Kennedy, J.F. (1963). 'What History Does for Us.' *The Boston Sunday Globe*, 21 April 1963.

List of Illustrations

1 Patrick Kennedy © Wikimedia Commons.
2 Bridget Murphy's house © Eamonn Hore.
3 Joseph P. Kennedy © Wide World Photos, Wikimedia Commons.
4 Pamphlet for the 1960 election campaign © John F. Kennedy Presidential Library and Museum, Boston.
5 Meeting with President Dwight D. Eisenhower © Abbie Rowe. White House Photographs, John F. Kennedy Presidential Library and Museum, Boston.
6 Meeting with J. Edgar Hoover © Abbie Rowe. White House Photographs, John F. Kennedy Presidential Library and Museum, Boston.
7 Senator Richard B. Russell © White House Photographs, John F. Kennedy Presidential Library and Museum, Boston.
8 Thomas J. Kiernan © Cecil Stoughton. White House Photographs, John F. Kennedy Presidential Library and Museum, Boston.
9 Caroline and Kerry Kennedy © Cecil Stoughton. White House Photographs, John F. Kennedy Presidential Library and Museum, Boston.
10 New Ross Quay, County Wexford © White House Photographs, John F. Kennedy Presidential Library and Museum, Boston.
11 Commodore John Barry memorial statue © White House Photographs, John F. Kennedy Presidential Library and Museum, Boston.
12 Nuclear Test Ban Treaty © Robert Knudsen. White House Photographs, John F. Kennedy Presidential Library and Museum, Boston.
13 Senator Ted Kennedy and President Ronald Reagan © White House Photographic Office, 1981–9. Ronald Reagan Library, California.
14 Senator Ted Kennedy, Vicki Kennedy and Bob Shrum © Bob Shrum's personal collection.
15 President Barack Obama with Cody Keenan © Official White House Photo, Pete Souza, Wikimedia Commons.
16 Bernie Sanders © Todd Church, Wikimedia Commons.

INDEX

de Valera, Eamon, 6, 25–35, 36, 37, 38,
78–9, 83, 84, 125
Deakin, Jim, 7
defence and national security, 73, 95, 96–7
Democratic Party, the, 13–14, 63, 211; and
National Conventions, 12, 13, 52, 68,
69, 136, 192
Department of Foreign Affairs, the, 164–5
détente, 91, 104
Devine, Tad, 174
Diem, Ngo Dinh, 108
digital communications campaigning, 211
Dillon, Denis, 167
Dirksen, Everett, 57, 67, 96, 97
DNC (Democratic National Committee),
the, 63, 211
Dobrynin, Anatoly, 98
Dodd, Thomas, 106
Donald, David Herbert, 145
Donaldson, Gary A., 62, 70
Donaldson, Sam, 184
Donlon, Seán, 165
Donnelly, Brian, 149
Douglas-Home, Sir Alec, 133
Downing Street Declaration, the, 133
Duc, Thich Quang, 108
Dukakis, Michael, 210
Dulanty, John, 31–2, 37
Dulles, Allen, 51–2, 104
Dunganstown, Co. Wexford, 1, 87, 130,
174, 213

East Boston Leader (newspaper), 44
East Milton, Boston, 148–9
economic modernisation of Ireland, the,
8–9, 78, 125–6, 129, 132, 134
Edwards, John, 185
EEC, the, 125, 126, 129, 134
Eisenhower, Dwight D., 10, 50, 62, 65,
95, 96–7, 105, 195; and the 1952
presidential election, 46, 48, 49; and
presidential ranking, 121, 144, 147;
and Richard Nixon, 58, 60

election expenditure, 44–5, 48, 54–5, 56,
59–60, 65
election polls, 111, 145, 185–6, 202
election strategies, 42–5, 46, 47, 48, 52–6,
57–8, 59–61, 63, 64, 69
emigration, 126, 133, 134, 189
Eskew, Carter, 186
ethnic composition of Boston, the, 152;
and Irish neighbourhoods, 148–9,
151, 159
Evening Herald (newspaper), 128
ExComm, 72

Fanning, Ronan, 35, 171
Farley, James, 29, 37
Favreau, Jon, 192, 194
Fay, Paul, 41
Ferdinand, Grand Duke Franz, 116
Ferguson, Don, 50
Fife, Gilbert A., 69
financial inducements and bribes, 41,
42, 43–4, 45, 48–9, 51, 52, 55,
62
Fitzgerald, F. Scott, 115
Fitzgerald, John F. 'Honey Fitz,' 41, 46
Fitzpatrick, James A., 87
Flannery, Mike, 167
Florida and the 2000 presidential election,
186–7
Fogarty, John E., 81
Ford, Gerald, 144
'Four Horsemen,' the, 166–8, 169, 171,
172 (*see also* Kennedy, Edward (Ted);
Moynihan, Daniel; O'Neill, Tip)
Fox, John, 49
'Freedom Crusade Committee,' the, 63
Freedom of Wexford, the, 1
Freeman, Orville, 67
Friends of Ireland, 172
Fulbright, J. William, 72
fundraising, 203, 204, 211
Future to Believe In, A (campaign slogan),
201, 204, 208, 212